THE VATICAN AND THE WAR

THE VATICAN
AND THE WAR

by Camille M. Cianfarra

LITERARY CLASSICS, INC.

DISTRIBUTED BY

E. P. DUTTON & COMPANY, INC.

NEW YORK, 1944

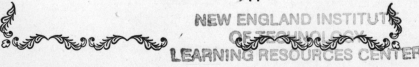

❦

FIRST EDITION

PRODUCING BOOKS IN WARTIME

This book has been produced in conformity
with war-time economy standards.

The amount of reading matter has in no
way been curtailed—when necessary more
words per page are used.

Thinner books and smaller books will save
paper, cloth, metals, transportation and stor-
age space and will conserve manpower.

The publishers will do their utmost in
meeting the objectives of the War Production
Board towards the successful prosecution
of the war.

AMERICAN BOOK—STRATFORD PRESS, INC., NEW YORK

TO

EDDA

THE VATICAN AND THE WAR

FOREWORD

AFTER spending seven years in Rome as *New York Times* correspondent, I returned to the United States in June 1942, and
one of the questions I was asked most often was: is the Vatican for us
or against us? The general belief at home seemed to be that Pope Pius
XII was sitting on the fence watching which way the war was going
while preparing to join the victorious nations. Why hadn't he openly
condemned the Axis powers? Why hadn't he joined the United
Nations? In other words, there was a deep-rooted suspicion that the
Vatican was playing both sides in the war, and that it had not taken
a firm, unswerving stand.

The covering of Vatican and Italian news for *The Times* gave me
the opportunity of being an eyewitness to the struggle that both
Pius XI and Pius XII waged against Nazism and Fascism, when it
became clear that the Axis powers were not to be deflected from a
policy of aggression aiming to enslave the free peoples of Europe.

Therefore, I did not base my observations exclusively on newspaper reports or on a cold analysis of papal speeches and decisions which could easily be misinterpreted, as it has happened with some critics of Vatican policy because of their lack of the background that one acquires only through immediate personal contact. I heard those two Pontiffs condemn time and time again the totalitarian system of government, and witnessed the birth and rapid growth of very close co-operation between the Vatican and Washington to prevent the war, and, later, to minimize it.

Yet, it seemed to me that all this struggle and indefatigable diplomatic work of the Holy See had received scant attention in the United States. In the following lines I have attempted to submit some facts and an interpretation of them based on personal knowledge. But, far from being the work of an expert, this book is only the chronicling of a reporter's experiences, for I am aware only too well of how vast and complex an undertaking an essay on Vatican policy is. Moreover, lest the reader might be led to think that I knew all along what was going to happen, let me explain that a considerable portion of the material contained in these pages was obtained long after the developments occurred.

To be sure, a great deal still remains to be told as to the part that the Vatican has been playing in World War II. The full story will be known only when the papal Secretariat of State and the lay powers decide to publish the documents they now jealously guard in their secret archives. Nevertheless, I believe that a study of the material available is sufficient to give an indication of the attitude of the Vatican towards the war.

I have been greatly aided in this task by private information gathered from friends who were connected with the Holy See and with the governments of the nations that had the power to decide the fate of the world. They helped to make clear to me the reasons behind decisions that ultimately affected the lives of millions of people.

I have paid particular attention to Italian affairs because they have had distinct repercussions in the tiny state on the other side of the Tiber, as is always the case between neighbor powers. Thus, I have endeavored to explain what in my opinion were the aims of Mussolini's foreign policy, and its domestic repercussions.

The fall of the Italian dictator, Italy's unconditional surrender, and the declaration of war against Germany by the Badoglio government, came as I was completing this book. Anyone conversant with Fascism must see that those three developments, although startling, sprang from the sandlike foundations built by Mussolini.

As a youngster, I was among the scores of thousands of people who witnessed the so-called March on Rome in 1922. I stood for hours at the corner of Corso Umberto and Piazza del Popolo watching "legions" of Blackshirts march through Rome's main avenue, between two thick lines of people jammed against the narrow sidewalks. During their millenary history Romans had seen parades far more impressive than the one organized by the Fascist Party. Displays meant nothing to them. An elderly man who was standing next to me looked at the Blackshirts as they were filing, and remarked: "Anche questo passerá." (This too will go.)

Fascism has gone. And it was in the order of things that it should be so because that movement was alien to Italian psychology and temperament. It never took root in the consciousness of the people, despite the fact that Mussolini had the opportunity of holding power for nearly twenty-one years—a generation!

Mussolini prided himself on the fact that Fascism was a "dynamic" movement that formulated its doctrine and program while it developed. This is a poor explanation, but obviously the best the dictator could find to justify seizure of power at a time when he knew that the problems he claimed still existed had already been solved by the natural economic readjustment that followed the upheaval wrought by World War I.

There have been many people who in past years have praised Mussolini for reforms he has made. What these people failed to see is that the former dictator, from the very first day of his regime, started to build the machinery to quench his lust for power. He sought to make Italy self-sufficient in every field, to prepare for war, and in doing so he bankrupted the country; he sought to imbue the Italians with a martial spirit, and thus created an artificial spiritual façade that crumbled at the first determined blow. Of course, there has been social progress in Italy, such as pensions for the aged, free maternity wards, improvement of hygienic conditions, and the like. But this progress was a natural product of the times and would have been achieved with or without Fascism, just as similar advancement occurred in England and in the United States, two democratic countries.

Mussolini was not a great statesman because his program was vitiated from the beginning by a fallacy. He failed to understand what even the humble farmer of the Abruzzi instinctively knew, that Italy and the Italians could not fulfill his mad dream of conquest of a Mediterranean Empire because, just as there are natural limitations to the physical strength of man, so are there natural limitations to the strength of a nation. Even with the complete marshaling of all her resources Italy cannot attain power greater than what her geographical position, demographic strength, natural resources, and industrial capacity permit her.

Fascism is now a historical nightmare; Mussolini, a Quisling. This is the fitful ending for a papier-mâché regime and its leader, who will be remembered as the man who wrote the darkest pages of Italy's modern history.

Before closing, I wish to express my thanks to: the publisher of *The New York Times*, for allowing me to use dispatches that appeared in this newspaper; the editors of *The New Yorker* and *The Sign*, for permission to reprint articles first written for those magazines; H. M. Lydenberg, former head of the Benjamin Franklin Library, Mexico City, who made available for me many useful reference books; Miss Alice Rohe, who has been an invaluable aid to me, with her knowledge of Italy which she acquired as correspondent in Rome for the United Press of America and for the Exchange Telegraph of London when she was the only woman in the annals of journalism to be bureau manager of a large news agency. Edda, my wife, who materially contributed to this book with the recollection and interpretation of joint experiences I might otherwise have overlooked.

At the same time, I should mention that I have followed Mario Bendiscioli's admirable book *La Politica della Santa Sede*, Luigi Salvatorelli's *Pius XI*, and Silvio Negro's *Vaticano Minore* in the explanation of the directives, aims and organization of the Vatican.

C. M. C.

Mexico City, November 1943.

THE VATICAN AND THE WAR

FIRST CHAPTER

Preparations were in full swing in the Church of St. Peter's. Pope Pius XI was to celebrate mass on Saturday, February the eleventh, to commemorate the tenth anniversary of the Lateran Treaty, which established normal relations between Italy and the Vatican in 1929, after an estrangement dating from 1870, when the troops of the newly born Italian Kingdom entered Rome and put an end to the temporal power of the Pope. For days, scores of carpenters and upholsterers had been decorating the basilica with huge gold-fringed drapes of red damask. Electricians had created an embroidery of thirty thousand lamps which were to bring out in glittering relief the noble contours of the "largest temple in Christendom." Romans were looking forward to the solemn *festa*. Tickets of admittance to St. Peter's, which the Vatican issued free of charge by the tens of thousands, were at a premium. Special invitations had been extended to sovereigns, ministers, members of the diplomatic corps accredited to the Holy See and of the Roman aristocracy. Crown Prince Humbert and the devout Maria Jose, his wife, were to represent the Royal House of Savoy; Count Galeazzo Ciano, Italy's foreign minister, the Fascist Government. All the bishops of Italy had been summoned to Rome and scores were arriving daily.

The Pope had prepared the address which he was to deliver to the Italian Episcopate that same Saturday. It was to be a conciliatory speech because, after months of violent polemics over Italy's anti-Jewish measures which conflicted with the Lateran Treaty, Pius XI and Mussolini had called a truce. In past weeks, Count Bonifacio Pignatti-Morano di Custoza, Italy's ambassador to the Holy See, and Cardinal Eugenio Pacelli, Secretary of State, had held frequent meetings to find a basis for understanding and allaying the tension between the two powers.

Although the Pope was not feeling well, his precarious state of health was generally attributed to the physical weakness proper to the aged. Well in his eighty-second year, Piux XI had shown remarkable stamina in withstanding the rigors of lengthy and tiring functions of recent months. Many times, when the world thought that he was about to draw his last breath, the stocky Pontiff had achieved a recovery which had surprised even his personal physician, distinguished, gray-haired Aminta Milani.

I had been going to the Vatican every day for the past four days, that is, since Sunday, the fifth of February, when the Pope suffered a slight heart attack which confined him to bed. All audiences, both public and private, had been canceled for an indefinite period. Officials of the Secretariat of State had told me that there was no cause for worry. Of course, the Pope was a very old man, and it was only natural that he should conserve his strength for the pontifical mass only two days away. He had tired himself in the preceding weeks by receiving hundreds of people daily and by making as many as five speeches to different groups of pilgrims despite the fact that he was suffering from asthma and other serious ailments which had almost wrecked his body but had not affected his strong will.

At one fifteen and four thirty, Thursday afternoon, February 9, the Pontiff was struck again by two heart attacks. To the doctors who stood helplessly at his bedside he begged that they prolong his life for two more days—just long enough to perform that ceremony, so near, yet, for him, so far away.

The telephone next to my bed rang at four thirty, Friday morning, February tenth. It was the tipster who was keeping the death watch.

"They gave him extreme unction," he said. "All hope is gone; better get dressed. I'll meet you at the Vatican."

Still not quite awake, I dialed ITALCABLE and dictated a flash for The New York Times.

"Pope critical. Extreme unction administered."

A few stray cats were the only signs of life as I walked from my house at 33 Via Margutta toward the garage just across that quaint, typically Roman, little street, a stone's throw from the Pincio.

"Romolo, the car. Please hurry."

"What's happening?" asked the surprised watchman. "It's a little early for you to get up, isn't it?"

"The Pope is dying," I said.

"*Poveretto* (The poor one.) Still he is quite old, isn't he?"

While Romolo was warming up the car, I telephoned Arnaldo Cortesi, former head of the Rome bureau of *The Times* who had been expelled from Italy five weeks before. Mussolini had found him too uncomfortably "nosey" for his liking. Cortesi, who had been covering Italian news for seventeen years, often unearthed stories in places where foreign correspondents were not supposed to go snooping. He had been told that he could no longer work in Italy and was now awaiting another assignment. To me, however, he was still the head of the bureau.

"Chief, the Pope is dying," I said. "I am going to the Vatican."

Shortly before five, I banged on the gate of the Santa Anna entrance, on the right side of the Bernini Colonnade. Vatican guards recognized me and, with an understanding smile, let me through without asking any questions. I drove up to the Courtyard of Saint Damasus, which is the heart of Vatican City. The vast enclosure, overlooked by three tiers of loggias designed by Bramante and frescoed by Raphael, had lost its usual atmosphere of calm and serenity. Cardinals, bishops, nuns, priests, civilians, guards hurried through it and headed for the elevator that took them to the private apartment of the Pope on the third floor. Big, black, Fiat limousines bearing hastily summoned cardinals and other prelates were arriving steadily. On the left corner of the courtyard, a group of Italian journalists and foreign correspondents stood in front of the cubbyhole office of Monsignor Enrico Pucci, who edited a Vatican news service.

"Pucci is up in the Pope's apartment," Reynolds Packard of the United Press told me. "He'll come down as soon as there is some development."

A few minutes after five, Monsignor Pucci emerged from the elevator and hurried toward the group of nervous, anxious newspapermen.

"He has lost consciousness and is sinking fast," Monsignor said. "I just came down to tell you that it is a matter of minutes now."

I telephoned Cortesi and gave him all the details available. Dawn was breaking. A faint, suffused, bluish light was creeping along the upper loggia and slowly coloring Raphael's frescoes. The courtyard was filled with cars and people. There was a murmur of repressed voices. We waited in silence, our brains figuring the best way to handle the tremendous story that was but a few minutes away.

At 5:40, Monsignor Pucci ran out of the elevator.

"The Pope is dead," he announced in a strangled voice.

"At what time?" we all shouted.

"5:31."

Upon the Pope's death, the authority of all the administrative bodies of the Vatican, such as the Secretariat of State, the Tribunals, the Chancellery, and the like automatically ceases. The Secretary of State personally retains only the authority of sending a circular notice to the members of the diplomatic corps, the nuncios, and other representatives of the Holy See, explaining that they must address all communications to the Sacred College of Cardinals during the period of "Vacant See," between the death and the election of the Pope. The power vested in the Pontiff is transferred to the cardinals, whose authority, however, is of a more temporal than spiritual nature. Headed by their dean, they solve only the most pressing problems facing the Church and leave to the new Pope any decision of great importance. Their principal task is that of attending to the daily administrative details of the Vatican. The Cardinal Camerlengo is the real provisional head as far as temporal matters are concerned. By virtue of his office, he holds the executive power and carries out the decisions of the cardinals who meet daily.

Even the members of the family of the defunct Pontiff, who, while their powerful relative is alive, enjoy general respect and prestige within the Vatican, find themselves relegated to the status of ordinary individuals, the power and influence they might have held, gone forever.

As soon as I finished covering the story of the Pope's death, I went up to the papal apartment. I found the hall filled with people who had no reason for being there except to satisfy their curiosity as to what was going on. Cardinal Pacelli, who, besides being Secretary of State, was also Camerlengo, was too busy attending to the many problems created by the Pope's death to pay any attention to the crowd of idle onlookers. For several hours, priests, seminarists, civilians, and even nuns crowded before the door leading into the private apartment hoping "to have a look at the Pope" as a young prelate confided to me. However, all their efforts broke before the polite but firm refusal of Monsignor Domenico Tardini, the energetic and brilliant secretary of the Congregation of Extraordinary Ecclesiastical Affairs, who stood in front of the door just as a common usher while the body of the former Pontiff was being clothed and prepared for its last earthly journey.

Italy was the first power to send condolences to the Vatican. A few hours after Pius' demise, Pacelli, as Camerlengo, received Morano di Custoza who conveyed the regrets of King Victor Emmanuel and of the Fascist Government.

The same evening, the Grand Council of Fascism put aside all scheduled political questions and paid a "respectful homage" to Pius. The event was commemorated in every Italian school where it was turned into a personal glorification of Mussolini. Italy's children were told by their teachers how Pius XI had called Il Duce "a Man of Destiny" because he had brought about the conciliation between Church and State.

Mussolini, in a personal telegram to Pacelli, said, "The disappearance of the Pope of the Conciliation has thrown not only the Church, but the whole Italian nation into mourning. Interpreting the sentiments of the Italian people, I send Your Eminence and the Sacred College the heartfelt condolences of the Fascist Government and my own personal ones."

That statement was nothing more than an official gesture on the part of the Prime Minister of a Catholic nation subsequent to the loss suffered by the Church. At the time, I thought Mussolini had been genuinely sorry to hear of the death of a Pontiff who had co-operated with him in the solution of the so-called "Roman Question." It had been one of Italy's thorniest problems, because the voluntary confinement of the Pope in the Vatican in protest for the "invasion" of Rome by the Italian troops in 1870, and the lack of official relations between the two powers deterred Italy's dictator from achieving what he hoped would eventually result in political and spiritual support of his regime by an almost one-hundred-per-cent Catholic nation.

Many months later, I obtained the real story. One day, in the fall of 1939, I was in the dressing room of the Parioli Tennis Club in Rome, relaxing after a hard game. There was an inter-club tournament going on, and Bruno Mussolini, one of Il Duce's sons, was among the players. Bruno had just won a match and was, therefore, feeling good. He was feeling good because, contrary to what might be supposed, the match had been "on the level." There were plenty of boys in the club who would have been happy to beat Mussolini's son, and one of them eventually did. While we were dressing, Bruno told me that the previous day, he had visited the Vatican museums. We started talking about the part which the Church had played in history, and I volunteered the statement that Pius XI had been a great Pope.

(I am relating the dialogue which followed as I jotted it down a few minutes after I left the club.)

"I suppose so," Bruno said, "although I thought it was time there was a change in the Vatican. I know that Father was rather glad to see him go."

"What do you mean?" I asked. "I thought your father admired and respected him. After all, Pius XI brought about the conciliation between Italy and the Vatican."

"Sure, sure, but that was ten years ago. I remember when the Pope died, Ciano [Count Galeazzo Ciano] telephoned Father early in the morning to give him the news. I was in Father's library when the call came. He broke into a big smile and said, 'Finalmente se n'e' andato! [Finally he is gone.] He then turned to me and explained, 'Quel vecchio ostinato e' morto.' [That obstinate old man is dead.]"

Bruno's words confirmed what Prince Clemente Aldobrandini told me almost a year before when Pius XI was thundering against Mussolini's racial laws.

This scion from one of Italy's most illustrious families had been received by Mussolini in a private audience. He saw Italy's dictator very rarely, although by virtue of his position and influence, he could have had audiences by the asking. But, as most of the members of the Italian aristocracy, he was closely connected with the Vatican and preferred not to identify himself too closely with the Fascist Government.

"As I walked into Mussolini's huge studio in Palazzo Venezia," Aldobrandini recounted, "Il Duce looked at me, and with a flicker of a smile said, 'I see you at every Pope's death—and this Pope takes such a long time to die.' "

The phrase, "at every Pope's death" ("Ad ogni morte di Papa,") is a colloquial expression used by the Italians to signify that events take place at very long periods. In this case, Mussolini's reference to Pius XI had a very definite political meaning.

Relations between the Fascist Government and the Vatican had become gradually more strained as Italy drew closer to Germany. Pius XI had opposed this policy with all the means in his power. Mussolini, who knew the strength and courage of the aged Pope, had a great deal of respect for him. Lately, however, he had found it impossible to collaborate with him. He felt that a new Pope could hardly be more intransigent than Pius XI, and there was always the hope that he might be more tolerant.

In the days following the Pope's death, Rome became the center of feverish diplomatic activity, both overt and covert. With more than three hundred forty million Catholics throughout the world, the choice of a Pope was a matter of great political importance to lay governments. It was more so at the beginning of 1939, when the major European powers were divided in two opposite ideological camps— Fascist and Democratic—each straining all their resources to prepare for a war which was regarded as inevitable. With his unequalled moral authority, a new Pope could influence millions of Catholics into supporting this or that government. He would be a factor of solidarity or dissension; he could be a powerful ally or a dangerous enemy.

Members of the diplomatic corps accredited to the Holy See, who during their years of residence in the Italian capital had built strong ties of friendship and valuable connections with cardinals and Vatican officials, set to work. They called on their friends, extended invitations to come to their residences; some of the representatives of the powers who were pursuing the same policy pooled their information. Cardinals, bishops, and prelates who were connected with important offices in the Vatican were sounded out as to who might be the successor of Pius XI. Cars bearing the C.D. (*Corpo Diplomatico*) license plate could be seen passing at all hours of the day through the Arch of the Bells, one of the Vatican entrances on the left side of the Bernini Colonnade. Ambassadors and ministers would drive up to the Court-yard of Saint Damasus and spend several hours in Vatican offices. Their work had become an active, sixteen-hour-a-day reporting assign-ment in no way dissimilar to that of the newspapermen who were working along the same channels for clues which might answer the query of hundreds of millions of Catholics: "Who is going to be the next Pope?"

An Italian cardinal, whose name I cannot mention because he always refused to be quoted, had known me for many years. He was, as a matter of fact, a friend of long standing of my family since the days in the early twenties when he was only a monsignor. He had often proved helpful to my father who had been the manager of the Rome Bureau of the United Press during the First World War, and who had covered the death of Benedict XV and the election of Pius XI. I had been calling on this Cardinal regularly for years, and he had, at times, volunteered information whenever his confidential state-ments did not conflict with the ethical and moral principles of the Church. In the days preceding the conclave, I managed to obtain an audience with him.

"There seems to be quite a great deal of interest in my person," His Eminence smilingly told me. "I have been showered with invita-tions on the part of certain representatives of foreign powers whose attentions I have not enjoyed for a long time."

The innate prudence and reticence of the clergy, trained all their lives to be discreet, create a mental habit which is often puzzling to the layman. His Eminence talked for some minutes on the same sub-ject with great circumspection. A word here and there, a vague allusion to people and situations were all he would give. At the end of the meeting, however, it was clear to me that when he had spoken of "two of our sons who, not content with having chosen the wrong path are now attempting to lead others astray and are using every device of their fertile minds to thwart the wishes of our Lord," His Eminence had meant to say that Mussolini and Hitler were exercising every pos-sible pressure to bring about the election of a cardinal whom they regarded as tolerant and less apt than others to take a strong anti-Fascist stand.

How right His Eminence was I saw three days later on February sixteenth, when Carl Ludwig von Bergen, German Ambassador to the Vatican and dean of the diplomatic corps, addressed the Sacred College of Cardinals in the customary presentation of condolences at the death of a pope. Von Bergen had been holding that post since the time of Pope Benedict XV. He was regarded very highly in Berlin and, shortly before Germany's annexation of Austria, his transfer to Vienna had been seriously considered.

"We live and act in one of the most decisive hours of history," von Bergen told forty cardinals gathered in the huge Consistorial Hall of the Vatican. "We are assisting in the elaboration of a new world which wants to raise itself upon the ruins of a past which, in many ways, has no longer any reason to exist.

"We want this evolution to be peaceful, and the Papacy, without any doubt, has an essential role. On the Sacred College, we are deeply convinced of this, most eminent Princes, weighs at this moment a most delicate responsibility of choosing a worthy successor for Pius XI —the choice of a Pontiff toward whom humanity may turn its gaze as toward a beacon shining in stormy and fearful anxiety for a common goal of peace and progress."

The speech caused a sensation and, needless to say, it was very frigidly received. Dead silence followed von Bergen's words. Many of the members of the diplomatic corps simply gasped at the audacity of their German colleague who so brazenly spoke of the Nazi concep-tion of a "New World." Sheared of its diplomatic language, von Ber-gen's speech contained Germany's demand that the cardinals choose a Pope in sympathy with Hitler's program of expansion so that he might use his great spiritual influence to induce England and France, the two powers which were opposing Germany's policy of aggression, not to take recourse to war. Substantially, Hitler asked that the new Pope favor the building of the "New World" at the expense of the "Old World" represented by the Western Democracies.

Granito Pignatelli di Belmonte, dean of the cardinals, not only ignored the personal appeal of the German Ambassador but clearly indicated that the Church would not be guided by political considerations in the election of a Pope.

"The Sacred College," he said, "in spiritual communion with the faithful the world over, raises most fervent prayer to the Lord that He may deign to concede to His Church for its good and the interests of the nations you so worthily represent, a supreme shepherd after His Own Heart."

The same day, I interviewed some members of the diplomatic corps to ascertain whether von Bergen had informed them of the contents of the speech before he delivered it. Nobody had seen it, I learned. As dean of the diplomatic corps, I was told, the German Ambassador had the duty of expressing the condolences of all his colleagues for the death of the Pontiff, but he had also the faculty of speaking in behalf of his own government and, therefore, of injecting a personal note in the address. The Sacred College had been fully aware of the political aims of the lay powers and had had no illusions about it since Pius XI's death, as I discovered during a conversation which took place when I was covering Pius' burial in St. Peter's four days after his demise.

The ceremony of the burial was private. The attendance was not nearly large enough to fill St. Peter's, but it did, nevertheless, create a warm and vibrant atmosphere. Many of the men were in full evening dress but wearing black ties as a sign of mourning. All the women wore the usual costume for Vatican ceremonies—an ankle-length, black dress with long sleeves, high collar, and a lace mantilla covering the hair.

The more distinguished among the guests were received at the bronze gates of the Vatican and escorted to their seats by Prince Camillo Massimo whose family dated back to the Punic Wars in the third century, B.C. He was hereditary Superintendent General of Vatican Posts, and it was part of his duties to receive visitors—a reminder of the days when his ancestors were required to meet all arriving stagecoaches carrying passengers and mail.

The ceremony before the burial took place between the Papal altar beneath the dome and the altar of the cathedra. Special tribunes had been built on either side of this space to accommodate the Pope's relatives, the diplomatic corps—all of whose members had been invited—the Roman nobility, the Knights of Malta, and other favored groups.

The basilica was completely bare and unornamented. Only twelve candles were lit—six on each of the two altars. The electric lighting was in operation only in the apse. The remainder of the basilica was dimly lighted by daylight filtering through dark rain clouds and was completely plunged in darkness as night fell. The body was placed on trestles not far from the place where the enormous triple coffin was waiting to receive it. The Noble Guard formed in a double line at its side.

Archbishop Roberto Vicentini, who was to impart absolution, took his place facing the altar of the cathedra on the far side of the body. He was flanked by half-a-dozen Swiss Guards standing at attention with their halberds and long serpentine swords. He recited the prayers for the dead to which the choir sang the responses.

As soon as he had finished, the ten *sediari* grasped the platform on which the litter was lying and carried it to the coffin a few feet away. Arriving there, they raised the body and lowered it, platform and all, into the coffin. The Pope's robes, which were too long, were folded under his feet. The whole operation was performed in a few seconds.

Monsignor Antonio Bacci, Secretary of Briefs to Princes, whom the Congregation of Cardinals had appointed to deliver the funeral eulogy, reviewed the principal events of Pius' pontificate. A copy of the eulogy, written on parchment, was enclosed in a cylindrical brass case and placed in the coffin at Pius' feet. Then three red velvet bags, one containing seventeen gold coins, a second, seventeen silver, and a third, seventeen copper—one coin of each metal for each year of Pius' pontificate—were also placed in the coffin.

After the various functions preceding the burial had been performed, Pius' two secret chamberlains, Monsignor Venini and Monsignor Confalonieri, who were perhaps closer to him than anyone else in the last years of his life, advanced together with Monsignor Federico Callori, Dean of the Participating secret chamberlains, and with gentle hands all three covered the Pope's face with a white cloth of the finest silk. A similar cloth was placed over the Pope's hands by Monsignor Carlo Respighi, prefect of pontifical ceremonies, who in this task replaced Monsignor Arborio-Mella di Sant' Elia, who was unable to attend because of illness.

Finally Cardinal Giovanni Battista Nasalli-Rocca di Corneliano, Archbishop of Bologna, covered the whole body with a crimson cloth. He owed this distinction to the fact that he was the first cardinal Pius had created after his accession.

Workmen in striped trousers and black coats advanced and began closing the triple coffin. Since the inner coffin was made of wood, the first lid was of wood also; it bore a large black cross on its outer surface.

Then came a bronze lid, which was soldered to the middle coffin, made of lead. This lid was elaborately decorated in relief. At the top it had a cross, beneath which were a skull and crossbones and then the Pope's arms, consisting of the papal tiara over an eagle and three spheres as well as a Latin inscription explaining that the Pontiff had lived eighty-one years, eight months, ten days, and that he was the head of the Universal Church for seventeen years and five days. These decorations and inscriptions were repeated on the lid of the outer coffin, which was of polished wood.

The first coffin was tied with two ribbons on which Cardinal Pacelli, the Papal Master of Ceremonies and the Dean of the Vatican Chapter placed wax seals. Six seals were placed in all—two by Cardinal Pacelli in his capacity as Camerlengo, one by him in his capacity as archpriest of the basilica, two by the Papal Master of Ceremonies and one by the Dean of the Vatican Chapter.

An equal number of ribbons and seals was applied to the leaden coffin, and by the same persons, the only difference being that the seals in this case were of lead.

A strange incident occurred when the workmen were soldering the bronze lid on the leaden box. The supply of solder was exhausted before the operation was completed, and everybody waited while a new supply was secured.

Just before the soldering of the leaden coffin began, the cardinals filed out silently and made their way toward the crypt, where they waited for the body to arrive. I followed them and found myself the only civilian among more than a score of the princes of the Church. Some knelt before the tomb of Pius X, and others before that of Benedict XV. A long time went by on account of the incident of the solder, and the cardinals, having finished their prayers, collected in small groups and began talking among themselves. I was standing in a corner of the low-vaulted, niche-like enclosure, not far from the place where Pius' coffin was to be immured, feeling somewhat out of place and expecting at any moment to be asked to leave, when Cardinal Tedeschini, who was standing next to Pius X's tomb, beckoned me to him. He and Cardinal Schuster were listening to Cardinal Nasalli-Rocca, who was proudly explaining to them that he was the author of the Latin inscription placed on Pius X's tomb. When I joined the group, Cardinal Tedeschini smilingly remarked, "You know, I have never seen such an interest in the Papacy. The world today is more conscious than at any other time in this century of the spiritual force of the Vatican. And," he added with a twinkle in his eye, "it will be more so in the forthcoming weeks."

Who was the Cardinal Italy and Germany wished to have elected? This was the paramount question in the minds of all those who had been watching the maneuvers of diplomatists and their agents. I spent day after day trying to find out, and although I could never obtain concrete proof, there is no doubt in my mind that Mussolini and Hitler had prelates with influential positions within the Church who had been charged with the task of securing support for their candidate. Both Mussolini and Hitler, I learned, never believed for a single moment that a non-Italian cardinal would be elected. They knew full well that the Sacred College was aware of the incalculable political repercussions which the election of a non-Italian would have throughout the Catholic world. In view of the grave tension between the Fascist powers and the Western democracies, if a French, English, or even American cardinal were elected, the Catholics and the governments of the Axis countries would undoubtedly feel that the new head of the Church was against them. The same reaction would obtain in democratic countries if a German or Spanish Cardinal were chosen. This was to be expected, especially in view of the fact that the election of a non-Italian cardinal would break a tradition which dated from 1522, when Adrian the Sixth, of Utrecht, was elected.

The choice of an Italian cardinal had on its side the overwhelming argument that it was in keeping with historical precedent. Moreover, the courage shown by Pius XI in combating neo-pagan doctrines in Germany, and the racial laws in Italy had shown to all Catholics that an Italian Pope was not influenced by nationalistic considerations and remained true to his universal spiritual mission. Consequently, Mussolini and Hitler concentrated their pressure on Italian cardinals. There were several of them who were regarded as less intolerant of Fascism and its political manifestations than others. The name of a certain cardinal was mentioned hopefully in Fascist circles. He was the prelate who had blessed Italian troops on their way to conquer the defenseless Ethiopians and, two years later, the Blackshirts who were sent to Spain to fight the Spanish Republicans. Even in the summer of 1938, when Pius XI was condemning Italy's racial laws, this man, unlike many other Italian cardinals, had kept silent. Another prince of the Church, as the members of the Sacred College were called, who was said to have stood high in Fascist favor, was a short, dark-haired, fiery titular of one of Italy's Sees. Pius XI had, at one time, appointed him papal legate to a Eucharistic Congress in French North Africa. The Pontiff reconsidered his decision when France informed him that, in view of the bad relations between Rome and Paris, the choice was inadvisable because the mere presence of such a cardinal on French territory might lead to incidents.

The Sacred College took some unprecedented measures to spike the efforts of the lay governments. Pacelli issued strict orders that, before being admitted inside the Vatican, callers should not only be questioned as to the reasons for their visit, but also identify themselves. Bona fide Italian newspapermen and foreign correspondents were furnished with identification cards. A special committee, composed of Cardinals Federico Tedeschini, Domenico Jorio, and Giuseppe Pizzardo, charged with scrutinizing the credentials of applicants for permission to remain inside the conclave and deciding which of the hundreds should be admitted and which excluded, displayed unusual severity.

In former conclaves, it was sufficient for the cardinals to submit the names of their conclavists and servants and they were approved without investigation. This time, the committee wished to know more about even the cardinals' personal attendants. They inquired into their antecedents and background, lest, when they were inside the conclave, they might have some means of remaining in touch with persons or interests outside on whose behalf they might attempt to influence their masters. The investigation, which was unusual considering that each cardinal vouched for the persons accompanying him, was very much greater in the cases of the humbler persons necessary for the proper functioning of the conclave. The majority of them, of course, did not have very close contacts with the cardinals, and, therefore, they were not in a position even to attempt to influence their decisions; but they might, nevertheless, have tried to send out news of the conclave proceedings and thus incite fresh intrigues. All these lesser people, therefore, were subjected to scrutiny so thorough that in some cases it extended to their parents, friends, and habitual companions as well as to possible contacts with embassies and legations.

The pressure on the Sacred College had become so widely known about a week before the conclave that Roberto Farinacci, editor of the extreme right-wing Fascist newspaper, *Regime Fascista*, and one of the strongest supporters of Mussolini's pro-German policy, thought it expedient to come out with an editorial in which he attempted to create an alibi for the Fascist Government. He accused the democratic press of trying to influence the Church by suggesting this or that candidate and ended with the statement, "All our adversaries have but a single hope: A political Pope who will compromise the Church and provoke a schism."

The influence and prestige American Catholics enjoyed in the Vatican was clearly demonstrated with the arrival of Cardinals George Mundelein of Chicago, and Dennis Dougherty of Philadelphia, ten days before the conclave. I went to Naples to cover the story for *The Times* and reached the pier just as the ship was docking. The first thing that met the eyes of the American cardinals when they came on deck was a large swastika flying from the masthead of the steamer, *Wilhelm Gustloff*, which had been hired by the Nazi Strength-Through-Joy Movement to send two thousand workers vacationing in Italy.

As soon as the gangplank was down, the newspapermen went on board. I was looking for the cardinals' cabins when I saw Roy Howard, chairman of the board of the Scripps-Howard newspapers, who was making a European tour. Despite the fact that he was a newspaper magnate, Roy Howard still liked "to cover" a story just like any regular reporter. In a few words he told me what the cardinals had been doing during the trip, where they were at the moment, and to whom I should talk as the best source of "dope."

It was late in the afternoon, and the cardinals were sitting at separate tables with their secretaries, finishing dinner. When they left the ship, Cardinal Dougherty received the noisier welcome because he was the first to land, and because he won the sympathies of the crowd by crying, "*Viva l' Italia! Sono mezzo Italiano!*" (I am half Italian.) Cardinal Mundelein, more reserved, only smiled in reply to the applause.

Upon their arrival in Rome, it became evident that the group of United States cardinals, which included William O'Connell of Boston, scheduled to arrive on the day of the opening of the Conclave, would play an important part in the election of the new Pope. The United States had consolidated its position as one of the great Catholic powers in the world as far as numbers were concerned, and its material contribution to the cause of Catholicism, not only easily exceeded that of any other nation, but was probably greater than that of all the rest of the world put together. So outstanding was the position of the American cardinals in the Sacred College, that the possibility of one of them becoming candidate for the Papacy was discussed in Vatican circles. An investigation, however, proved that such an occurrence was very unlikely. First of all, the United States had taken a decisive, anti-Axis stand, and, therefore, the election of an American cardinal would without any doubt be resented in Germany, as well as in Italy. It was not to be doubted that even the German cardinals, despite the fight between the Holy See and the Nazi Government, would refuse to vote for the American candidate. Such a refusal was certain on the part of cardinals from those nations which had, whether they liked it or not, to live harmoniously with the German Government. These included Poland, with one cardinal, Hungary, also with one, and Spain, with three. Even under the most favorable circumstances, an American candidate could not count on more than twenty votes of non-Italian cardinals. To obtain the two-thirds majority necessary for the election, he would, therefore, need the votes of more than twenty Italian cardinals, since sixty-two members of the Sacred College were scheduled to participate in the conclave. In other words, more than half of the Italian vote should have been switched from an Italian to a foreign candidate. This was generally agreed to be inconceivable.

Three days before the conclave began, foreign correspondents were invited to visit the Sistine Chapel where the cardinals were to meet, beginning March first, to elect the successor of Pius XI. As I entered the chapel, I saw sixty-two thrones installed alongside the walls on which the cardinals would sit during the voting. In the middle of the hall was a large table on which the votes were to be counted. Seven four-hundred-candle-power lamps were hanging from the ceiling. At the far end of the chapel, five steps led to a temporary altar, set up directly facing Michelangelo's *Last Judgment*. I was observing the scene when I heard an angry voice ring out loudly.

"Get out of that throne! And don't take any pictures!"

I turned around and saw Monsignor Arborio-Mella di Sant' Elia, papal master of the chamber, who, in those days, combined functions equivalent to those of a chief of police and of a mayor, walk threateningly towards Frank Gervasi of International News Service. Gervasi had blithely sat on one of the thrones and had told his photographer to snap him in a pose of profound meditation. He said later that he had been hunting for cardinal robes to put on, but could find none, so the picture had to be taken in civilian clothes.

In those last three days, many foreign correspondents, and especially the heads of the press services, worked feverishly to enlist the services of conclavists who might give them a "beat" on the election of the Pope. Reynolds Packard of the United Press mobilized his large staff of Italians to approach someone who would remain immured in the Vatican during the conclave, promising a reward of several thousands of lire to anyone who contrived to let him know before anybody else the name of the cardinal elected. On the eve of the conclave, the bar of the Foreign Press Club, which was the correspondents' meeting place after the day's work, presented the strange spectacle of listless and unusually laconic newspapermen morosely sipping drinks. Everyone was thinking of the big story that was going "to break" in the next few days and was wracking his brain to find some means with which to score a "beat."

On the morning of the opening of the conclave, all the cardinals were in Rome except O'Connell. He arrived in Naples at 9 A.M., March 1, and was the last cardinal to enter the Vatican, early that afternoon. I was standing next to Monsignor Domenico Tardini in the Royal Hall, between the Sistine and Pauline Chapels, when a Vatican attendant informed him that O'Connell had arrived. Monsignor left hurriedly for the apartment assigned to the Boston cardinal, and I followed him. We took the elevator and went up to the third floor where we found O'Connell standing in the middle of his room in woolen underwear and entirely alone.

O'Connell was quite angry.

"Here I have been for the last half hour," he said to Monsignor Tardini in Italian, "and there is no one to receive me or tell me where my apartment is. E' incredible."

Monsignor Tardini made profuse apologies. He explained that there was a ceremony going on in the Sistine Chapel, and that all Vatican officials were attending it. He helped His Eminence to put on his cardinalitial robes and escorted him to the Royal Hall just as the cardinals were filing out of the Sistine Chapel where they had taken the customary oath to obey all the constitutions regulating the conclave, safeguard the Church's interests and to vote as conscience dictated.

The closing ceremony was truly impressive. As each cardinal came out singly from the Sistine Chapel, the master of ceremony called out his name. A Noble Guard would detach himself from the group standing by the door. After giving a formal military salute, he would fall into step by the cardinal's side and accompany him to his cell. The princes of the Church, clad in their purple robes, passed through a double row of Noble Guards behind whom were prelates, newspapermen, and members of the Roman aristocracy and of Italy's royal family, including Crown Princess Maria Jose of Piedmont, as well as relatives of some of the cardinals.

Edda, my wife, who was witnessing the ceremony from one corner of the Royal Hall, told me later that, when Cardinal Pacelli appeared from the door of the Sistine Chapel, the maid of one of his nephews whispered to a friend next to her, "He is a holy man, but his family hopes he will not be chosen because of his frail health and the grave responsibilities he would have to face."

Twenty minutes after the last cardinal left the Sistine Chapel, the bell in the Courtyard of Saint Damasus began ringing. This was the signal for a great bustle of activity. Masters of ceremonies toured the Vatican calling out "*Extra Omnes*" (Everybody out) and making sure the order was promptly obeyed. A dozen groups of Swiss Guards inspected all the buildings inside the conclave area from cellar to roof in search of "stowaways." Workmen closed the last passages from the Parrot Courtyard to the Courtyard of St. Damasus by means of movable walls of sound-proof material prepared beforehand. Finally, Prince Chigi-Albani, who was marshal of the conclave, led the party that inspected the enclosure from the outside, while Cardinal Pacelli, as Camerlengo did the same from the inside, to ascertain that all connections with the rest of the world were thoroughly severed. At six fifteen, both parties were back at the entrance of the Courtyard of St. Damasus. Two minutes later, the door swung on its hinges, closing with a loud report. The three keys on the inside and the three on the outside turned in their locks. The papal flag at the top of the royal staircase, built by Bernini, was hauled down and replaced by a silken banner showing the arms of the Chigi family on a white field.

I left the Vatican a few minutes before six with Monsignor Joseph Patrick Hurley, the only American prelate attached to the Secretariat of State, who is now Bishop of St. Augustine, Florida. We stood in

St. Peter's Square watching the lights appear through windows belonging to the cardinals' bedrooms.

"Who will be the next Pope?" I asked him.

"You'll know fairly soon, I think. I should not be surprised if you'll have the answer tomorrow."

The conclave had begun.

SECOND CHAPTER

The arrangements made by the American press to cover the election of the Pope surpassed anything that had been seen in Italy since the advent of Fascism. Reynolds Packard, of the United Press, Richard G. Massock, of the Associated Press, and Gervasi, of the International News, hired rooms in some of the buildings in Piazza Rusticucci, which is the vestibule to the majestic St. Peter's Square. They had windows facing the center loggia on which the new Pope was to appear to bless Rome and the world. Assistants, armed with binoculars, kept a permanent watch. They had prepared themselves for a long wait. Extra telephones had been installed and an army of messenger boys, who were to take the dispatches to the cable office, hired. Early in the morning of March second, the press associations kept their lines to London open for hours. To prevent the operators from butting in and cutting them off, which often happened if one did not keep on talking, the correspondents read chapters from American books or newspapers while waiting for the first *fumata* that was to issue from the pipe on the roof of the Sistine Chapel. The smoke resulting from the burning of the ballots in the stove would signal to the world outside whether or not a Pope had been elected. If the smoke were a thick black, it meant that the balloting had not been decisive; if it were white, the election had taken place. The stove had been tested before the beginning of the conclave and had proved to be in perfect working condition. A supply of wood shavings had been placed next to it in order to produce black smoke.

Under the loggia, at the foot of the wide granite steps leading to the main entrance of St. Peter's, a score of photographers had installed cameras with telescopic lenses which looked like medium-size antitank guns. The big American photo associations had promised handsome rewards for the first telephoto pictures of the new Pope, and competition was very keen. "Wide World," which was the photo service of *The Times*, had instructed me to spend any amount of money in order to flash the pictures to New York, via London. I had hired a covered truck and built a dark room inside it. Three of our photographers had been placed at strategic points, in order to snap the Pope from different angles. The photographers were to take the pictures to the truck and develop them while en route to a small hotel in front of the telephoto station in the main post office at Piazza San Silvestro. In the hotel, our chief photographer, Armando Bruni, had taken a room where he was to make copies from the already developed negatives and rush them to the post office. The rival organizations had conjured up tricks of their own, and, as it later happened, we filed our pictures at intervals of less than a minute.

In the afternoon, Cortesi and I went to St. Peter's to wait for the second *fumata*. There was a comparatively small crowd looking expectantly at the roof of the Sistine Chapel. We had been there only a few minutes when shouts rent the air. Smoke was issuing from the pipe, white and fleecy at first, then black like the one in the morning, leaving everybody in doubt whether a Pope had been elected or not. The first visible proof that the Roman Catholic Church had a new head was afforded by the appearance on the terrace over the entrance to the Vatican of a number of ecclesiastical conclavists and lay attendants, several of whom were carrying cardinal's cloaks, which they waved excitedly and with obvious jubilation. The fact that they had been able to leave the section of the Vatican so carefully sealed the previous evening proved that the conclave was finished and a Pope elected.

At exactly one minute after six, the large hall above the portico of St. Peter's, known as the Hall of Benedictions, which has windows along both sides, some overlooking the basilica and others, the square, was suddenly flooded with electric light. The door leading to the balcony was thrown open, revealing the gilded columns and capitals inside and marble friezes with large, black inscriptions. Four attendants, one in full evening dress and three in simple black, appeared on the balcony. From the balustrade they suspended an enormous cloth of velvet sheen. It had a wide blood-red border, and in the center, the papal arms on a snow-white field.

No sooner was this done than a golden cross borne by a white-surpliced acolyte appeared, followed by Cardinal Camillo Caccia Dominioni, Dean of the Cardinal Deacons, still wearing the violet robes known as *croccia*, which are donned only in the conclave. In a magnificent, musical voice that twenty loud-speakers, placed at various vantage points, caused to reverberate throughout the square, he said and half-sang the centuries-old formula:

"*Nuntio vobis gaudium magnum: habemus Papam.*" (I announce to you a great joy. We have a Pope.)

"My most Eminent and most reverend Lord, the lord Cardinal Eugenio Pacelli!"

Italian Government troops who had been kept in reserve at the side of the square and near the famous colonnade were now rushed out and prepared to present arms when the new Pontiff appeared to impart the apostolic benediction.

They cleared a space between the point where the two halves of the colonnade began their vast sweep toward the city of Rome and the bottom of the steps leading to the entrance to St. Peter's. The crowd thus became divided into two sections, one in the body of the square and the other on the steps. Facing the basilica, the troops were drawn up in long lines of infantry, Fascist militia, grenadiers, and carabineers. A few minutes later, the Vatican radio made the first announcement that was audible to the crowd in the square. It informed the world, still awaiting the blessing, that Cardinal Pacelli's election had occurred on his birthday. Meanwhile, a large group of cardinals took positions at the window on the left of the central balcony. Their coming made it evident to everyone that the new Pope was about to appear. A hush fell on the square, the silence being broken only by a sharp word of command bringing all the soldiers to attention.

The sun had already set, and the completely cloudless sky was taking a dark blue tinge in the coming twilight. On the left of St. Peter's and in the body of the square, the sea of black was punctuated by the white, upturned faces. In the middle, between the two waiting crowds, stood the double line of soldiers, their bayonets fixed, reflecting the last rays of the light of day. On the right, the terrace over the entrance to the Vatican was filled with members of the diplomatic corps, among whom a group of Noble Guards standing at attention with drawn swords added a touch of color. The façade of St. Peter's was scarcely visible in the fading light and seemed to throw into even bolder relief the open center window silhouetted by the illumination of electric light. On it, all eyes were centered.

The new Pope appeared, preceded by a golden cross and surrounded by a group of cardinals and monsignori in ecclesiastical robes. On his head he had only a little white skullcap. He was dressed in the usual white cassock familiar to anyone who has seen a Pope, and over it, he wore a white rochet and red mozzetta edged with ermine. Around his neck he had a red stole embroidered in gold.

Another command was shouted, and the soldiers presented arms. More than half of the people present fell to their knees on the cobblestones. The new Pope raised his hand thrice, making the sign of the cross and repeating the sacramental formula, "May Almighty God, the Father, the Son, and the Holy Ghost bless you." The crowd crossed itself, and everyone rose to his feet cheering and singing. Pius XII stood for several seconds making little, friendly gestures with both hands. Then suddenly, he turned and disappeared into the recesses of St. Peter's. A few minutes later, the light in the Hall of Benedictions was extinguished, and the basilica was plunged into darkness. The crowd streamed slowly out of the square in the gathering dusk.

I had missed my guess completely on the election. Of all the cardinals, I was convinced that Pacelli had the fewest chances to be chosen for the Papacy. One of the reasons was that I thought I had an "inside" track in the Vatican. In my childhood I had gone to a Roman school where one of my classmates had been Marcantonio Pacelli, nephew of the present Pope. We had remained good friends and, in the days preceding the conclave, I had had several talks with him. We discussed the possibility of his uncle's election, but Marcantonio never gave me the slightest indication that he believed such an event was likely to occur. He pointed out that there was only one instance of a Secretary of State becoming Pope, in the whole his-

tory of the Church. This was the monk, Hildebrand, secretary to Pope
Alexander II, who became Pope Gregory VII in 1073. Being secretary
to the Pope was equivalent, in those days, to being papal Secretary of
State, but it was necessary to go back almost eight hundred fifty years
in the history of the Papacy to find even a partial precedent to
Cardinal Pacelli's election, which was unusual also in that no cardinal of the Curia had been elected Pope for more than one hundred years. All the Pontiffs since Gregory XVI, in 1831, in fact, had
gone to the Vatican straight from an Italian See. On the contrary,
Pacelli had spent all his life as a churchman in the papal Secretariat
of State and diplomatic service. Another point distinguishing his
election was that for more than two hundred years, no Roman had
sat on St. Peter's throne; that is, since Innocent XIII, who reigned
from 1721 to 1724.

Days later, one of the conclavists explained to me how the election
had taken place, although he himself had not been able to ascertain
how the voting went. He knew, however, that when the cardinals
left the Sistine Chapel after the morning balloting, Pacelli returned
to his apartment and did not touch any food. Later, he walked in
the Courtyard of St. Damasus, showing on his face signs of profound
emotion. At four in the afternoon, when the bell summoned the cardinals for the third balloting, Pacelli, visibly moved, missed a step
and fell along the stairway of the Ducal Hall which lead to the
Sistine Chapel. The general impression in Vatican circles was that
the cardinals had unanimously chosen Pacelli from the beginning of
the conclave, and that he had been elected in the morning. The fact
that a third balloting was taken in the afternoon was due to his
request, I was told, that the Sacred College repeat once more the
voting after meditating on its choice. The confirmation came in the
form of sixty-one votes for him; that is, all of them except his own
which he cast for Cardinal Granito Pignatelli di Belmonte, Dean
of the Sacred College. This seems to be borne out by a statement
by Cardinal Jean Verdier, Archbishop of Paris, who said that "the
value of Cardinal Pacelli was indisputable, and that his exceptional
personality impressed all of us since the first moment we entered
the Sistine Chapel for the balloting. The Sacred College—I may

say this without violating the oath of secrecy which applies to the activities of the conclave—could not hesitate to choose Pacelli for the Papacy."

On the other hand, the officially inspired Italian press, the day after the conclave said that Pacelli received twenty-eight votes on the first ballot, thirty-five on the second, and sixty on the third. The fact that those figures were printed in many newspapers led observers to believe that reliable intelligence reached Italian official quarters from authoritative sources. Pacelli's election caused no surprise in Vatican circles according to information which I gathered in the weeks following the conclave. It was explained to me that the choice of the Secretary of State was a logical one. Since 1936, when Pius XI was gravely ill—so ill, in fact, that his recovery was regarded as miraculous—the feeling in the Vatican was that Pacelli was being groomed for the Papacy. This does not mean that he personally aspired to become Pope, it meant only that Pius XI felt his closest collaborator was the best possible successor. He saw the war coming, and, therefore, wished a man of outstanding diplomatic gifts to be at the helm of the ship of St. Peter rather than a churchman who was unfamiliar with political questions. Of all of the princes of the Church, Pacelli was, without any doubt, the one who had the diplomatic experience necessary to steer the Church through the stormy international waters. The same thing happened in 1914, when Benedict XV was elected. Unlike his predecessor, Pius X, Benedict was a "political" Pope. His election was the natural result of world conditions brought about by the war.

From 1936, when Germany was already preparing her program of world conquest, Pius XI left nothing undone to place his Secretary of State in the forefront of the Catholic world. He sent him as his Papal Legate to the International Eucharistic Congress in Buenos Aires in 1934, to the famous French shrine of Lourdes in 1935, to the United States in 1936, again to France in 1937 and to Budapest in 1938. Pacelli traveled more than any other Italian cardinal and had, therefore, become the most widely known.

As everyone knows, the Pope is forbidden by the laws of the Church to designate his successor, and therefore, all that Pius XI could do was to give the man he thought best fitted to cope with the great responsibilities facing the Papacy an experience which was unmatched by any other cardinal.

Pacelli's visit to the United States was a part of his plan. The prestige of American Catholics increased as our country gradually became a great power during the first World War and the period following it. American Catholic organizations, such as the National Catholic Welfare Conference, were being studied and imitated in Europe. They were in the vanguard of many missionary and pastoral fields, while their large financial contributions to the Church played an important part in the expansion of the Catholic faith throughout the world. The United States was making its influence felt in Central and South America, and the Vatican, which had no diplomatic relations with Washington, was relying more and more on the action of American Catholics to bring about favorable conditions for the spreading of the faith, not only in the Western Hemisphere, but also throughout the Pacific. In view of their solidarity, wealth, and strength, the Catholic organizations in the United States performed important work and obtained guarantees and valuable assistance in behalf of the Church from the Government.

During the Pontificate of Pius XI, the Vatican had been following very closely the manifestations of religious life in the United States and had been able to gauge the concrete results obtaining from the loyal collaboration between Church and State. In the United States, the Church was free from the persecutions, the diffidence, and the anticlerical feeling which impaired its work in some European countries, such as Germany and Russia. For this reason, the Vatican had always scrupulously abstained from gestures which might mar the excellent relations with the American Catholics, giving them great freedom of action and leaving it to the local episcopate to guide their activities.

However, Pius XI had realized that his pro-Fascist attitude at the time of Italy's conquest of Ethiopia had caused strong resentment among American Catholics. In the face of strong opposition on the part of the Anglo-Saxon world to Italy's expansionist policy, the Pontiff abstained from condemning Mussolini and left the Italian clergy free to co-operate with the Fascist Government. One of the reasons for this attitude—and perhaps the most important—was that the conquest of Ethiopia would open a new missionary field for the Roman Catholic Church. As a result, there were innumerable cases of clergymen, from the humble parish priest to cardinals, who made speeches in favor of the war. Among the outstanding examples, there was the one furnished by Cardinal Alfredo Ildefonso Schuster, of Milan, who went so far as to call the campaign a "Catholic Crusade." Of course, Pius XI, as Head of the Church, which claims to be supra-natural in character, could not take an open stand since he had to consider the international repercussions of the conflict. Therefore, in referring to it, he used circumspect statements which, while showing his concern not to compromise the moral position of the Holy See, were so carefully phrased as not to offend the feelings of the Italians or of the Fascist regime.

On August 27, 1935, five weeks before Italian troops invaded Ethiopian territory, the Pontiff addressed a group of Catholic nuns in Castel Gandolfo. He urged them to pray for the maintenance of peace, but he also made clear that he did not regard the forthcoming outbreak of hostilities in East Africa as "only a war of conquest because in this case it would evidently be an unjust war." Italy, he continued, held that it was a just war, because of her need for expansion and defense. "If the need for expansion is a fact that must be taken into account," Pius said, "the right to defense has limits and moderations that must be respected." In other words, the Pontiff opposed the war on principle and admitted the aim of conquest, but did not refute the Fascist contention which justified the war on the ground that overcrowded Italy needed more land on which to settle her surplus population. Ten days later, speaking to a group of war veterans, he formulated wishes for the fulfillment of the rights and needs of a "great and good people," which, he said, was his own. These rights and needs, he stressed, should be satisfied equitably and peacefully (con la giustizia e con la pace). This could only mean that Ethiopia should submit to Fascist pressure, since the Pope had implicitly accepted Italy's "need for expansion and for defense," in East Africa. When Italy overran Ethiopia and the unequal struggle ended, the Pope spoke on May 12, 1936, at the inauguration of a Catholic press exhibition and remarked that the event coincided with "the triumphal joy of a whole and great people over a peace which should be an effective contribution and a·prelude to lasting peace in Europe and the world." It was, of course, normal that a religious leader should express his gratification for the cessation of hostilities, but strong criticism was caused by the fact that Pius not only did not deplore the subjugation of Ethiopia, which had been an independent country, but he himself shared the joy of a nation which had been almost universally condemned as an aggressor.

Pacelli's trip to the United States had many purposes: to strengthen the relations between the resentful American Catholics and the Vatican; to investigate the activities of Father Charles Edward Coughlin, parish priest of the Shrine of the Little Flower at Royal Oak, Michigan, whose broadcasts on social questions had caused considerable alarm in Rome; to interest the American Government in the crisis which the Church was traversing in Mexico; to give the Secretary of State an opportunity to make himself widely known throughout the United States, and to meet American political leaders—especially President Roosevelt.

How the information gathered by Pacelli and the personal contacts he made proved invaluable to the Vatican and resulted in very close co-operation between Washington and Rome will be seen later. Pacelli achieved all these aims, except one. He did not succeed in inducing Washington to interfere with Mexico's anticlerical policy. In April, 1936, Pius XI issued an encyclical in which he spoke of the "enemies of God and Christ who have succeeded in winning over many of the lukewarm and timorous . . . now participating in the de-Christianization of a people that owes its most beautiful glories to religion." He regarded the situation of the Church in Mexico as one of the most serious problems to be solved, and it is not to be wondered that Pacelli attempted all in his power to enlist Washington's support. He failed because United States' interference in the internal affairs of another country conflicted with Roosevelt's Good Neighbor Policy and would have caused unfavorable reaction not only among the highly susceptible Mexicans, but throughout

Latin America. Conditions in Mexico remained, therefore, pretty much as they were while the Holy See was forced to await improvement of conditions from the action of the Mexican clergy themselves.

Upon his arrival in New York, Pacelli displayed great interest in the activities of Father Coughlin. Some months before, L'Osservatore Romano had published editorials containing a certain amount of criticism of the parish priest from Royal Oak. The Vatican, however, had carefully abstained from issuing an official statement. It was feared in Rome that any action on the part of the Holy See tending to curb the activities of Coughlin would be unwise in view of the very large number of the Coughlin followers. On the other hand, Vatican officials did not conceal their uneasiness over the fact that Coughlin's social views might sooner or later prove harmful to the interests of the Church in the United States. Pacelli investigated the situation thoroughly. One evening, at a dinner given in his honor by the late Papal Duchess, Mrs. Nicholas Brady, at her estate in Long Island, he questioned some American political leaders at great length as to the political and social repercussions of Coughlin's broadcasts. He apparently convinced himself that the parish priest should be silenced. Several months later, strong-willed Archbishop Edward Mooney was appointed Bishop of the Diocese of Detroit, which includes the parish of Royal Oak.

Mooney attempted to halt Coughlin, but there was little he could do since the parish priest had the right to broadcast and express his personal views on current affairs just as any other citizen. Many Americans felt that the Pope should have forbidden him to talk, but anyone who is conversant with Vatican affairs knows that one of the main concerns of papal diplomacy in regard to the United States is to leave the American clergy absolutely free to solve their own problems, when the latter do not affect Church tenets and spiritual interests. Had the Holy See officially condemned Coughlin, millions of Americans would have certainly resented what could be regarded as interference in a purely national question of a temporal nature.

The day after his re-election on November 5, Roosevelt invited Pacelli to his home in Hyde Park. That was undoubtedly the most important meeting the Papal Secretary of State had in the United States. From the personal contact, there arose a mutual liking and respect which materialized in close co-operation between the two men.

I was at Rome's railroad station when Pacelli arrived from his American tour. Some cardinals, all the members of the diplomatic corps accredited to the Holy See, high Vatican dignitaries, and officials, as well as his three nephews, Carlo, Giulio, and Marcantonio Pacelli were at the station. Marcantonio introduced me to his Uncle as a former schoolmate, and I seized that opportunity to ask him whether he had discussed with President Roosevelt the re-establishment of diplomatic relations between the Vatican and the United States.

"I cannot speak," he replied smiling.

That was enough. If he hadn't, he would have said so. He told me that he was very happy over the results of his American trip and the welcome he had received from the "great American people."

The morning after the election, I went to the Vatican to cover the first official acts of Pius XII. Arturo Felici and his nephew Carlo, official Vatican photographers, took me through the gates as one of their assistants because Monsignor Arborio-Mella di Sant' Elia, Papal Master of the Chamber, had barred all newspapermen from the Courtyard of St. Damasus. He thought they had sensationalized Vatican news. Fortunately, I had always steered clear of Monsignor Mella. He knew me only by sight as someone he had frequently seen about the Vatican. He looked at me that day as I was standing with Felici in the Courtyard of St. Damasus but asked no questions since I had taken the precaution of equipping myself with a camera tripod. It was a nuisance, but it proved to be a very effective safe-conduct, for I was able to walk all over the Vatican grounds and witness undisturbed the ceremonies of the day.

After taking a brisk walk up and down the "second loggia" which is known as the Raphael Loggia, the Pope appeared about eleven o'clock before the many persons who crowded his anterooms. Amidst a murmur of respect, he moved between two deep lines of kneeling ecclesiastics and laymen on his way to the Sistine Chapel, where he was to receive the "obedience" from the cardinals.

The Pontiff found the Sacred College gathered in the Chapel awaiting him. Only Cardinals Tommaso Pio Boggiani and Francesco Marchetti-Selvaggiani were absent. The princes of the Church appeared in the full glory of their vestments, crimson robes and ermine capes. They were lined around the chapel walls, each standing in front of the throne he had occupied in the Conclave. In the center of the altar's top step, a throne had been placed, facing the chapel and with its back to the altar. On this throne, the new Pope seated himself while his court formed around him at the bottom of the steps.

First, Cardinal Camillo Caccia Dominioni, dean of the cardinal deacons, and then, Cardinal Nicola Canali, sub-dean of the same order, rose from their thrones to make their "obedience." As they moved, they threw over their shoulders the enormous cappa magna, a mantle of scarlet silk which, being more than twenty-five feet long, trailed on the floor behind them. The two cardinals, in turn, knelt before the throne, reverently bending over the cross embroidered in gold on the toes of the Pope's slippers. Then they placed themselves just behind the papal throne, one to the left and the other to the right. One by one, while the choir sang the triumphal notes of a Te Deum of thankfulness, other cardinals repeated the obeisance performed by the first two. After prostrating themselves at the Pope's feet, the cardinals returned to their thrones, their long capes sweeping the floor behind them.

When two of the oldest cardinals, Granito Pignatelli di Belmonte and Donato Sbarretti, approached the altar for their act of "obedience," the Pope rose from his throne and, before they could kneel, embraced them affectionately, in order to spare the two octogenarians the effort of bending.

A microphone on a movable tripod was then brought close to the papal throne, and into it the Pope delivered in Latin, his first radio appeal to the people of the world. He read the message from a typewritten text handed to him by the Papal Master of the Chamber. The lucid style in which the message was written, however, left no doubt that it flowed from the Pope's own pen. In a clear ringing voice Pius called on mankind to forget its quarrels and enjoy the "sublime gift of peace which is desired by all honest souls and which is the fruit of charity and justice."

All the traces of mourning in the Vatican for the death of Pius XI had disappeared that day. Gone were the half-staffed flags, the black crepe, and the violet robes. Every palace was gay with the yellow and white colors of the Holy See flying in the warm breeze of an unusually early spring.

The choice of Cardinal Pacelli for the Papacy was welcomed in every country in Europe and in the Western Hemisphere, with the exception of Germany. Nazi newspapers pointed to the fact that Pius XII had been Secretary of State to Pius XI, the Pontiff who had been constantly attacking the Nazi movement and doctrine. They assumed an attitude of diffident reserve, despite the fact that the new Pope had been for many years, nuncio in Munich and, therefore, knew the German psychology, customs, and language.

France, England, and the United States voiced their undisguised satisfaction, which was based on the same reasons that had prompted the Nazi coolness. The French press stated flatly that the new Pope was "Franco-phile," a statement which aroused the ire of the Italians. Polemics went on for days between the newspapers of the two countries. The Fascist press hotly refuted what it called a "base and impudent attempt on the part of atheists and Freemasons" to create difficulties for Pius XII at the very beginning of his Pontificate. It saw in the French attitude a maneuver to commit the Pontiff to a policy favoring the democracies instead of the totalitarian states and predicted that the "facts will speak for themselves."

It is to be doubted whether the election pleased Mussolini. If one must judge from the Nazi reaction, it seems clear that the Axis was hoping to see on the throne of St. Peter's, a man other than Pius XI's closest collaborator. However, Italy's dictator instructed the Italian press to play up the fact that the new Pope would have no interest in causing an open breach with Fascist Italy, "which has solidly created the nation's spiritual and political unity." Virginio

Gayda, Fascist mouthpiece, wrote in the *Giornale d'Italia*, that an improvement of relations between the Vatican and the Axis was to be expected if for no other reason than that the affairs of the Church would now be directed by a "younger man." In an effort to hide the official feeling of discomfiture over the election of the cardinal who was not Mussolini's candidate, he interpreted the Pope's first message to the world as expressing support of Italy's policy of aggression. Pius XII, he wrote, spoke of "peace, which manifests itself in Christian charity, but not in the abstract themes of democratic pacifists who use pacifists' theories to preserve their privileges and illegitimate possessions."

The attitude of the Italian Government on the election was summed up by Guido Rocco, head of the Information Bureau at the Ministry of Press and Propaganda. When I asked him what he thought of it, he said, "It could have been worse."

The Germans took the same attitude. "A careful diplomat is, undoubtedly, better than an impulsive, irascible old man as Pius XI was," Count Von Plessen, chancellor of the German Embassy said.

Amidst all the polemics, and the biased interpretations of the papal speech on the part of the international press, which betrayed the intention of the lay governments to present Pacelli as a Pontiff in sympathy with their political views, Anne O'Hare McCormick, of *The Times*, wrote what perhaps was the most authoritative comment on the election in a dispatch from Berlin to *The Times* on March 2. She had been received several times by Pacelli when he was Secretary of State. She saw him again about two weeks before the death of Pius XI and was the only journalist who talked to him before he became Pope, five weeks later. What impressed Mrs. McCormick most was the warm support which Pacelli gave to Pius XI's "heroic fight against the terrible heresies of the times," and the enthusiasm he evidenced for the United States. "Pacelli," she said, "implied that American tolerance and largeness of view were more conducive to the free practice of religion than any other atmosphere."

Disappointed in the election of Pacelli, the Axis powers, on the days preceding the coronation of the new Pontiff, started a new drive to secure the appointment of at least a Secretary of State who would show understanding for their policies. In this case also, the activities of Mussolini's and Hitler's emissaries were jealously guarded. Count Bonifacio Pignatti-Morano di Custoza, Italy's ambassador to the Holy See, was received by Pius XII, as was Diego von Bergen, the German ambassador, and many other diplomatists. It was, of course, impossible to learn what was discussed in those meetings, but, as subsequent events showed, the efforts of Italy and Germany were again frustrated.

Michael Williams, Catholic writer, who was in Rome in that period on a special assignment for *The Times*, carried out a personal investigation of the Axis maneuver and stated in a dispatch that Mussolini had instructed the Italian Ambassador to oppose the nomination of the handsome, blue-eyed Neapolitan fisherman's son, Cardinal Luigi Maglione, for Secretary of State. The Axis opposition against Maglione, who had been nuncio to Paris and was reputed to be a Francophile, was so strong that some Vatican quarters doubted his appointment. However, Pius XII showed that, like his predecessor, he was not going to subordinate the interests of the Church to those of the lay powers. On March 11, he announced Maglione's appointment.

Apart from whatever political implications this step might have had, Pius XII's decision was the right one. Pacelli, as Secretary of State, had been Nuncio to Germany and knew that country thoroughly. Maglione, on the other hand, had spent many years as Nuncio to Paris, which he left in 1935, when Pius XI created him cardinal, and he had a first-hand knowledge of France. In addition, Pius XII and his new Secretary were tied to each other by a friendship that began when they were classmates in the Capranica College in Rome, where they studied for their priesthood. That feeling had been cemented by long years of collaboration in the period of Pacelli's tenure of the Secretariat of State. Needless to say, the appointment was hailed in the democratic press as another example of the Pope's pro-democratic leanings. This rejoicing proved to be so irksome to the Axis powers that *L'Osservatore Romano* was forced to throw some cold water on French enthusiasm by pointing out that the Vatican was neither for nor against this or that form of government, since its attitude is that it accepts and recognizes legally constituted lay authorities provided their policies are not harmful to the interests of the Church.

The importance which the civilized world attached to the Papacy at a time when Europe was in a state of ferment and the shadow of war hovered ominously over the international horizon had an eloquent proof in the care taken by many nations in choosing the special missions that were to attend the impressive coronation ceremony in St. Peter's on March 12, 1939. This interest was dictated chiefly by political motives. Many governments realized that the Vatican was a great spiritual force and coveted its support because it would materially strengthen their internal and international positions.

A few days before the coronation, the special missions of the lay powers began to arrive in Rome. For the first time in the history of Vatican-American relations, the United States designated a representative in the person of Joseph P. Kennedy, Ambassador to London, who is Catholic. The Duke of Norfolk, also Catholic, and the leading member of England's aristocracy, was to represent King George and the British Government. France sent Paul Claudel, former French ambassador to the United States and an eminent Catholic writer and poet. Deeply religious Ireland paid the greatest possible homage to the Pope—her Prime Minister, Eamon de Valera attended the ceremony personally. Italy delegated Crown Prince Humbert and Foreign Minister Galeazzo Ciano.

Germany was the only one of the great European powers who refused to pay special attention to the Vatican. She merely instructed her ambassador, Diego von Bergen, to represent her. On the day of the coronation, the members of no less than thirty-five special missions and the entire diplomatic corps were to be seen in the special tribune erected on one side of the central nave in St. Peter's.

It was still pitch dark when I arrived in St. Peter's Square on the morning of March twelfth, but people were already gathering. The first light of dawn was tinting the dome of the basilica with violet as the massive iron gates were thrown open, admitting the first comers. They had a long wait ahead of them, for the ceremony was scheduled to start at eight-thirty. However, the Pope did not actually appear in St. Peter's until almost nine. The people flocked in such numbers and so continuously, that by seven o'clock, the church was almost completely full, and half an hour later, the gates had to be closed—there was no more available space.

A magnificent procession, gay with the colors indicated for such a joyous occasion as a coronation, accompanied the new Pope to the throne, which was placed in the apse with its back toward the Altar of the Cathedra. The Swiss Guards were in orange and yellow, Noble Guards in red tunics and white knee breeches, the choristers in violet, and monsignori in purple; the cardinals in vermilion and ermine, the friars in brown, and the priests in black. They were strung out in a double line all the way up the nave from the entrance to the throne and were merely the brighter tones on the already motley palette of the basilica.

The lighted candles glinting from burnished breastplates and bared swords, the flash of jewels in pectoral crosses and precious rings, the glitter of the Papal triregnum and the miters, carried on cushions by the chamberlains in red robes and crmine capes, the sheen of velvet and silk added to the scene's richness and luster.

All branches of ecclesiastical activity, all ranks of the Catholic hierarchy were represented in the procession. There were priests, bishops, cardinals, monsignori, bearded missionaries and sandaled Capuchins, patriarchs of the Eastern Rites, Jesuits, black-skinned clergy from Africa and slant-eyed priests from the Far East, choir boys and acolytes, judges of the Ecclesiastical Tribunal and mitred abbots, soldiers and gentlemen-in-waiting.

The Pope sat on the sedia gestatoria, which rested on the shoulders of the twelve sediari in red damask. The sedia itself was a throne of red velvet and gold, bearing at the back the cypress, which was the emblem of Pope Leo XIII, for whom it was originally built. Over the Pope's head floated a white canopy embroidered in gold, resting on eight poles carried by eight ecclesiastical Advocates of the Tribunal of the Signatura, each in a rochet and purple cape.

On either side of, and slightly above, the Pope's head, were two semi-circular, ostrich feather fans. These, perhaps, recalled to many minds the similar fans used in the procession of the emperor under whose reign St. Peter, the first Pope, suffered martyrdom.

The Pope wore his full pontifical vestments, but they were completely hidden from sight by his enormous cape, richly embroidered in gold, which was so long and ample that it covered most of the floor of the *sedia gestatoria*. On his head was a silver miter studded with jewels. His hands were covered with white gloves and on the third finger of the right hand, the Fisherman's Ring, emblem of Papal authority, could be seen.

He was very pale, and his eyes looked weary and shrunken behind the lenses of his spectacles, as if he had spent a sleepless night. As he was carried up the nave, he blessed the people to the right and left, lifting his hand with a slow gesture, and conveying the impression that he was mortally tired.

The faithful in the church greeted him with tremendous handclaps, cheers, and shouts of "*Viva il Papa*," but not a muscle of his face moved, nor did he give the slightest indication that the applause had been either heard or appreciated. Only his hand, ceaselessly making the gesture of blessing, showed that he was aware of the crowd's presence.

Surrounding the Pope in the *sedia gestatoria* were members of the ecclesiastical and lay courts. Mingling with the Pope's ecclesiastical privy chamberlains, with the two principal masters of ceremonies in violet cassocks, surplices and rochets, and with the three cardinals, who were to assist the Pope in celebrating the mass, in cloaks of silver lamé over vermilion robes, were gentlemen of the ancient princely houses of Rome who occupied the highest posts of honor in the Vatican court.

Here were Prince Marcantonio Colonna, prince assistant to the pontifical throne; Prince Giovanni Battista Sacchetti, quartermaster major of the apostolic palace; Prince Camillo Massimo, superintendent of the pontifical posts; Marquis Giacomo Serlupi-Crescenzi, equerry major of the Pope, together with a number of privy chamberlains of the Cape and Sword.

Their names, their appearance, and their costumes all harked back to centuries long past, and they seemed to have stepped out of a portrait by Velásquez. All wore doublet and hose, medieval ruffs at their throats, and chains of gold about their necks and shoulders supporting glittering decorations. They had long velvet capes hanging down their backs and rapiers at their sides.

With them walked the Commander of the Swiss Guard, Colonel de Sury d' Aspremont, resplendent with shining breastplate and plumed helmet and officers of the Noble Guard in scarlet tunics with golden epaulets, burnished helmets with long black horsehair plumes and black and white egrets, buckskin breeches and top boots.

Before the papal court came six mace bearers in black doublet and hose, with white lace at their wrists, violet capes, and rapiers hanging from their belts. On either side was a single row of Swiss Guards —representing the Catholic Cantons of Switzerland—carrying long serpentine swords with heavy hilts resting on their shoulders and the points straight up.

When Pope Pius reached the papal altar, he descended from the sedia and celebrated Mass. He was at the papal altar only to recite the opening prayers, then for the elevation of the Host, and at the end, for the final benediction. All the rest of the time he was seated on the throne at the other end of the apse from the altar.

The culminating point of the ceremony came at the elevation of the Host. While the Pope was at the high altar, which is placed under the dome of the basilica in such a position that the officiant faces the people in the nave over the altar itself, a word, in German, as sharp as the crack of a whip, resounded through the church, causing all the Swiss Guards with halberds who stood in a circle around the altar, to drop to their right knees, at the same time bringing their left hands to their helmets in the salute. They were imitated by the Noble Guards near the papal throne and by the Palatine Guard in the body of the basilica.

When the Pope lifted the Host on high, the cardinals, bishops, and other prelates and ecclesiastics assisting in saying the mass fell on the altar steps, prostrating themselves in prayer. At the same instant, music filled the Basilica, pervading it with a mellow, yet vibrant melody. This music came from the famous Vatican Silver Trumpets, whose players were hidden in the highest point of the dome of St. Peter's. So deceptive were the echoes caused by the dome that the music seemed to spring out of the air itself.

The Pope, having given his final blessing, remounted the *sedia gestatoria* and was carried out of the basilica amid cheers and applause even more deafening than that which greeted his arrival. Shortly after, he appeared on the outer balcony of St. Peter's for the actual ceremony of coronation.

The scene at St. Peter's Square when the coronation reached its climax was almost overwhelming in its dramatic and stirring qualities. The whole piazza and the adjacent Piazza Rusticucci were packed tight, as was also about half of the newly cleared Via della Conciliazione—a very wide avenue connecting St. Peter's with the Castel Sant' Angelo.

This sea of black was punctuated here and there with islands of a lighter hue indicating the presence of nuns in white headdresses, ecclesiastical students in red or violet or mauve robes, according to their nationality, monks and friars in brown or white according to their order, and women wearing hats of all colors of the rainbow. From this mass of humanity rose hails and cheers.

Various as were the tongues in which the crowd expressed itself, there was in every mind only one thought. Every eye was riveted on the central balcony in the façade of St. Peter's, every ear strained not to miss a word of what was being boomed out by the metallic voice of loud-speakers disposed at various points around the piazza.

In the brilliant sunshine, framed by the huge door leading to the balcony from the mysterious recesses of St. Peter's, and against a background of silver lamé draperies embroidered with a pattern resembling the fleur-de-lis in gold, the actors in the supreme scene of the coronation could not have stood out in bolder relief if they had been on a stage.

To the majority in the piazza, the figures of the Pope and those standing around him appeared tiny, dwarfed by distance and the immensity of their surroundings. Yet, the Pope could be seen clearly by all. He was enveloped from head to foot in a magnificent cape of cream-colored silk, which fell in lazy folds from his shoulders to his feet. He sat on a throne, the red velvet of which could be seen behind his head and under his hands at the armrests.

Above the Pontiff's head floated two flabella, or semi-circular ostrich feather fans, lending to the scene a touch of barbaric splendor and Eastern opulence. From the edge of the balcony at the Pope's feet hung a tapestry with a wide edge of red, and in the center, the arms of Pope Pius IX on a white field. At the Pope's elbows were two cardinals in crimson robes under white capes and wearing white miters. Surrounding him were a few members of his ecclesiastical court in cassocks and surplices.

Before the Pope, though on a lower level, stood the Auditor of the Tribunal of the Sacred Roman Rota in a white tunicle holding aloft a golden spear-headed cross. In the background, the glittering helmets, bared swords and scarlet tunics of two resplendent Noble Guards made a bright splash of color. For the first time since 1870 the red flag of the Holy Roman Church was seen on this occasion. It was carried by the pontifical standard bearer, the Marquis Patrizi Naro Montoro.

Suddenly, there was a brighter flash from the balcony as the sun lit the jewels adorning the triregnum which the Dean of the Cardinal Deacons was holding suspended above the Pope's head. At the same moment, the Cardinal's voice filled the piazza through the loud-speakers.

"Receive the tiara adorned with three crowns," he said in Latin, "and know that thou art father of princes and kings, rector of the world upon earth, vicar of our Lord Jesus Christ to whom be honor and glory, world without end."

The silvery voices of the hidden Sistine Choir were drowned by the crowd's loud "Amen," and at the same instant the triregnum descended slowly upon the Pope's head.

THIRD CHAPTER

How does the Vatican live? Where does it obtain the means necessary to finance its huge administration and to foster its spiritual mission?

These questions will never be given a satisfactory answer because the Holy See does not publish budgets as the lay governments, and it guards jealously all data concerning its economic situation. However, a certain amount of information is available which, though incomplete, gives a general idea of the various sources of income.

The Pope, as already stated, is an absolute sovereign and the sole owner of all Vatican property. In his person are concentrated the three powers: legislative, executive, and judiciary. A commission of cardinals, which has under its jurisdiction the Governor of Vatican City aided by a group of technical advisors, represents the Pope in the exercise of the first two, while three tribunals attend to the latter. The first of these tribunals is a lower court, the second, called Sacra Rota, the Court of Appeals, and the third, the Apostolic Signatura, the Supreme Court. These institutions control incomes, expenditures, monopolies, taxes, registration of acts granting Vatican citizenship or residence, and the issuing of birth and death certificates.

The State of Vatican City is financed with proceeds derived from the sale of stamps, the slight charge on legal acts, the extra price placed by the papal monopoly on goods received in bond, and by direct subsidies on the part of the Holy See which before the outbreak of the present war amounted to nearly two hundred thousand dollars a year. Stamps are a large source of the income. The first time they were issued, soon after the Lateran Treaty, sales totaled one hundred fifty thousand dollars. Since then, they have averaged fifty thousand dollars a year, for there was hardly a pilgrim who, on visiting the Vatican, did not stop at one of the four papal post offices to mail cards and letters to the folks back home.

The income from the other Vatican activities is kept secret, as is that of the so-called "obolo," or "Peter's Pence," for Saint Peter's, namely, the offering of the faithful at collections taken in churches throughout the world for the upkeep of the Holy See. The proceeds from these collections are turned over to the Pope personally, who disposes of them as he sees fit. Since there is no administration for these funds, it is impossible even to hazard a guess as to their amount, which before the war Vatican experts estimated at many millions of lire. The income from the "obolos," however, varies with economic conditions. In the past decade, I was told, it had suffered greatly from the general depression. Moreover, financial restrictions imposed by many governments had also directly affected the flow of money to Rome. For instance, Monsignor Cesare Orsenigo, papal nuncio in Berlin, was said to have in custody millions of marks which couldn't be sent to the Vatican because of the Nazi laws prohibiting the exportation of currency.

The financial position of the Holy See was immeasurably strengthened by the signing of the Lateran Treaty whereby Italy handed over to the Vatican one billion lire's worth of state bonds and seven hundred fifty millions in cash, or what at that time was the American equivalent of about one hundred fifty million dollars, as compensation for the economic loss of the papal states incorporated in the Italian Kingdom in 1870. Pius XI created a special commission to administer this fund which, as far as is known, is still intact.

The Pope is his own treasurer and has to account to no one. As a result, even his most intimate collaborators have no idea of the financial situation of the Vatican. When Benedict XV, who was noted for his prodigality, died, Cardinal Gasparri, as Camerlengo during the period of Vacant See, made an inventory and found that the Holy See was literally broke. His first task was to negotiate a fifty thousand lire loan to defray the expenses of the conclave. To avoid a repetition of this humiliating situation, Pius XI, soon after his election, set aside an unspecified amount to be used only for conclave expenses.

Benedict XV spent money as fast as he received it. He kept huge sums in a drawer of his desk and disposed of them personally for the creation of Catholic schools, convents, missionary settlements,

and the like. A bishop who intended to ask the Pope to finance a
project for the building of a convent in Palestine was warned not
to mention the subject because, on seeing the request for the audience, Benedict had remarked:

"I am sure he is going to ask me for money to carry out his plan,
and I don't have it."

Therefore, when he was received, the bishop talked of general
subjects such as the condition of the Church in Palestine, the number of converts, etc., without even hinting at his project. Finally, as
he was taking leave, Benedict said,

"Well, what about your plan? I am sure that the estimate must be
prohibitive."

"It's about one hundred thousand lire, Your Holiness," stam-
mered the embarrassed prelate.

"In that case, We shall contribute," said the Pope. He opened a
drawer and handed the surprised bishop a packet containing one
hundred one-thousand-lire bills.

The population of the Vatican consists of nine hundred sixty-three
residents, according to an unofficial census in 1942. The residents account for a third of that number. The ecclesiastical population is
slightly above one hundred, including nuns. However, there are
many more employees of the Vatican who are neither citizens nor
resident and have been granted by the Italian Government exemp-
tion from military service because of the special nature of their tasks.
Four-fifths of the Vatican citizens are Italian-born; the other fifth is
composed of the Swiss Guards, the Vatican-born, and a sprinkling of
citizens of other nations. In 1939, the United States, for instance, was
represented in the Vatican by only one prelate; able, esteemed Monsignor Joseph Patrick Hurley whom Pius XII, in recognition of his
qualities, appointed Bishop of St. Augustine, Florida, in 1940.

Except for the cardinals who acquire it automatically, Vatican citizenship, as distinguished from nationality, coincides always with one's
functions and residence within the borders of the midget state. The
son of a Vatican citizen has no hereditary right to citizenship; it is
granted him only by the Pope personally. He loses it when he is of
age, at which time he automatically becomes Italian. The residents

are those people such as servants, whose presence in the Vatican is not necessarily permanent.

Before Pius XI's reign, Vatican clerks were very much envied by the Italian bureaucrats. They worked from nine until one and had the rest of the day to themselves. The jobs demanded so little effort that they were invariably bequeathed from father to son, generation after generation. There are any number of jokes about the Vatican employees. A classic remark made by Pius IX was told me by Silvio Negro, one of Italy's ablest Vatican experts.

An old and trusted clerk asked to be received by the Pope in a special audience.

"Holy Father," he said, "I have come to ask for a favor. I have a grown son who does not want to study and loafs from morning until night. All he thinks about is going hunting. . . ."

"I understand," Pius interrupted, "you think he is qualified to enter our administration."

(The son got the job.)

Pius XI, whose father had been an industrialist in the north of Italy, believed in efficiency. He really put the Vatican employees to work with regular office hours and changed many of their personal habits. However, as a compensation, the Vatican civil servants, today, still enjoy a number of privileges very much coveted by the Italians, in spite of the fact that they are under a one hundred per cent totalitarian form of government. They buy the necessities of life at what before the war was half the price charged in Italy, pay no rent and taxes except on letters and telegrams, and are exempt from military service although the Vatican is jokingly referred to as the most militarized state in the world, more than 50 per cent of its population being soldiers.

The temporal army of the Vatican is composed of the Swiss Guards, Papal Gendarmes, Palatine and Noble Guards. It totals about five hundred men. The Swiss Guards, whose colorful uniform with blue, red, and yellow stripes was designed by Raphael, were first brought to Rome in 1506, by Julius II, who found his kingdom and his own life were in danger because of the frequent political crimes and invasions of the papal states by foreign powers. The members of this corps are recruited from four Catholic Swiss cantons—Uri, Schwyz, Unterwalden, Lucerne—and must be bachelors between eighteen and twenty-five years of age, five feet eleven inches tall, and with no physical defects. They are one hundred twenty-two in number, including the "General Staff." The whole corps is composed of a commander-in-chief with the rank of colonel, a lieutenant colonel, a major, a captain, a first lieutenant, a second lieutenant, four sergeants, ten corporals, one hundred halberdiers, and two drummers. The Papal Gendarmes, with a black tunic, white pants, and fur busbies, are the Vatican police and number one hundred eighty-four. The Palatine Guard, sky-blue jacket, red band at the waist, red side stripes on the pants and fur shakos, consists of a regiment formed by two battalions in addition to a band. It is the guard of honor in the papal antechamber and at solemn ceremonies in St. Peter's. The Noble Guards, in red tunics and white knee breeches, are the escort of honor of the Pope. They are cadets of patrician families from all parts of Italy and are commanded by a Roman prince.

Being not only a spiritual but temporal ruler, the Pontiff has his own court which, to a large extent, is still faithful to tradition. Today, it is substantially an Italian court of the Renaissance type, with titles and costumes used in the sixteenth century, despite a religious character which is proper to the unique figure of its sovereign. It is composed of what are called the papal "chapel" and "family." The former, which is the religious court, includes all the representatives of those ecclesiastical bodies which make up the cortege of the Pope during public functions, such as cardinals, patriarchs, archbishops, bishops, abbots, and prince assistants at the Papal throne, who are the first-born of the Roman houses Orsini and Colonna; the latter, all persons who hold an office recognized by protocol. The "family" is regarded as the court proper, and among its most important members are cardinals, prelates, and laymen who perform duties in the Vatican, including the Secretary of State, the Master of the Chamber, and Secret Participating Chamberlains as well as Privy Chamberlains of the Cape and Sword.

As a sovereign state, the Vatican also issues its own currency which is minted in Italy. It is of the same alloy, size, and weight as the corresponding Italian coins. Those of gold and silver bear the effigy of the reigning Pope and those of brass and nickel his coat-of-arms and the papal keys. They have par value with Italian currency but not in the rest of the world, and, since the amount in circulation totals only one million lire, the Holy See uses Italian bank notes in addition.

The Vatican is the smallest sovereign state in the world with a one-hundred-eight-acre area which can be comfortably toured in a forty-five minute walk. Its borders, marked by a tall brick wall built by Paul III as a defense against invasions in the sixteenth century, are within the city of Rome. Although it is commonly referred to as a "state," the seat of the papacy is hardly more than a group of palaces befitting the residence of a sovereign, with a few modern unpretentious office buildings, for the administration of Holy See property, and apartment houses, scattered throughout its huge gardens. The palace where the Pope lives is a continuation of St. Peter's Church with which it is connected through internal passages so that the Pontiff attends functions without stepping outside his domain. Inside the tiny state are also the famous Vatican museums.

After the Lateran Treaty, Pius XI undertook a full-fledged public works program to give his people some of the facilities and conveniences of modern life, but he forbade both citizens and residents to engage in any form of private commercial activity. So, one finds no shops in the Vatican, except a general store, where only the local population and the members of religious institutes residing in Rome, may buy all the necessities of life; a pharmacy, which is managed by monks; and a bar which sells Italian soft drinks and excellent pastry.

Another bar is in the sacristy of Saint Peter's. It does a thriving business on days when solemn functions are held in the basilica, especially during pontifical Masses, which last several hours. I invariably slipped in with some colleagues for a fast, mild drink or a cup of coffee, and had to fight my way through prelates, seminarists, as well as laymen who packed the small room.

Among other services, the papal city has its own newspaper, L'Osservatore Romano, which is extremely well-informed and a library containing many thousands of volumes which was completely reorganized under Pius XI with the assistance of experts from the United

ministration of dioceses, and with affairs concerning Catholics of various Oriental rites. At the head of the others are cardinals of Curia, thus called because of their offices in the government of the Church. When the Pope is the prefect, then a cardinal is the Secretary.

According to statistics I was able to obtain before leaving Italy, Catholics of all rites totaled 348,507,000, of whom 341,500,000 were of the Roman rite. Evangelical Christians were estimated at 235,000,000, and Oriental Christians at 140,000,000, making a total of 723,500,000 Christians of all denominations. If to this figure are added 18,000,000 Jews and 243,000,000 Mohammedans, the grand total for all members of monotheist religions is about 985,000,000, as compared with 814,-000,000 politheists in Eastern Asia and India, and including 94,000,000 pagans.

Because of the fact that they are the most important members of the Roman Catholic clergy, the cardinals are the natural advisors of the Pope, and, in some cases, his principal collaborators in the central government of the Church. The cardinalate, incidentally, is not a rank in the true sense of the word but a title which may or may not be conferred according to circumstances. The hierarchical scale ends with the bishop—and the Pope himself is Bishop of Rome. The cardinals form what is called the Sacred College which theoretically consists of seventy members but in reality falls short of that number. One of the reasons for the vacancies is that, should the Pope die suddenly, his successor will be able to fill the vacant places with men whom he wishes to have as his own collaborators. In spite of the fact that the Sacred College in 1943, had only forty-four members, Pius XII created no new cardinals, probably because any appointment would have been given a political significance, which the Church wished to avoid in view of the war.

The cardinal who holds the greatest power within the Church is the Secretary of State. He is not only the foreign minister of the Pope, but sole minister for all that does not deal directly with religious matters. He confers with the Head of the Church at least once a day, receives ambassadors and other personalities whom the Pope does not see personally, signs treaties in his name, and is the only cardinal who resides in the Vatican Palace. In short, the Secretary of State is the exponent of papal political activity, and direct heir to the tasks which during the Renaissance period were performed by the "cardinal nephew." That was the time when cardinals were often created by the Pope at the suggestion of kings and princes and who, therefore, were more concerned with furthering the political interests of the lay sovereigns than those of the Church. For this reason, the Pope felt that only a member of his immediate family could be the loyal and faithful interpreter of his decisions.

Invariably the Secretary of State is a man who has had experience in the diplomatic service of the Church, and who, as a result, is acquainted with its methods, aims and problems. On the other hand, the Pope may have no diplomatic experience. He may have been chosen from among the heads of a See, or may come from a congregation dealing with purely religious matters. In this case, the power of the Secretary of State is even greater. Pius X, who was Archbishop of Venice before his elevation to the Papacy, left the entire direction of Vatican policy to Cardinal Merry del Val, one of the greatest Secretaries of State in modern times. He merely gave broad directives and relied on the experience and judgment of his collaborators. Benedict XV, instead, was an experienced diplomatist and his control of Vatican policy was much stricter as was that of Pius XI, by nature and temperament an authoritarian, who was for a time in the Vatican diplomatic service as nuncio to Warsaw. Cardinal Maglione, Secretary of State under Pius XII found himself in the same position as his predecessors, Pacelli and Gasparri. He merely executed instructions, the initiative for any major political move resting with the Pontiff. But, even in this case, the power of a Secretary of State is unmatched by that of any other cardinal.

The Church considers itself a society which has within itself all the characteristics and elements of lay organizations and claims to be superior to any other because of its spiritual and universal nature. Its aim is to "save souls," that is, to make converts, regardless of race and nationality. The constant task of the Church is to obtain the best possible conditions for the development of its program within the framework of the lay state. The directives for her policy come from the Vatican which, as the guiding body of the Church, gives the official decisions as to what to believe and how to act as well as practical rules for religious activities in the lay world, formulates new programs and develops those already existing, defends the religious life of the Catholics, and is, finally, the supreme organ possessing the means with which to fight internal and external pressure. When the state interferes with its program, the Holy See, in common with lay governments, resorts to diplomacy in its dealings with the civil power, not only to protect its rights, but also to prevent forces hostile to itself from influencing the policies of the State. In this case, its activities become purely political since it attempts to negotiate with the lay government an agreement called "concordat" which will permit the coexistence of both the spiritual and lay powers.

Of all the organs of the Roman Curia, those which deal more specifically with Vatican policy are the Secretariat of State, the Congregation of Extraordinary Affairs, and the Congregation of the Ceremonial. The Secretariat of State has the task of negotiating with foreign governments. This is done either directly or through the nuncios and internuncios who are the Vatican permanent diplomatic agents accredited to the lay powers, and with the assistance of the Congregation of Extraordinary Affairs which deals mainly in agreements made with civil governments. The Congregation of the Ceremonial concerns itself with questions of precedence and of protocol for cardinals and lay diplomats accredited to the Holy See. In 1943, the Vatican had regular diplomatic relations with thirty-seven nations, not including twenty-five apostolic delegates.

The Nuncios have the rank of ambassador and the internuncios that of minister. Since the Congress of Vienna in 1815, they have been granted the right of being deans of the diplomatic corps, regardless of their length of service. In addition, there are the apostolic delegates, who are the Pope's representatives accredited to the clergy of foreign countries. They have no diplomatic standing in theory but often, being the Holy See's only representatives on the spot, they in actual practice act as intermediaries between the Vatican and the civil government.

Specifically, the nuncios and internuncios must: secure the respect of the Church interests by political powers; reconcile whenever pos-

sible the divergent viewpoints of Vatican and lay authorities on matters of interest to both; cement relations between the individual countries and the Holy See; ensure the carrying out of papal instructions,
and the application of canon law and decisions rendered by the
Roman congregations as well as immediate obedience to papal wishes;
maintain and consolidate unity of faith, discipline, feeling, and action
in keeping with the directives from Rome.

These objectives are attained not only through diplomatic relations
with the lay powers, but also through the local bishops and clergy,
influential Catholic personalities, and organizations in the political,
economic, cultural fields. The carrying out of the program and the
means to be used are left to the initiative of the nuncios, who, through
their personal contacts and the Catholic organizations, attempt to
exercise their influence on the civil administrative bodies and the
faithful themselves.

The Vatican is probably the best-informed power in the world.
News both political and ecclesiastical pours into its various offices
through a gigantic machine which extends to the farthest corners of
the globe. Nuncios and apostolic delegates have access to the same
sources of information as ambassadors and report to the Secretariat
of State just as ambassadors report to their foreign office. When their
dispatches contain data which the Secretariat of State deems important, they are submitted to the Pope in concise form.

By far the most copious information comes to the Vatican from
the bishops. There are more than thirteen hundred bishops in various
parts of the world who send periodical reports on all matters they
consider of interest to the Holy See. Of course, wars hamper the
smooth functioning of this machinery because of the dislocation of
international communications. But in peace time, an enormous amount
of correspondence reaches the Vatican every day in the year. Reports
from little-known parts of the world also are sent by missionaries.
Moreover, archbishops and bishops in ordinary, as distinguished from
"titular" bishops who are granted that title because of special missions, must see the Pope personally at least once every five years if
residing in Europe, and every ten years if residing elsewhere. These
are called visits "ad limina." The same obligation extends also to the

vicars apostolic. Upon arrival at the Vatican, each visitor must submit
a report of his diocese based on a specific set of questions and giving
a very detailed statement of spiritual, social, material, and ecclesiastical
conditions among the clergy and the faithful. The information is ex-
traordinarily accurate, especially as far as sentiments and feelings of
people in the various countries are concerned. The diplomat comes in
contact with only a limited section of the population of the country
in which he lives, and it is usually a section which does not represent
the mind of the country as a whole. The bishops instead, live among
people of all classes and have daily meetings with priests within their
diocese who report the slightest variation in public opinion. Nuncios
and internuncios send any reports of an urgent nature in code by
cable or wireless; reports from bishops and missionaries are mailed.

One of the advantages the Vatican has over temporal government
is that while the policy of the latter follows clear-cut lines on bases of
easily discernible interests, that of the former cannot be clearly identified or defined. The Vatican places no limit of time on the achievement of its ends. It thinks of itself in terms of eternity, and its dealings with foreign powers are, therefore, based on the assumption that
the Holy See can afford to wait since men are mortal and the Church
is eternal.

Formerly, all people took their religion seriously, and there were no
attacks against religion as such. The Church fought against heresy and
schism but not against governments which deliberately wished to de-
stroy Christianity. The wars against the Turks were among the few
examples of conflicts against non-Christian powers in which any religious state was involved. Today, some powers want to abolish religion altogether or replace it with new nationalist doctrines, and
others are trying to force the Church into line with their lay policies.

The weapons have changed as radically as the fight itself. In the
past centuries, the Church had temporal power and could enforce the
religious edicts of the Pope with armies either of its own or of powerful Catholic rulers who were ready to unsheathe the sword in defense
of the Church. When Rome became the capital of the new Italian
Kingdom in 1870, the Vatican was deprived of the last possibility of
ever having the temporal force necessary to play a part as a political

factor and was obliged to rely to a large extent upon public opinion for the attainment of its objectives.

Paradoxically enough, the moral strength and power of the Church has increased in modern times because of its temporal weakness. Catholic solidarity with the Church is so strong that the words of a Pope, though backed by no power of ultimatum, invariably evoke profound subterranean moral energies which, in the long run, affect mass consciousness. The Pope's prestige is such that even if he makes political mistakes or carries out an unsuccessful policy, he can always count on the loyalty and devotion of the clergy and the faithful.

The army of the Vatican is composed of the Catholics themselves; its leaders are the priests; its weapons, the written and spoken word, which wield the power of persuasion. In other words, the Vatican relies not only on diplomacy but on propaganda among the faithful and on moral sanctions for the furtherance of Catholic interests.

Despite the fact that it has no temporal threat of force to fall back on, the influence of the Holy See in the international field today is a factor with which even strongly authoritarian powers such as Germany must reckon. Bismarck, who was defeated in the *Kulturkampf*, would very likely acknowledge this if he were alive. Mussolini himself, in an article he wrote for the French newspaper, *Figaro*, in December 1934, stated that the "history of Western civilization from the time of the Roman Empire to our days shows that every time the State clashes with religion, it is always the State which ends defeated. The simple, passive resistance of the clergy and the faithful is sufficient to foil the most violent attacks on the part of the State."

Napoleon, however, did not know this and had to discover it by the process of trial and error. He harbored a profound dislike for Cardinal Consalvi, one of the greatest Papal Secretaries of State, who invariably succeeded in undoing all that the French Emperor had obtained from the weak Pius VII. One day Consalvi was summoned by Napoleon.

"Do you know that I am capable of destroying your Church?" shouted the exasperated Corsican.

"Your Majesty," was Consalvi's humble reply, "not even we priests have achieved that in eighteen centuries!"

FOURTH CHAPTER

Across the Tiber from Saint Peter's, in one of the oldest quarters of Rome near Piazza dell'Orologio, there is a narrow street not more than three hundred feet long, named Via degli Orsini, after one of the old Roman princely families. On it stands a nineteenth century, four-story, brownstone building called Palazzo Pediconi. In the third floor apartment of that archaic mansion, Eugenio Maria Giuseppe Giovanni Pacelli was born, March 2, 1876, the second son of Filippo Pacelli and Virginia Graziosi.

The Pacellis belonged to what was called the "black" nobility, the members of which were granted their titles by the Pope and not by the king. They were loyal servants of the Vatican for generations. The family came originally from Oriano, a village near the medieval town of Viterbo, not far from Rome. The grandfather of the present Pope, Marcantonio, moved to Rome in 1819, at the invitation of his uncle, Cardinal Caterini. Marcantonio studied canon law, and, in 1851, Cardinal Giacomo Antonelli, Pius IX's Secretary of State, appointed him under-secretary of the interior for the papal domains. Marcantonio held this post until the end of the temporal powers of the Pope in 1870, when Italian troops occupied the city which was subsequently proclaimed the capital of the young Italian Kingdom. In 1861, he founded *L'Osservatore Romano*, official organ of the Holy See to this day.

Marcantonio had seven children. His third son, Francesco, a consistorial lawyer, was the father of Pius XII. Among other tasks, consistorial lawyers prepare causes for beatification and interpret canon law before the Vatican tribunals. Virginia Graziosi, Eugenio's mother, came from the upper Roman bourgeoisie. Besides Eugenio, she gave birth to three other children: the elder son, named Francesco, like his father, Giuseppina, and Elisabetta. Francesco followed his father's footsteps and was a lawyer of outstanding ability. He was chosen by Pius XI as his personal representative in the secret negotiations with

Mussolini preliminary to the signing of the Lateran Treaty of 1929. In recognition of his services, Pius XI bestowed on him the title of Marquis. He died in 1934. One sister married Luigi Rossignani, who was employed in the administration of the Holy See, and the other, Doctor Arnaldo Mengarini, head of the Vatican-owned hospital of the Infant Jesus in Rome. Francesco's three children, Carlo, Marcantonio, and Giulio, held positions in the government of the Holy See. Carlo, the elder son, became counselor general of Vatican City, one of the highest administrative posts, and his two brothers, attorneys-at-law of the Sacra Rota, a Vatican tribunal. On December 14, 1941, King Victor Emmanuel conferred on Carlo the hereditary title of Prince, a distinguished addition to those of marquis, and Nobles of Acquapendente, and Sant' Angelo di Vado, already held by the family.

From his early childhood, Eugenio was profoundly religious. Members of his family recounted that he was no more than a tot when he built a small altar in his room and decorated it with candles, flowers, and pictures of saints. Every day he spent hours in prayer. In the morning, he usually went out with his brother who was due at school one hour earlier than he. Walking as far as a small chapel called Madonna della Strada a few yards away from his home, he would pray until the servant came to take him to school. His religious fervor was rather unusual for a small boy growing up at a time when Rome was seething with anti-clerical feeling since the clash between the Papacy and the Italian Kingdom in 1870, was still fresh in the memory of the people. Groups of socialists often stood in front of the Vatican's bronze door, waving flags and shouting insults at the Pontiff, whom, of course, they never saw. Pacelli was five years old when one of the most disgraceful incidents in the modern history of Italo-Vatican relations took place.

In July, 1881, the Holy See asked the Italian authorities for permission to take the corpse of Pius IX, the Pope who fought against Italy in 1870, from St. Peter's, where it had been temporarily buried, to its permanent resting place in the Church of St. Laurence outside the walls. The Italian Government acquiesced and promised the necessary protection. Thousands of devout Catholics, who had remained loyal to the Holy See, gathered in St. Peter's Square. Bearing torches, singing liturgical hymns, and reciting prayers for the dead, they formed a procession and headed slowly towards the church which was at the other end of the city. They had hardly moved when anti-clerical mobs appeared from side streets with shouts of "Down with the Pope" and "throw him in the river."

The faithful ignored the provocations and dodged the stones hurled at them as best they could, while the police, instead of intervening, looked on with obvious enjoyment. In the Via Nazionale, which is one of Rome's main streets, the demonstration reached its climax when the anti-clericals massed for a large-scale attack. Along one of the side-walks there were heaps of cobblestones which were being used for street repair. They proved useful to the assailants who rained them on their foes. Many people were wounded, but the procession still went on. A short, coarse-looking barber, who had left his shop near-by, acted as a self-appointed leader. He approached a tall, bearded, distinguished-looking gentleman in a top hat, morning coat, and striped trousers, who, heedless of the turmoil, was reciting prayers as calmly as though he were in St. Peter's, and shouted under his nose: "Down with that lousy Pope."

The Catholic did not even as much as look at the hotheaded anti-clerical, but when the latter turned, he kicked him in the pants so hard that the barber was lifted clean in the air, described an arc and landed with a heavy thud on the opposite sidewalk. The distinguished gentleman, whose name unfortunately is lost to history, performed this feat without even interrupting his prayers. The kick was so masterly that some of the barber's friends, roaring with laughter, applauded in appreciation.

Pius IX's body finally reached its destination, but its tribulations were not over. In July, 1943, St. Laurence outside the walls, was hit by large-caliber bombs during an air raid on Rome. The coffin was not damaged, however.

Signor Filippo Pacelli wanted both his boys to become attorneys-at-law in the state courts and for this reason took the almost unprecedented decision for the head of a family closely connected with the Vatican of sending Eugenio to a government-supported lay school.

Although he felt a strong vocation for the ecclesiastical career, young Pacelli bowed to his father's wishes. A brilliant student, he received a diploma cum laude at the end of his classical education. His fellow students of those days still remember how Pacelli in his early teens challenged his professor of history to a public debate over one of his compositions.

The professor, who was known for his anti-clerical feelings, had instructed his pupils to write an essay on *The Greatest Heroes in History*. As he was correcting the compositions, he came upon one which extolled the life of St. Augustine.

"It seems to me," the professor sarcastically remarked, "that one would hardly list St. Augustine along with Caesar, Napoleon, Alexander the Great, and other historical figures."

"I disagree with you, sir," said young Pacelli rising from his seat, his face pale but determined. "I am ready to support my thesis now."

The professor scowled at the boy who dared to defy him and was, therefore, guilty of insubordination. The whole class expected Pacelli to be expelled for the rest of the term. There were a few seconds of profound silence as everyone held his breath.

"I am sorry to have wounded the religious feelings of one of my pupils," the embarrassed professor finally said, and went on with his lesson, ignoring the challenge.

By the time he left the "lyceum," which is Italy's equivalent to the American prep school, Pacelli's mind was made up. He wanted to be a priest and not an attorney. He had no difficulty in convincing his parents who were aware of their son's religious feelings, and in 1894, he entered the Capranica College, a Roman seminary founded in 1457, by Cardinal Domenico Capranica. During the first few months, he studied so hard to prepare himself for an ecclesiastical career, that at the request of his worried mother, he interrupted his education and left the city for the family farm at Oriano to restore his delicate health.

It was a gloomy trip. The chances of pursuing his life's vocation seemed shattered since his physican doubted whether he had the physical strength necessary for the many years of intensive study ahead of him. Pacelli felt he was a failure. The ancestral home he had loved was now the tomb of his dead hopes. For many mornings he sat in the rustic courtyard wistfully watching rural life unfold before him. Sometimes he took long walks through the fields, still green in the early fall, or visited the village church. He went horseback riding with farmers who, though they had known him since his birth, were puzzled by his melancholy air and felt they would never understand this austere young man who seldom smiled. Then, strength returned, and with it, hope for the future. The crisis passed, and a few weeks later, Pacelli was back in Rome.

After graduating in theology from the Gregorian University, he was ordained priest on April 2, 1899, and celebrated his first Mass in the Borghese Chapel of Basilica Santa Maria Maggiore. Pacelli wanted to be a "shepherd of souls." For two years he spent many hours in a confessional in the Chiesa Nuova, a church almost around the corner from his home. However, the Vatican needed young men to train for its diplomatic service. Students who attended the Academy of Ecclesiastical Nobles, an institution which had for a long period supplied a great number of Vatican diplomatists, were very few. At the time when the Pope was a temporal sovereign, scions of Rome's patrician families were trained in that school and became accomplished Holy See representatives in foreign courts. But with the end of the temporal era, the luster of such a career dimmed, and the young Roman nobles were gradually absorbed by the lay professions of the rising kingdom.

One evening in February 1901, Pacelli was playing the violin. He had studied it as a young boy, and it was for him a cherished form of relaxation. He was interrupted by the startled maid announcing the visit of Monsignor Pietro Gasparri, who was at that time Secretary of the Congregation for Extraordinary Ecclesiastical Affairs, a section of the Papal Secretariat of State.

The puzzled young priest was still clutching his violin as Gasparri, who was to become Cardinal Secretary of State under Benedict XV, entered the Pacelli salon. A hardy mountaineer from a village of the marches, one of Italy's central regions, Gasparri was of a disconcerting frankness. He tackled every problem as a football player does his opponent—with force and directness.

"I have come to ask you to join the Congregation's office," said

Monsignor without even waiting to sit down. "We need promising young priests there."

Pacelli was not enthusiastic. He appreciated the honor of Monsignor coming personally to invite him, but he wished to dedicate his life to purely ecclesiastical activity. Gasparri was not to be denied, however. He pointed out that the Church may be served not only by active proselytizing but also by defending its rights and existence with diplomatic means. Pacelli entered the Congregation.

His career was rapid. Within three years, he was *minutante*, which in its literal translation means the employee who writes minutes of letters and documents. His immediate superior at that time was Monsignor Giacomo della Chiesa, Under-Secretary of the Congregation, who later became Benedict XV. While he worked at the Secretariat of State, Pacelli continued his studies, and whenever he had a few hours to himself, he went to the Chiesa Nuova, his favorite church, and sat behind the confessional, or taught catechism to the children.

In 1909, he was appointed professor of canon law at the Apollinare Academy in Rome and, shortly afterwards, professor of ecclesiastical diplomacy, at the Academy of Nobles. During that period, he collaborated closely with Gasparri who had embarked on a gigantic task—the codification of canon laws. Aim of the work was to sift and gather the countless number of papal bulls, decisions, and decrees issued throughout the centuries and co-ordinate them into one compact organic code which would simplify the application of ecclesiastical rules. For years, five thousand clergymen in every civilized country collaborated under oath of secrecy. The loyalty and abnegation of the priests was such that the whole work cost the Church fifty thousand lire, or what at that time was roughly five thousand dollars, for unavoidable office expenses and postage. Not one of the collaborators received a penny for his labor!

Shortly after the outbreak of the first World War, Benedict XV succeeded Pius X. The new Pope, who had had the opportunity of appreciating Pacelli's ability when he himself was at the Secretariat of State, appointed his erstwhile collaborator, nuncio to Munich in April, 1917. As a sign of his benevolence, Benedict also personally consecrated Pacelli, Titular Archbishop of Sardi. It was Pacelli's fourth mission abroad. He visited England three times, the last in 1911, when he went to London, as counselor of the papal delegation headed by Cardinal Granito Pignatelli di Belmonte, representing the Vatican at the coronation ceremonies of King George V.

Munich was at that time a very important post for the Holy See, because it had the only nunciature in Germany and, therefore, the only means of diplomatic contacts between the Vatican and Emperor Wilhelm II. Moreover, there was the war. The position of the Holy See, which both groups of belligerents were attempting to influence in their favor, was a delicate one. Benedict XV was accused by the Allies of being pro-German, and by the Central Powers of being pro-Ally. Pacelli's first political task in Munich was to prepare the ground for Benedict XV's peace proposal of August, 1917. The Pope and Secretary of State, Gasparri, felt that if Germany gave guarantees of restoring Belgium's independence there would be a basis for a compromise peace.

Pacelli made frequent trips to Berlin and was received by Emperor Wilhelm, but he could obtain only vague promises. Germany still believed that she was going to win the war and suspected the Allies of being behind the papal offer. When, because of German unwillingness to give concrete pledges, the peace plan was rejected by the Allies, the Emperor realized his mistake, but it was too late. From that time on, Benedict XV abstained from diplomatic initiatives and confined himself to general appeals for peace.

The loss of the war swept the Hohenzollern dynasty and the Bavarian House of Wittelsbach from their thrones. Those were dark days for the Church in Germany. Revolution, with all its excesses and violence, made the life of the clergy very difficult. In April, 1919, the flags of the newly formed and short-lived Bavarian Socialist Republic were flying on top of all government buildings in Munich. Troops sent by the Reich Government to crush the revolt were besieging the city, which was in the hands of the socialists. Many of the ambassadors and ministers accredited to what at that time was an independent kingdom, fled when the revolution broke out. Pacelli stayed.

Cavalry Captain, Francesco de Luca, former Italian military attaché in Munich, wrote in a March 1939 issue of the Roman newspaper,

Il Messaggero, that in April, 1919, he received a telephone call at the Italian Embassy.

"This is the secretary of the Nuncio speaking. Please come immediately. Red soldiers are here."

De Luca jumped in his car and alighted five minutes later in front of the nunciature, in Brienner Street. Seven men, brandishing revolvers and daggers, were in the grounds. Standing before them under the portico of the building, he saw Pacelli, one hand over the gold pectoral cross worn by all bishops as a sign of their rank.

The men demanded money, whatever precious objects the Nuncio had, and, especially, his automobile. Pacelli knew that he was risking his life with a refusal. Nevertheless, he calmly addressed the threatening group and protested against the invasion of what was a property with diplomatic immunity. The men aimed their revolvers at him, but he stood firm. They finally went to the garage and attempted to start the car. But they found the battery gone, no gasoline, and the tires deflated. They left, uttering ominous threats.

When the revolutionary storm finally abated, Pacelli showed that the Vatican was ready to collaborate with any form of government provided it is given essential guarantees for the carrying out of its spiritual mission by signing a concordat with Bavaria which was hailed in the Vatican as a masterpiece of diplomacy. His mission completed, Pius XI, who had succeeded Benedict XV in 1922, sent Pacelli to Berlin. There the papal nuncio began negotiations for another concordat with Prussia, which was concluded in June, 1929, and lasted until the advent of the Nazi regime.

As a result of his diplomatic successes, Pacelli's prestige was very high in the Vatican. He had fulfilled all the missions assigned to him with a skill all the more remarkable because of the adverse conditions he had had to face in a predominantly non-Catholic country with a socialist government ideologically opposed to the Church.

When he was nuncio, Pacelli spent every summer vacation in Stella Maris, a convent built at the foot of Mount Rorchasch in Einsiedeln, Switzerland. He preferred the mountains to the sea or the country. It is a well-known fact, for instance, that he never particularly liked Castel Gandolfo, the papal summer residence, seventeen miles from

Rome, which overlooked the sapphire-blue lake by the same name, and had an unbroken view of the Alban Hills in the Roman campagna.

Almost every afternoon, he left the Swiss convent and climbed to the top of Mount Rorchasch. It was upon his return from one of these walks in November, 1929, that he found a telegram waiting for him from a friend in Rome. It read: "Heartiest congratulations."

"Do you understand what this means?" Pacelli asked Father Tomas Jungt, the spiritual director of the convent and his habitual walking companion.

"The message is very clear to me," Father Tomas replied. "May I also congratulate you upon your elevation to the cardinalate?"

Pacelli was recalled to Rome a few days later, and on December 16, received the cardinal's hat.

Gasparri, who had successfully brought to conclusion the complex and prolonged negotiations for the Lateran Treaty with Italy in February, 1929, was forced to resign at the beginning of 1930. The strong-willed Pope had been carrying on violent polemics with Mussolini over the interpretation of that treaty and had felt for some months that his Secretary of State, a man of great intelligence and with a personality as strong as his, did not approve of his views and methods in dealing with that particular phase of Italo-Vatican relations. Pacelli, who had been for years Gasparri's right hand before his diplomatic missions, was chosen to replace the man who, twenty-nine years before, had invited him to enter the Vatican diplomatic service.

Pacelli conformed with the traditional role of the Secretary of State, that is, he scrupulously followed papal directives and instructions. In the nine years that preceded his election to the papacy, he brought himself even more forcibly to the attention of the Catholic world. Assisting Pius XI in his "concordatarian" policy, he signed agreements with Baden, Austria, Prussia, and Yugoslavia. All, except the latter, were ratified. However, the concordat with Prussia lasted only a few months, although it was never denounced by either power. It was the result of expediency on the part of Hitler who, as soon as he became Chancellor, placed under his control all the forces of the state and suppressed all parties. The Center, which was the traditional supporter of the Church in Germany, broke up with surprising docility. This caused a strong reaction among the Catholic clergy and faithful. To placate them, Hitler signed the concordat and violated it as soon as he felt securely in power.

It was, undoubtedly, due to Pacelli's diplomatic ability, moderating influence on Pius XI, and knowledge of world affairs that the Holy See succeeded in preventing the rupture of relations with Germany despite Hitler's repeated and flagrant breaches of the concordat. This was in keeping with the modern tradition of the Vatican, which is of the opinion that, if a contact, no matter how ephemeral, is maintained, there is always the possibility of influencing the civil government and of protecting Catholic interests. For this reason, the Holy See avoids, whenever possible, formal severance of relations.

Another instance in which Pacelli showed his diplomatic skill was during the Spanish Civil War, 1936–39. The Vatican condemned the hunting of clergymen, the sacking of churches, the persecution of Catholics fostered by the Loyalists, but it kept its nuncio in Madrid and did not formally recognize the Franco regime until the end of the revolution.

During his tenure of office as Secretary of State, Pacelli became the greatest single propagandist of the Catholic Faith in the civilized world. He visited North and South America, France, and Hungary.

In 1934, Pius XI appointed him Cardinal Legate, that is, his personal representative to the International Eucharistic Congress in Buenos Aires. The reception which the Argentine Government accorded him, and the display of religious feeling on the part of the people surpassed anything of the kind ever seen in that part of the world. Pacelli was treated with honors far greater than those usually rendered a visiting sovereign. All the members of the government participated in the religious ceremonies. The President of the Republic, Agustin P. Justo, took communion in public and dedicated the country to Christ King, as symbolic of the nation's loyalty to the Catholic Faith. The closing function in Palermo Park was attended by one-and-a-half million people, who represented thirty-two nations. Five cardinals and one hundred eighty bishops were present.

Pacelli's departure for Italy was witnessed by the entire population of Buenos Aires. As the liner started down the River Plate, hundreds of white doves were released, and the sirens of all ships at anchor were blown for one minute in a final gesture of farewell. At night, powerful reflectors designed a luminous cross over the capital in memory of the final blessing Pacelli had imparted to the city in the morning.

The Cardinal Legate was profoundly impressed, I was told in Rome. The honors and attentions heaped upon him placed a great strain on his modesty. He accepted them because they were an homage, not to him, personally, but to the representative of the Pope.

The following year, he went to the shrine of Lourdes and in October, 1936, to the United States, where he visited twelve of the sixteen ecclesiastical provinces. France welcomed him again in 1937, with honors unprecedented for that country, when he attended the Eucharistic Congress at Lisieux. The last trip he made as Papal Legate was to Budapest. Admiral Nicholas Horthy, Regent of Hungary, who, incidentally, was a Protestant, offered Pacelli the hospitality of the Buda Royal Palace, and participated in the opening and closing ceremonies. Two thousand special trains brought scores of thousands of faithful representing fifty-seven nations to Budapest. One million people were stated to have attended that Eucharistic Congress.

FIFTH CHAPTER

There was universal rejoicing among the Vatican officials and residents over Pacelli's ascension to the papacy. They all knew his habits, mentality, method of work, and did not, therefore, have to make the effort of adapting themselves to the personality of a comparative stranger as was the case when the holder of an Italian See was elected, such as Pius X.

Tall, lanky, with dark hair graying at the temples and black penetrating eyes behind gold-rimmed spectacles resting on an aquiline nose which emphasizes his thin ascetic face, Pius XII gives the impression of being a man who has divorced himself from the materialistic needs of life to attain the highest possible form of spiritual and intellectual development. As Henry Bordeaux once wrote, "He has the sublime greatness of a mortified, almost translucent body which seems destined to serve only as the cover for his soul."

Pius XII is gifted with an extremely agile and logical mind. Diplomatists who have known him for years have been impressed by the fact that in a meeting he eliminates all digressions by constantly reverting to the main subject until it has been exhaustively discussed. He is aided in this by a truly formidable memory. He very seldom reads a speech; every word has been written beforehand and memorized. After reading the text twice, he usually knows it by heart, not only when it is in Italian or Latin, but also in any of the other languages he knows—English, French, German, Spanish, and Portuguese.

In the early days of his pontificate, Pius once addressed a group of Hungarian pilgrims. Despite the fact that he had only a smattering of Hungarian, which is admittedly one of the most difficult languages in the civilized world, the Pontiff memorized the phonetics of every word, so that, much to the surprise of his listeners, he spoke to them in their own language.

His speeches betray his humanist culture. One often finds in them references to Homer, Sophocles, Herodotus. Born a Roman, he was imbued with "Romanism," that is, he admires the pagan beauty of the City of the Caesars, the high level of civilization reached by Roman genius. To him is attributed the phrase, "To live heroically is better than to live comfortably" which later inspired Mussolini to say, "It is better to live one day as a lion than one hundred years as a sheep." He is also a student of contemporary literature. His literary style has been likened to that of the French ecclesiastical writer, Bishop Jacques Bossuet. From ancient Greece, he acquired a highly developed feeling for artistic eurythmy and his love for aesthetics; from Imperial Rome, the judicial knowledge, the science of government, and a practical outlook in the approach to problems. Many of his sermons and addresses in the Italian language are texts in the religious schools and seminaries because of the purity of expression, the lyricism of the images, the impeccable style, and the loftiness of thought.

He speaks with a clear, moving, and pleasantly toned voice. His slim arms, elongated and aristocratic hands with which he sometimes emphasizes a phrase or a word, the strikingly spiritual features, the slender fragile-looking body clad in the white papal robes give him the hieratic appearance of an apostle.

He is not what one would call a popular pope in the sense that the average person is made to feel he is in the presence of a human being with impulses, emotions, passions, virtues, and defects common to all men. The depth of his mind, his habit of meditation, natural aloofness, and austerity of life have made him solitary. Endowed with an iron will, Pius XII, by the constant application of self-discipline, has achieved complete control of mind and body. Thus, at times he impresses one as being a cold and distant man whose gestures and words lack spontaneity.

However, this control, discipline, and training is not the result of personal ambition—an end in itself. For Pius, it is the weapon and the means with which best to defend and further the interests of the Church. Since his early youth, his actions have been subordinated to this purpose. So, when the challenge is not there, when he is among members of his immediate family and people he knows well, the affective qualities of the man break through the barrier of reserve and austerity. He becomes affable and interested in the thoughts, feelings, and problems of others.

Soon after his election, he paid a visit to Cardinal Francesco Marchetti-Selvaggiani, an old friend, who had fallen ill during the Conclave. Wearing the white robes of the Pope, which he had just donned for the first time, he approached the suffering Prince of the Church, who, surprised and confused at the unexpected visit, made an effort to rise from his bed.

"I beg forgiveness of Your Holiness," Marchetti-Selvaggiani said, falling back on his pillow, "If I am unable to render due homage. . . ."

"Do not fatigue thyself," interrupted the Pope smiling. "For this evening let us be only Eugenio and Francesco."

"*Come ti sta bene quella tunica!*" said the Cardinal, who thus conveyed his satisfaction over Pacelli's election.

A shadow of sadness appeared for a moment in the eyes of the new Pontiff, who, looking through a window of the bare cell at the city of Rome, sighed:

"Perhaps I'll never be able to travel any more."

Pius loves the humble, ordinary folk because of their simplicity, naïveness, and lack of sophistication. After a general audience, he walks through the crowd and mingles with it. He listens to family troubles, wants to know the name of wide-eyed, awe-struck children who clutch at their mother's skirts, promises that he will pray for the dear ones who are ill, or, as during the war, on the battle fronts. On those occasions he acts just as any small town parish priest. He learned mass psychology from meeting people in all walks of life, during the years spent in the diplomatic service of the Vatican. Many times have I seen him almost mauled by women who begged him to give their infants a special blessing and who pulled at his tunic, grabbed him by the arm, almost tore his hand in a display of uncontrolled emotion, while his entourage vainly attempted to protect him. Once, I was told, his pectoral cross was broken and his ring disappeared during one of these manifestations of popular enthusiasm.

At the end of one audience, I watched an Italian peasant step up to him as he was making his way through the crowd in the Clementine Hall, and express the desire to be confessed by him. Giovanni Stefanori, his private butler and faithful bodyguard, and Monsignor Aborio-Mella di Sant' Elia, Papal Master of the Chamber, were appalled at the audacity of the request. But, before they could intervene and drive the man away, the Pontiff took the farmer by the arm and retraced his steps to a corner of the hall. For a few minutes he listened in an attitude of profound concentration, and finally raised his hand in a blessing of absolution over the kneeling man.

Pius XII is the psychological opposite of Pius XI. Cautious, suave, tolerant Pius XII; impulsive, bristling, authoritarian Pius XI. The former, the quintessence of statesmanship, a man whose temper and reactions are controlled by an acute, brilliant, intuitive mind trained in that most rigid of schools—the diplomatic service of the Vatican. The latter, a fighter, sometimes even careless of consequences, who often listened more to the dictates of his generous heart and hot temper than to political expediency. Despite their differences, or indeed, because of them, these two men fought side by side with perfect teamwork against the increasingly strong enemies of the Church in the past decade. Their relationship was far closer than the one arising from the loyalty and obedience which a collaborator usually feels for the Heads of the Church. It was the blending of friendship, devotion, mutual respect, and admiration. The aged Pius XI valued the profound understanding of political situations, the foresight, and quick brain of his Secretary of State which very often tempered his obstinacy and impulses. He once remarked to Cardinal Michael de Faulhaber, Archbishop of Munich, "If the Catholic world knew how much Pacelli means to the Church!" More than that, the gruff, intransigent, authoritarian Pontiff fully appreciated the merits of a collaborator who could interpret his wishes and execute his instructions with a smoothness and thoroughness of which he himself was incapable, undoubtedly because of the serious illness which slowly disintegrated his body and somewhat affected his nervous system for many years before he died. No wonder that, before Pacelli left as Papal Legate for the Eucharistic Congress in Budapest in 1938, Pius XI said to a meeting of Cardinals, "Pacelli always speaks for Us."

According to the men who have worked with him since the time he began his career, Pius XII was never found unprepared to tackle a major problem. He studied with great care for all the tasks he performed. For a full year before being sent as nuncio to Bavaria, he acquainted himself with the customs and various problems of the country to which he was to be assigned. He takes a long time to make a decision of importance. Once it is made, however, one may be sure that it is the result of profound analysis and meditation.

An assiduous reader, he follows closely Italian as well as international events. Every day he methodically scans the newspapers of many countries, a task which is made easier for him by his knowledge of languages. Foreigners received in private audiences marveled to me at the Pontiff's knowledge of issues and events purely local in character of which he had learned through his constant reading of the press.

Despite the many hours he spends at his desk every day, Pius invariably takes one hour in the afternoon for a daily walk. This habit dates back to the day when Cardinal Gasparri, shortly after Pacelli's entrance into the Secretariat of State, seeing his young assistant grow pale and emaciated because of overwork and lack of relaxation, said:

"Dear Pacelli, you need some fresh air. Look, I go out every day for a little while. Moreover, for the priest who speaks so much of Heaven, it does no harm to feel a bit of earth under his feet."

When he was Secretary of State, Pacelli was a familiar sight to Romans in the Villa Borghese, the beautiful park in the heart of the capital. At 4 P.M. a black limousine would stop in front of the monumental gate in Piazzale Flaminio. Dressed in the garb of a simple priest, Pacelli and Monsignor Pio Rossignani, his private secretary who was also the brother-in-law of one of his sisters, would climb out of it and start walking briskly through green, sheltered, almost solitary bypaths, in the general direction of Piazza di Siena where every year in May, riders of many nations participated in an international steeplechase. They would be invariably followed at a discreet distance by two plain-clothes men assigned to their protection by the Italian Government. After a few hundred yards, Pacelli would slow up and read his breviary. One afternoon, I was having tea with Edda, my wife, in the Casina delle Rose, nestled among the trees of the Villa, and popular among Romans as well as tourists, when I saw the Secretary of State look with a somewhat startled face at the people sitting near us who were nudging each other and whispering, "Look, look, Cardinal Pacelli!" He had become so absorbed in his reading that he had failed to note where he was going and had thus found himself in the midst of a gay crowd.

When a cardinal is elected Pope, he loses his nationality, his name, and whatever civil ties bind him to his country of birth, and becomes the representative of Christ on earth, the head of a spiritual empire, and the citizen of every nation where there are Catholics. There is no ruler who is so much a slave of his mission and, at the same time, the most absolute monarch in this world, as the Pope. Before he is elected, the white robe he must wear until his death is prepared for him. In fact, before the conclave begins, three white tunics are made: short, medium, and large, so as to fit temporarily any type of body. Moreover, the new Pope finds that his daily life is already regulated to the minutest details by a tradition perpetuated by the people who form part of his court and government. The men around him may change but those who replace them will have the same tasks to perform and will be chosen from the same environment according to deep-rooted custom. For instance, the Pope's confessor—an ordinary priest who visits the Vatican once a week at fixed hours and who alone may absolve the Supreme Head of the Church of his sins—is a Jesuit; the master of the apostolic palace, a Dominican; the sacristan, an Augustinian. Should the Pope break this tradition without sound reasons, a whole religious order would regard such a gesture as an affront— a serious complication even for a Pope, in view of the strong spirit of solidarity, and the pride characterizing the members of religious orders. Pius X, a saintly man of simple tastes and habits whose cause for canonization has been under way for sometime, was terrified, at first, to find himself at the Head of the Church. One day, he pointed to the Swiss Guards on duty outside his apartment and whispered to an old friend, "There are my jailers!"

The Pope's daily life has become even more monotonous since the end of the temporal power of the Holy See in 1870. Before, a Pontiff, as in the case of Pius IX, could take drives in Rome's Pincian Gardens or walk in the streets talking with people, imparting blessings, and bestowing favors. He could move from the Vatican to the Quirinal which was one of his palaces and later became the official residence of the King of Italy. But, by voluntarily shutting himself up in the Vatican in sign of protest against the seizure of Rome, the Pope confined his life to one hundred and eight acres of ground —the total area of his midget state. Even after the conclusion of the Lateran Treaty, which released the Pontiff from his voluntary imprisonment, the daily routine changed but slightly. The only difference up to the present is that the Pontiff goes to his villa in Castel Gandolfo for a period of rest in the summer time, and to solemn functions in the Roman churches. Nor can it be otherwise since every time he crosses Saint Peter's Square, which is the boundary line between Italy and the State of Vatican City, he is on foreign soil.

Like Benedict XV, who, ten minutes after his election was walking about the Vatican as though he were in his family home, Pius XII had no need of "breaking in" to his new job, because of the experience he acquired in the nine years he was Secretary of State. He knew practically every resident of the tiny city as well as all the intricacies of administration, physical characteristics and problems which confronted the Holy See, so that he took over control without the commotion usually attending the death of one sovereign Pontiff and the arrival of another. He was, as always, extremely reserved and continued to live with the same simplicity which characterized his life as Secretary of State. The only changes were those forced on him by his new office, such as the audiences with pilgrims.

Pius XII rises at about 6:30 A.M. A modern Pope, he shaves himself with an electric razor which he bought during his trip to the United States. His manservant, Giovanni Stefanori, who has been with him since his appointment as Secretary of State, does not enter the private apartment on the third floor of the palace until the Pontiff has finished dressing. I have not seen the apartment since Pius XII took possession of it. However, when I was in Rome, Monsignor Enrico Pucci, head of a Vatican news agency, told me that few alterations had been made to it after Pius XI's death. The bedroom, which has two windows overlooking St. Peter's Square, is furnished with great simplicity. It has a plain brass bed with a damask cover, a medium-size rug, a common dresser, a small mirror which is the only one existing in the whole apartment, and a mahogany desk. A painting of the Virgin hangs from one wall. The dining room is equally unpretentious, with two cupboards, and a simply carved walnut table. A small study, a modern bathroom built during Pius XI's reign, and a large hall complete the apartment proper which, however, comprises many other rooms used by the members of the household. It also has a guest room although under the last three Popes, it was used only once —when Pius XI returned to a humble Polish priest the hospitality that the latter had extended to him many years before in a small town when the then Monsignor Ratti, was nuncio to Poland. The private apartment came into existence under Pius X, who, after his election, continued to live in the small room assigned to him for the conclave, instead of using the state apartment on the second floor as had all his predecessors. When Vatican officials saw that he was determined to remain where he was, they began adapting several rooms next to his in order to give him at least a minimum of comfort. A bed which belonged to Pius VII was unearthed from one of the warehouses, repainted, and substituted for the plain iron bed in the Pontiff's chamber. When it arrived, one of the intimates said:

"It's a beautiful bed."

"No doubt," Pius X replied rather sadly, "but I shall have to die in it."

At seven-thirty, Pius says mass in his private chapel, which is next to his bedroom, and before retiring to his library in the official apartment spends fifteen or twenty minutes eating a frugal breakfast consisting of coffee, milk, and rolls. The library is a beautiful corner room with windows overlooking Saint Peter's Square. It is in this room that all private audiences take place, where cardinals, sovereigns, princes, bishops, ambassadors, and laymen render homage to the Head of the Roman Catholic Church. The Pope works at a large walnut desk on the top of which stands a white statue of Christ and a Crucifix. Against three of the walls are tall bookcases, their panes covered with gray cloth. White curtains are on the windows, with the exception of the center one, immediately behind the Pope's chair, which has panes of colored glass depicting the Virgin Mary sitting on a throne with the Infant Jesus on her lap.

Secretary of State Maglione, the first person the Pope receives daily, is usually in the library waiting when Pius arrives at eight-thirty. As first collaborator of the Pontiff, he takes the private elevator reserved for the Pope and his relatives. This stops on the first floor, where the apartment of the Secretary of State is located, and he is thus able to see his sovereign in absolute secrecy. The day's work begins with this audience during which are examined the most important questions being considered by the Secretariat of State at that particular moment. Maglione, armed with a large brief case bulging with papers, reports on the meetings he has had the previous day with diplomatists, prelates, and other visitors. He discusses with the Pope whatever events are affecting the Church in the various countries, as well as news contained in dispatches sent by the diplomatic representatives of the Holy See accredited to the lay governments, and in the press. Usually the audience with the Secretary of State lasts a long time. It is followed by others granted to cardinals, who have precedence over all others, and high-ranking prelates at the head of congregations. These audiences are so arranged that chiefs of departments are received at least once a week. In addition, the Pontiff sees visiting bishops who report periodically on the affairs of their dioceses, and other prominent churchmen as well as laymen who have a claim on his time. The private audiences average about ten per day.

The Secretary of State may call on the Pope whenever he thinks it necessary and without a prearranged audience. Everybody else, however, must wait for his turn in the anterooms of the official apartment where he is welcomed by the Swiss Guards and the court attendants with the honors due his rank.

Woodrow Wilson, the last President of the United States to visit a Pope, caused a sensation in the papal antechamber. On entering the Clementine Hall, which is on the second floor of the state apartment, he handed his top hat to one of the attendants and started for the library where Benedict XV was waiting for him. The members of the court, who had received Wilson at the foot of the majestic marble

staircase in the Courtyard of Saint Damasus, built during the reign
of Pius IX, and had escorted him to the hall, were petrified because
Wilson had forgotten to take off his overcoat. The "dean" of the
attendants, who, in the twenty years of service at the Vatican had
escorted practically all the crowned heads of Europe and dozens of
prime ministers, was the only one who saved the situation. With two
quick steps he approached Wilson as he was about to enter the
library, and gently placed his hands on the surprised President who,
before he knew what was happening, found himself minus the overcoat. A sigh of relief was heard about the hall: protocol once again
had been observed.

The audiences invariably end at 1 P.M. At this time, Pius receives
his Master of the Chamber who submits to him a list of requests for
audiences and the Pope decides the visitors he will see the next day.
Half an hour later, the Pontiff has lunch in the dining room of his
private apartment. Stefanori serves his table, and German nuns, who
have cooked his meals since he was nuncio in Berlin, are in charge of
his kitchen. Pius' diet is very simple, not only because he has no preference for particular kinds of foods, but also because he suffers from
stomach trouble. The cooking is in the traditional Italian style. He
drinks ordinary wine and does not smoke. In accordance with an
ancient custom, the Pope eats alone. The only companions of Pius XII
are two canary birds which are released from their cage as soon as he
enters the room and allowed to fly undisturbed during the meal. They
are trained so that when he calls them by name, they often perch on
his shoulder or jump on his table to peck at the food prepared for
them in two small saucers. On very rare occasions when there are official guests for lunch, the Pope still eats alone at a table which is
higher than the others, and is, of course, served first. Even as Secretary
of State, Pacelli never had any guests, Monsignor Pucci told me, and
he observed this custom also during his trips.

After lunch, Pius takes a brief rest and at 4 P.M., his daily walk. One
afternoon I was in the Courtyard of Saint Damasus when I heard
subdued clapping. It was the papal gendarme on duty at the state
apartment who thus signaled that the Pope was about to go out. The
signal was relayed immediately all along the itinerary. Cars were

stopped and casual visitors asked to leave. I hid behind a column of the portico in the courtyard and saw Pius XII, who was wearing a light white overcoat and red hat with upturned brim, appear a few minutes later. He climbed into the waiting black limousine with the chamberlain who happened to be on duty that day. Pius always rides as far as the Vatican Gardens where he leaves the car and begins his one-hour walk with a quick, elastic step. He is followed at some distance by his chamberlain and the Esente of the Noble Guards, who is entrusted with the duty of watching over the person of the Pontiff.

A tour of the Vatican Gardens is something that one does not easily forget. Pius XI, who was a great lover of nature and an enthusiastic follower of technical and scientific progress, gave his private park the beauty of perennial spring. One hot summer day, I was walking through the gardens when I met Engineer Enrico Galeazzi, general director of the Vatican technical services, and asked him how it happened that, at the time the whole countryside was withered, flowers blossomed and fields were emerald-green in the Vatican.

Galeazzi laughed, pleased.

"Pius XI," he said, "had ninety-three hundred irrigators installed, which required fifty-five miles of pipe lines. Moreover, he had two reservoirs built which contain one million five hundred thousand gallons of water flowing directly from Lake Bracciano (forty miles from Rome). If you are here this evening you will see scientifically regulated rain, water every inch of the park."

Upon his return to the Vatican palace, the Pope prays for a few minutes and then retires again to his study. Unlike Pius XI, who granted special audiences also in the afternoon, the present Pope spends the rest of the day working alone. At that time, he prepares the speeches he will deliver the next day, makes notes for future encyclicals and answers an incredible amount of correspondence. He writes on an American made typewriter, and, occasionally, dictates to one of his secretaries, although before I left Rome in the spring of 1942, I was told by an official of the Secretariat of State that Pius XII had for some time been using an ediphone. Late in the afternoon, he summons Monsignor Giovanni Battista Montini, Substitute Secretary of State for Ordinary Affairs, or Monsignor Domenico

Tardini, Secretary of the Congregation for Extraordinary Ecclesiastical Affairs, and gives them instructions concerning whatever matters must be attended to the next day. Before partaking of some light food, the Pontiff recites the Rosary in his chapel with the private secretaries and secret chamberlains who form part of his household. He then grants himself a few minutes of relaxation conversing with his collaborators and at 10 P.M., he is back in the library. Many times on passing through Saint Peter's Square, I saw lights burning in there as late as 1 A.M.

No one knows what he does at that time, but, according to some Vatican prelates close to him, Pius spends a few minutes writing his diary and then works on a theological treatise which he began many years ago. He keeps the manuscript locked in one of the drawers of his desk and never speaks about this work, not even to the members of his family.

Pius allows no variation in his daily routine, except, of course, when he participates in religious functions and in ceremonies which are an essential part of his mission. Punctuality is for him a duty to himself and to others. The visitor who has been granted an audience is pleasantly surprised when he is ushered into the presence of the Pope at exactly the appointed time. In this also, Pius presents a striking contrast with his predecessor. When I was covering general audiences scheduled for 12:30 P.M., because Pius XI was expected to make an important speech, I often had to wait as late as two-thirty, and even three o'clock. This was due to the fact that the Pontiff had been detained by a number of private audiences. Instead, Pius XII first attends to the public audience which occurs every Wednesday at 10 A.M., and then receives private visitors. He appears on the dot, allows a reasonable amount of time for his personal contact with the crowd after his speech and is back in his library before noon.

Pius XI supervised directly all the activities of the Vatican administration. In the afternoon, he usually received Marquis Camillo Serafini, Governor of Vatican City, and many other officials who reported daily to him. After the Lateran Treaty, he also attended personally to the diplomatic relations with Italy and had granted a fixed audience on Sunday to the Italian Ambassador. Pius XII has freed himself of all bureaucratic matters, delegating his power to trusted officials, so that he may dedicate himself exclusively to the affairs of the Church. The Italian Ambassador is treated exactly like all the other members of the diplomatic corps accredited to the Holy See and has his contacts with the Secretariat of State.

SIXTH CHAPTER

Pius XI left to his successor a very heavy heritage. At the beginning of 1939, the Roman Catholic Church in Europe was beset with enemies. Atheist Bolshevism, for many years arch foe of religion, was temporarily relegated to second place by the neo-pagan doctrine fostered by Nazi Germany. An offspring of anti-Semitism, the neo-pagan theories condemn the Catholic religion as a foreign importation of Jewish origin and uphold that blood and race are the supreme human values because they forge the soul, character, and body of man. This has resulted in an anti-religious policy affecting all the Christian churches in Germany.

Even in Catholic Italy relations between Church and State were tense on account of the Fascist racial laws which invalidated religious marriage and violated the 1929 concordat. On the other hand, England, France, and the United States had joined efforts to maintain peace against the aggressive policy of Germany and Italy, and had drawn closer to the Vatican which approved of Chamberlain's appeasement drive, encouraged France's growing solidarity with the national clergy as a reaction against steady German pressure, and found a natural ally in freedom-loving United States, which had strongly criticized Nazi aggressiveness and religious persecutions.

As the most militant enemy of the Church, Germany, then, was the gravest source of worry for Pius XI in the last years of his pontificate. Shortly after his advent to power, Hitler embarked on a policy of de-Christianization which was in open conflict with the doctrine of the Catholic Church. The concordat he signed with the Vatican in 1933, in order to obtain the support of the Catholics and clergy for his young regime, proved to be a mere scrap of paper since the ideology of the Nazi totalitarian state could not be conciliated with Catholic doctrine.

For many centuries the Church has advocated jurisdiction over a number of social activities including education and marriage. However, since the evolution of the modern state, the lay authorities exercise greater control over the activities of the individual which formerly had been left to private initiative. To avoid an open clash, the Church has chosen the lesser of two evils. It has sought to compromise by signing an agreement with the State designed to remove all points of friction in fields where both the lay and religious powers claim jurisdiction. Thus, while never abandoning its theoretical claims, the Church has in practice recognized certain exigencies of the State when the latter has in turn acknowledged some essential needs of the Church and of its religious bodies.

The purely diplomatic activity of Pius XI aimed at guaranteeing through bilaterally defined juridical understandings the life of the ecclesiastical bodies in various countries, while making all possible concessions in fields where the specific spiritual function of the Church was not affected. Also, Pius XI never yielded the right of the Vatican to appoint bishops and parish priests, although he granted to the State the faculty of approving or rejecting such appointments for political reasons. He insisted on complete freedom of action of the Church in its religious, educational, and pastoral activities. In many cases he also obtained civil recognition of religious marriage and equality of the confessional schools with those supported by the state. Where the fiery Pontiff, who had to face the growth of the modern authoritarian state during his long reign, showed great intolerance was in the field of education. In many speeches and encyclicals he affirmed the right of the Church to supervise this social activity independently of the temporal power. He maintained, as all his predecessors, that teaching is a matter of public interest which concerns both the individual and the community; that the Church, because of its spiritual mission, has the right to judge whether education is beneficial or contrary to Christian principles and whether it is in keeping with the tenets of the faith.

In view of this doctrinal stand, the clash with Hitler was inevitable, for Nazism, in common with other totalitarian forms of government, placed the interests of the nation above those of the individual. But, unlike Fascism, it excluded the Church from participation in any form of social activity on the ground that it was an alien force which did not share its ideology and was, indeed, antithetic to the spirit and aim of the political party whose power was so great as to identify itself with the state. According to its ideology, religion was a purely private question of an internal character. The German citizen was taught to know how to find the fulfillment of his needs in the State's conception of life, national history, tradition, rites, and festivals. If he failed, then the Nazi explanation was that he had not reached the full maturity of his social responsibility.

When Hitler, in the fall of 1933, began his attacks against not only the Catholic Church but all other churches as well, the Vatican kept an attitude of reserve. It entrusted to the German clergy the task of carrying the struggle against Nazism, which, in its early stage, was only on doctrinal grounds. Cardinal Michael Faulhaber, Archbishop of Munich, led the fight with a series of sermons during which he refuted the Nazi thesis that Germany should return to its pre-Christian origins because Christianity was a spiritual movement foreign to the national tradition. Soon, however, Hitler launched a strong campaign to induce parents to prefer government-supported schools to the confessional ones and enacted a series of measures aiming at placing Catholic youth organizations under the control of the Nazi party. In other words, the struggle transcended from the doctrinal to the practical ground and the issue with the Vatican was squarely joined.

Alfred Rosenberg's racial theory set forth in his book, *Myth of the Twentieth Century* was bitterly decried by the German episcopate since it branded Christianity as a corrupting force because of its Jewish origin. For Rosenberg, blood is the factor which, through a mysterious process, determines the physical and moral make-up of the individual. Race mixture, according to him, brings about a collapse of values and moral disintegration. Only by keeping the race pure may a nation attain greatness. The aim of Nazism, he says, is, therefore, that of eliminating all foreign influences from national life and of reverting to the purely German or Nordic traditions. Christianity is a corrupting force because it has aided the mixture of races by virtue of its universalistic philosophy which makes no distinction between Jews and Aryans.

The Vatican placed the book on the Index in February 1934, thus forbidding all Catholics to read it under penalty of religious sanctions. But since Hitler had declared that it was a private work and had not the official approval of the government, there was no formal conflict with the Holy See. The Natzi putsch of July 1934 in Austria, during which Chancellor Dollfuss was murdered, aggravated the tension between the Vatican and the Reich. The former viewed with deep concern Hitler's attempt at annexation. While abstaining from any official pronouncement on the political question of the anschluss, the Vatican was, nevertheless, directly interested in supporting the independence of Austria, which was a bulwark of Catholicism in Central Europe. For the Holy See, that country represented the ideal form of lay government since it had adopted Christian corporativism, granted freedom of action to the Church in all social and cultural activities, and curbed communism as well as socialism while the Nazi regime that attempted to supplant it, upheld ideologies of an anti-Christian character.

The birth of the Rome-Berlin Axis was still two years away. Mussolini was at that time a staunch supporter of Austria's independence, the only barrier between Italy and a Germany that was growing in power and rapidly recuperating from the 1918 defeat at the hands of the Allies. Mussolini mobilized troops on the Italo-Austrian border and was ready to intervene if the Nazi putsch were successful. Only a few weeks before, he had met Hitler in Venice in an effort to dissuade the German dictator from menacing Austria's security. The meeting was a complete fiasco because the Führer refused to commit himself to a hands-off policy in regard to Austria as well as the South Tyrol, which had been annexed by Italy under the Versailles Treaty. He merely agreed not to interfere with Austria's internal affairs for ten years, but warned his Italian colleague that the anschluss was inevitable. An Italian diplomat who attended that meeting told me that he overheard the enraged Duce say to Dino Grandi, Ambassador to London, as he was coming out of the conference room, "He (Hitler) is a stubborn fool."

Thus Vatican and Italian interests on the Austrian question coincided. The former warmly supported an Anglo-Franco-Italian declaration in September 1934, to guarantee Austria's independence and used all its influence to induce the Vienna Government to accept it.

Germany's rising strength united England, France, and Italy in what was called the Stresa front, after the name of the place in Northern Italy where the parley was held. The three powers affirmed their determination to protect Austria, and condemned German rearmament. The Vatican again showed its satisfaction for this political development by sending Cardinal Pacelli to the imposing religious celebrations at the Shrine of Lourdes. I learned at the time that Pius XI had decided to go personally to that ceremony, but finally abstained on the advice of his physicians who feared that the trip might prove too fatiguing for a man in his late seventies. Pacelli's presence in Lourdes, that is, in a country which was more directly threatened by German rearmament, was tantamount to a moral participation of the Vatican in the Stresa front. The French Government was quick to seize the political implications of that gesture and treated the visiting Prince of the Church with unprecedented honors.

However, Hitler's attempt to de-Christianize the Reich continued unabated, despite the protests of the German episcopate. In February 1934, Faulhaber threatened with excommunication Nazi leaders who were responsible for the campaign against the confessional schools. His words received papal approval by the presence at the sermon of Monsignor Orsenigo, papal nuncio to Berlin. Undaunted, Nazi leaders decreed that membership in the party was incompatible with membership in Catholic organizations. They disbanded the Catholic boy scouts, while Hermann Goering, president of the Prussian Government, issued a circular against the so-called "politically active clergy." L'Osservatore Romano, official organ of the Holy See, published a scathing editorial in which it talked of a renewal of the Kulturkampf, the struggle between Church and State in the time of Bismarck. In August, the German bishops met for their annual conference in Fulda, Germany, and signed a collective protest against the ecclesiastical policy of the Nazi Regime. Hitler, one month later, not only ignored the protests but gave new impetus to the anti-Catholic campaign by accusing the clergy of political activities against the government.

It looked as though Germany and the Vatican were heading for a showdown, but several political considerations stayed the hand of the Pope. First of all, the Holy See found in the Hitler regime a powerful ally against Communist expansion, and secondly, the Stresa front had been smashed by Mussolini's attack on Ethiopia. The isolation of Italy as a result of the economic sanctions voted against her by the League of Nations had brought about a rapprochement between Fascism and Nazism. At the same time, the first half of 1936, saw the advent to power of Communist-supported Popular Front Governments both in Spain and in France, that is, of regimes which the Vatican feared because of their socialist ideology and anti-clerical policy.

Throughout 1936, the Holy See abstained from any direct attack against Germany. The outbreak of the Spanish Civil War, which was followed by anti-religious persecutions, destruction of churches, and banishment of religious functions, dictated an attitude of extreme reserve towards Hitler. Italy's and Germany's aid to Generalissimo Francisco Franco, leader of the Rebels, allied the papacy with Nazism in Spain, against the Loyalist Government and its supporter, Russia— the paramount reason for Vatican caution in its dealings with anti-Bolshevist Germany.

Despite the fact that the attacks against the Church in the Third Reich were increasing, the German episcopate made a supreme attempt at conciliation with the government by issuing a pastoral letter at the annual Fulda convention warmly praising Hitler's anti-Communist campaign and pledging the full support of the Catholic clergy to it. However, the bishops pointed out that the struggle against Communism could not be successful unless the Nazi Government abandoned its attempt to eradicate the Christian faith from the consciousness of the Catholics by restricting the mission of the clergy to the walls of churches and by opposing religious influence on the people. Hitler's reply was that the Church should be grateful to Nazism for having saved it from the fate it had suffered in Spain.

In December 1936, Monsignor Orsenigo lodged a strong protest with the Reich because of a Nazi measure which made enrollment in the Hitlerjugend compulsory for German youth. Pius XI retaliated by denouncing "leaders who pretended to be the defenders of order and civilization" while they were destroying the Church and the Christian faith which he said were the strongest conservative forces. The old Pontiff was forced to his bed by an attack of arteriosclerosis a few days before Christmas and practically never left his private apartment until the middle of March. During that period of comparative idleness he had the opportunity to meditate upon the situation of the Church in the world. Prelates attached to the Pontiff's household told me that each day Pius spent many hours sitting in an armchair next to the window of his bedroom in complete silence. Then, at the end of February, I was informed that he was preparing two encyclicals. Only his secretaries knew of their contents, however. The documents were issued almost simultaneously in March, 1937. One discussed the situation of the Church in Germany, and the other dealt with Communism.

The Berlin Bureau of the New York Times telephoned us to ask whether we had the text of an encyclical just released in Germany. Cortesi, who was head of the Rome office at that time, and I were astonished. Not a word had come from the papal Secretariat of State. I inquired at the Vatican and found that a prelate who enjoyed the confidence of the Pope had left two weeks before for Berlin with the text of the document. Copies of it had been made in Germany and sent to all the bishops for distribution among the parish priests in their respective dioceses to be read simultaneously from all the pulpits on Palm Sunday. The secrecy with which papal instructions were carried out caught the Nazi Government off guard. The encyclical was read to millions of Catholics who thus heard the case of the Church versus Nazism. However, the Nazis did prevent its publication, seized the presses which had made copies of it, and arrested the printers.

The encyclical condemned, among other things, the campaign of defamation of the clergy arising from the "immorality trials" of ecclesiastics who had been accused of illicit relations with nuns in

Catholic convents as well as with members of their own sex; denounced the systematic attacks on Catholic schools and especially the Nazi pressure on heads of families to prevent their children from attending religious functions; and decried the neo-pagan theories fostered by the Nazis and the exalting as "God-like" of Hitler and the German race.

However, even in that strongly worded document, Pius showed considerable caution. He did not even mention national socialism by name, and merely intimated that the neo-pagan doctrines were "supported or favored" by the civil authorities. From the political point of view, therefore, the Vatican limited itself to exposing a situation hostile to the Church without officially censuring the Nazi Government.

Hitler, who had played a number of successful tricks on his enemies, for once found himself bested by a power whose political wisdom springing from millenary experience was superior to his own. Pleased Vatican prelates told me that when he heard of the encyclical, he was beside himself with fury. He called Baron von Neurath, who was then the foreign minister, to his office and dictated to him a stinging note of protest. The Führer objected to the fact that the Vatican, instead of discussing the situation of the Church in Germany directly with his government, had appealed to world public opinion. The Holy See blandly explained that all its efforts to arrive at a solution of the conflict between Church and State had up to that time met with no co-operation from the government.

While relations were strained almost to the breaking point, a serious incident, which added more fuel to the fire, was wilfully created by the late Cardinal Mundelein of Chicago, who, in a speech he delivered in May, called Hitler a "paper hanger" and attacked his anti-religious policy. The Führer was more enraged by Mundelein's words than by any other insult—and there had been quite a few choice ones—addressed to him since his seizure of power. He protested both to Washington and to the Vatican. While the former pointed out that citizens of the United States enjoyed freedom of speech, the latter countered with the argument that since the Third Reich had never disavowed attacks made by Nazi leaders against the

Church, the papacy on its part saw no reason why it should disavow a cardinal. These replies only served to make Hitler angrier. In another note published on May 29, he threatened to denounce the concordat because, he said, the attitude of the Holy See rendered impossible the maintenance of good relations, and he ordered the recall of Diego von Bergen, Ambassador to the Holy Sea. Von Bergen left Rome for an "indefinite leave" but returned unobtrusively a few months later when Hitler realized that his gesture of protest was not only futile but to his disadvantage. Monsignor Orsenigo remained at his post since Hitler failed to carry out his threats.

Pius XI proved more than a match for the German dictator. He refused to be intimidated, indeed his censure of Nazism became more bitter as disheartening news reached the Vatican of progressively intense anti-religious persecutions in Germany. At a general audience which I attended in Castel Gandolfo, in the summer of 1937, the Pontiff fired a broadside at Hitler by paying a high tribute to Mundelein who, he said, was so "bravely defending the rights of God and the Church." Shortly after this statement, Pius had a series of talks with Monsignor Orsenigo, whom he had called to Rome for consultation. The result was an editorial in L'Osservatore Romano which branded Hitler as a man without honor for officially approving Rosenberg's ideology at the year's congress of the Nazi party in Nuremberg "despite repeated assurances in writing and orally that Rosenberg's works were his private affair." Thus, the Vatican newspaper continued, the "declarations and assurances of the German Government have lost their value."

The worst was still to come, however, for the conflict between State and Church in Germany, caused by Nazi racial ideology, extended in the following months to Italy, as a result of increasingly strong German political influence on the Fascist Government arising from Mussolini's policy of collaboration with Hitler.

This policy was a direct outcome of the Ethiopian War. The economic sanctions applied against Italy by the League of Nations had given to a war, which at the beginning was undoubtedly unpopular, the wholehearted support of the Italian people. Mussolini shrewdly exploited that reaction by enacting a series of "emergency measures" which gave him even greater power in every field of national activity. In this way, the democracies made Mussolini not only more powerful but strengthened the Italian domestic front by temporarily creating national support to the Fascist Regime.

At the end of that war, Italy found herself politically and economically isolated. In an interview granted to Ward Price of the *London Daily Mail*, in the summer of 1936, Mussolini held out a sprig of olive to Britain and France, the two powers which had engineered the sanctionist move and were chiefly responsible for Italy's forced isolation. Now that Ethiopia has been conquered, the Italian dictator said, "Italy considers herself among the satisfied nations." In a conversation he had in June, 1936, with Bertrand de Jouvenel, son of a former French ambassador to Italy, Mussolini again expressed his desire to renew collaboration with the two Western democracies. I met de Jouvenel one evening at the Taverna del Quirinale, a de luxe open-air cabaret, a few hours after he had seen Mussolini. He told me that a rapprochement between Italy and France was very probable. Mussolini, according to him, was willing to come to an understanding because he was anxious to reform the Stresa front.

When Italy declared war on England and France, de Jouvenel published an account of his meeting with the Italian dictator. He said that the day after the Popular Front victory in France which gave Leon Blum the premiership, Mussolini promised Italy's collaboration to restrain Hitler's expansionist policy provided Paris recognized the Ethiopian Empire. Mussolini pointed out that France had herself to blame for her inability to intervene in Central Europe, since she had let Germany reoccupy the Rhineland, which was being fortified. A French army could pass through Piedmont, cross Austria, and thus help Czechoslovakia—the only way to check Hitler's conquest of Central Europe. Blum turned a deaf ear to the proposal.

One late afternoon in October, a photographer of Luce, the Italian official photo service, tipped me off that Count Ciano was leaving Rome the same evening. He did not know for sure where he was going, but he thought it was Berlin. The Luce boys were among our most valuable tipsters because, whenever any important event was scheduled, the Ministry of Foreign Affairs would notify their chief

in order to have photographers on the spot and record the ceremony
in a news reel. The Government Press Bureau refused to give me a
confirmation. Andre Rabache, Rome correspondent of Paris' *Le Matin*,
with whom I discussed the rumor, suggested that we go to see Count
Charles de Chambrun, the French Ambassador, who, in those days,
was one of the best diplomatic sources of information.

We were climbing the wide stairway of the Michelangelesque
Palazzo Farnese, seat of the French Embassy, when we met Maurice
Ingram, counsellor of the British Embassy, who had paid a call on
de Chambrun. Rabache told him about the rumor. Ingram broke
into a hearty laugh, shook his head and said, "Just another one of
those mad stories. I can't see how it can be true, you know. Italy and
Germany together?"

De Chambrun, who had been steadily working for a Franco-
Italian rapprochement, did not think it was so funny, however. He
said that he had heard nothing about it, but since France and
England had ignored Mussolini's repeated offers to reach an understanding, well, he would not be too much surprised. . . .

That evening at nine o'clock, Ciano departed for Germany. And
on October 24, 1936, the Rome-Berlin Axis was born.

France's and Britain's refusal to recognize the Ethiopian Empire
in the months immediately following the end of the war; the Franco-
Russian mutual assistance pact concluded in May, 1935; the Austro-
German rapprochement of July 11, 1936, which brought about
economic collaboration between those two countries based on Germany's pledge to respect Austria's integrity; and Russia's active
propaganda in Spain and in France were the factors that caused Mussolini to turn his eyes on the man whom only two years before he
had called a stubborn fool. Moreover, Germany was the only big
power which had given moral and material aid to Italy's Ethiopian
adventure. She had supplied the culprit nation with goods that
fifty-two member states of the League of Nations had refused her,
and had given press support to Il Duce's claim that forty-two million
Italians needed more land in which to live.

After preliminary conversations with von Neurath in Berlin, Ciano
went to Berchtesgaden where Hitler was waiting for him. A few

hours later they issued a joint declaration whereby Italy and Germany agreed to consult each other on all questions affecting their mutual interests and affirmed their intention to work for "general peace and reconstruction."

The general impression in Rome was that what the press termed the Berchtesgaden protocol did not go beyond a superficial manifestation of solidarity. Speaking in Milan on November first, Mussolini once more made unmistakable peace overtures to Britain and France, and for the first time used the word, "Axis" to describe the Italo-German understanding reached eight days before. Contrary to what is generally believed, he did not coin that word. It was the late Premier Gombösz of Hungary who first adopted it as a political expression in one of his speeches. "This Rome-Berlin protocol," said Il Duce, "is an Axis around which all European states, animated by a desire for peace, may collaborate."

The rapprochement with Germany was viewed with considerable coldness not only among Italian officials and military leaders who could not forget that they had fought the Teuton barely twenty years before, but also among the people. When Italy entered the war in June 1940, some pro-democratic friends in the Ministry of Foreign Affairs told me that if France and England had recognized the Empire in the months immediately following the conquest of Ethiopia, Mussolini would have gladly collaborated in the encirclement policy which Paris and London were pursuing in Central Europe to offset the growing German peril. Although quite sincere in their belief, these men were wishful thinkers. Very likely Mussolini would have resumed for a time the Stresa partnership, but would not have remained permanently aligned with the two Western democracies. His ambitious dream of a Mediterranean Empire envisaged domination of Jugoslavia, Greece, Turkey, Egypt, North Africa, and Spain, and was in direct conflict with British and French interests in that sector.

There is an Italian proverb which says, *L'appetito vien mangiando.* (The more you have the more you want.) Mussolini felt very cocky at that time, and so did a very large percentage of Italians who believed what their Duce and his press, radio, and Fascist supporters had been steadily hammering into their brains—that Italy had come out victorious against the economic siege of fifty-two nations. The Italians failed to see that sanctions were applied only to certain types of war materials, and that, despite the loyal solidarity shown by the members of the League of Nations, the newly devised sanctionist machinery was on the whole defectively applied. Although Mussolini knew better, the Italian people, in general, mistook as proof of Italy's might, the Anglo-French political blunders which permitted ship after ship loaded with Italian troops, tanks, planes, guns, and mustard gas to pass through the Suez Canal on their way to Eritrea and Italian Somaliland whence they proceeded to annihilate Haile Selassie's badly led and equipped armies.

As a result, Mussolini was in those summer days of 1936, at the height of his popularity. The physical privations, the curtailment of personal freedom, the innate Italian adversion to the systematic regimentation of the individual, the stifling taxes—a situation which had been endured since early in 1925, when Mussolini definitely crushed the constitutional opposition and securely established his regime—were temporarily forgotten in the joy of triumph. The average Italian chest expansion increased by several inches; wherever I went I heard only ridicule for England. Because of democratic hostility, even well-known anti-Fascists such as Vittorio Emanuele Orlando, Liberal Premier of Italy during the first World War, made peace with Mussolini and changed overnight into warm supporters of the Ethiopian War.

The evening of May 9, 1936, a crowd of at least two hundred thousand people filling Piazza Venezia, Corso Umberto, Via del Plebiscito, Via Quattro Novembre, Via dell'Impero and all the other side streets as far down as the eye could see, listened to Mussolini read the decree that announced the creation of the Ethiopian Empire. On this occasion, I witnessed the first and last real demonstration of popular enthusiasm in Rome. At the end of the speech, people just went crazy. According to my count, Il Duce appeared forty-two times on the balcony of Palazzo Venezia—a record in curtain calls he never even remotely approached in subsequent years.

Having depleted his resources in the Ethiopian War, and being still distrustful of Hitler's expansionist policy, which included as its ultimate program the annexation of Austria and of Italian-held South Tyrol, Mussolini played a two-handed policy with the signing of the Berchtesgaden protocol. He laid the groundwork for Italo-German collaboration and, at the same time, acquired a political weapon with which he hoped to coerce France and England into recognizing the Ethiopian Empire.

The first and most important result of the Axis was Mussolini's support of Hitler's anti-Bolshevist policy, and for this reason the attitude of the Vatican towards that political development was favorable. For months, Fascist and Nazi planes, troops, and equipment had been helping Generalissimo Francisco Franco in Spain, in his fight against the Loyalist Government—a move that coincided with the interests of the Holy See in that country. In perfect harmony, L'Osservatore Romano and the Fascist press vied with each other in publishing harrowing tales of Loyalist persecutions of the clergy and faithful. But the aims of the Church and those of the Fascist Government were quite different. The Pope merely wished to re-establish peace and tranquillity in the Iberian Peninsula by supporting a government which would allow the Church to fulfill its spiritual mission. Mussolini, instead, saw in the Spanish Civil War an opportunity to establish his influence over a Mediterranean power. He hoped to tie Franco to his chariot as an invaluable ally for the time when Rome would feel ready to make her bid for supremacy in what the Italians like to call, Mare Nostrum. He expected to obtain from Spain certain political and strategic advantages that would materially improve her position both in the Mediterranean and in Continental Europe. The cardinal motive for his policy, as he repeatedly stated, was to have freedom of entry into and exit from the Mediterranean. He could not, however, attain this freedom without having control of the key positions—the Suez Canal, Gibraltar, Malta—and of other strategic points from which the lines of maritime communication could be controlled.

Mussolini knew that in the event of war, Britain and France would seal the Mediterranean hermetically, that British-held Gibraltar and Suez Canal would prove insurmountable barriers, and that Malta,

Bizerta, Corsica, and other Anglo-French bases would become formidable centers of operations against Italy. In addition to the fact that a Spain allied to Italy would have meant an extra frontier for France to defend, Mussolini had hopes that Franco would make bases in the Balearic Islands available for his submarines and airplanes. Thus he would be in a position to threaten Gibraltar, bring under the range of his air force, Anglo-French shipping in the Mediterranean, and even operate effectively in the Atlantic by using as bases the many harbors of the Basque coast.

The Vatican soon found out, however, that the Rome-Berlin Axis was developing from what it had thought would be a fundamentally anti-Bolshevist alliance, into a powerful weapon in the hands of two ambitious men bent on enslaving Europe. It saw with dismay that pagan Germany, which at the beginning was only a brilliant second to Catholic Italy, was gradually asserting her political influence on the weaker partner through increasing economic penetration. During the sanctionist period, Italy had been forced to buy goods from Germany, and when sanctions were finally lifted, Germany was firmly entrenched in the Italian market.

An unequivocal sign of Holy See displeasure concerning Italy's pro-German policy was had when Mussolini paid an official visit to Hitler. On September 24, the day he departed aboard a train composed of nine armored coaches, Italian newspapers came out with eight column headlines. They extolled the virtues of the German race, which three years before they had described as composed of "pederasts and nothing else," and waxed lyrical over the "great historical event" which would cement the friendship of two "young and virile nations."

L'Osservatore Romano announced the event with fourteen words.

"Today, at twelve-twenty, His Excellency, the Chief of the Italian Government, left for Munich."

As one prelate put it, the impression of the Vatican in regard to the Hitler-Mussolini meeting was that "relations between the Catholic Church and Nazi Germany are not apt to be improved." There was considerable chagrin over the fact that Mussolini had ignored the tenseness of Church and State relations in Germany and had refused to act as mediator between the two powers. The German Embassy confirmed this by saying that the question would not be raised during the conversations in Berlin since Hitler felt that it was purely a German internal affair and outside the scope of the Rome-Berlin Axis.

Mussolini returned to Italy deeply impressed by Germany's strength, which Hitler had taken care to show him on a tour of war plants and in military maneuvers. Two days later, Edda and I met an Italian cavalry captain named Giorgi at a diplomatic party. He was a very close friend of Achille Starace, Secretary of the Fascist party, who had accompanied Mussolini on his trip. Giorgi told us that Starace summed up his impressions of Germany in one sentence, "When those people start moving, they will be a steam roller." Mussolini's impression, according to Starace, was the same. In fact, hardly a month had gone by before Mussolini, in his new-born love for Prussian efficiency, presented to astonished and mildly amused Romans his edition of the German goose step which he called *passo Romano*. It was the first time since the beginning of his rule that the Italian dictator had stooped to imitate a German military custom. The sophisticated and peace-loving Romans failed to be impressed as hastily trained detachments of troops goose-stepped self-consciously through Via dell' Impero, the spacious avenue studded with remains of Imperial Rome between the Coliseum and Piazza Venezia. A middle-class Italian standing next to me, whose innate thriftiness was apparently outraged, turned to a friend as the soldiers were vigorously banging their feet on the immaculate asphalt and sighed, "I bet you those boots won't last two months . . . and to think that they cost so much."

The political effect of the Mussolini-Hitler talks was soon apparent. On November 6, 1937, Italy joined the alliance against Communism which Germany and Japan had concluded a year earlier. On December 11, she withdrew from the League of Nations, after a meeting of the Grand Council of Fascism, Italy's supreme constitutional body.

According to the version given me by one of the council members, it was a very heated session despite the fact that most of the thirty-odd men present were hardly more than sycophants. Mussolini opened the meeting in a salon of the Palazzo Venezia with a detailed exposition of his trip to Germany. He stated that, in view of England's and France's failure to recognize the Ethiopian Empire, he had decided to withdraw from the League of Nations and to strengthen the alliance with Germany. Dino Grandi, Italian Ambassador to London, who had come to Rome solely to attend the session, explained to the council that he expected to obtain British recognition of the Empire very shortly. He advised against a too close collaboration with Germany which, in his opinion, was not sufficiently strong to match the Anglo-French resources. Roberto Farinacci, former secretary of the Fascist Party and editor of the newspaper *Regime Fascista* which was being subsidized by the German Embassy in Rome, declared himself in favor of a pro-German policy. Carlo Maria de Vecchi, Italo Balbo, and Emilio de Bono, who, with the late Michele Bianchi, had been the quadrumvirs, or leaders, of the so-called, "March on Rome" in 1922, supported Grandi. All of these men were anti-German and told Mussolini that it would be a mistake to abandon the traditional pro-British policy which counterbalanced the weight of the German colossus of the north. Their contention was that Italy, since she was potentially weaker than Germany, could not tie herself to a much stronger ally which would ultimately dominate her because of its continental position.

Marshal Pietro Badoglio, Chief of the General Staff of Italy's armed forces, wound up the discussion by saying that a middle-of-the-road policy, between Germany on the one hand, and England and France on the other, was the wisest course since such a policy would allow Italy to pursue a badly needed rearmament program without creating distrust and obstacles of an economic nature on the part of the other three powers.

After listening to these arguments, Mussolini rose from his chair and sealed Italy's tragic fate with these words:

"Signori, I am convinced that this is the century of the Germans, and I am sure you will agree with me that it is better to be with them than against them."

SEVENTH CHAPTER

Italy's withdrawal from the League of Nations came as a shock to the Vatican because it was a proof of Germany's influence on Italian policy and a blow at an institution which, despite its many faults and practically extinct usefulness, still remained a body for the promotion of peace. However, the Holy See abstained from any official gesture that might imply criticism of Mussolini's collaboration with Germany. It had, at that moment, far greater problems affecting the Church and hoped to enlist Italy's support for their solution.

Three German cardinals and two bishops visited Rome in January 1938, and gave to Pius XI a complete report on the religious situation in their country. The picture was very black indeed, since Hitler's policy of de-Christianization was being relentlessly and more aggressively pursued than ever. Monsignor Borgongini Duca, according to what I learned at the Vatican, had several meetings with Ciano and suggested to him that Mussolini intercede with Hitler to ameliorate the conditions of the Church in Germany. The Holy See's contention was that Berlin's position in the fight against Bolshevism would be immeasurably strengthened by a mutually satisfactory agreement with the Catholic Church, which was ready to give its wholehearted co-operation in the campaign.

Nothing came of it, however. Cardinal Faulhaber told twenty thousand Catholics on February 30, the sixteenth anniversary of Pius XI's coronation, that eighty-two Catholic schools had been closed in his diocese and fifteen thousand children thus deprived of Catholic training. He accused the Nazi Government of misleading and misinforming the people as to the policies and aims of the Church by forbidding publication and circulation of papal messages. The same month, the *Schwarze Korps*, official organ of the Elite Guards, published an editorial that advocated the denunciation of the concordat with the Holy See as incompatible with the "modern idea of a totalitarian state's sovereignty." From the viewpoint of organization and ideology, it said, confessional schools and freedom of education for children are an anachronism in the new Reich—remnants of the bygone era of liberalism and individualism. Adolf Wagner, Bavarian Minister of the Interior, followed this Nazi blast by retorting to Faulhaber that "there will be no peace in Germany until all the political priests are driven out and exterminated."

The religious struggle in Germany was superseded temporarily by one far more serious—the erasing of Austria from the map of Europe.

Both the Vatican and Italy looked on with grave concern as Hitler forced the Austrian Chancellor Kurt Schuschnigg to include Nazi elements in his cabinet early in February, 1938. Mussolini grew wary of his partner. While still officially professing to regard with favor what *Informazione Diplomatica*, the bulletin of the Ministry of Foreign Affairs, called the "natural development of the relations between Austria and Germany based on sincere and mutual collaboration," he opened conversations with Chamberlain for an Anglo-Italian accord to reconcile the interests of the two powers in the Mediterranean which had been unsolved by the so-called gentlemen's agreement signed in January, 1937.

To make even clearer to Hitler, as well as to England and France, that Italy, despite the Axis, was not 100 per cent behind Germany, Ciano on February 16 gave assurances that the rights of Jews would be respected. That communique, which asserted that the "Fascist Government has never thought and is not now thinking of adopting political, economic, or moral measures against Jews as such, except, of course, in the case of elements hostile to the Fascist Regime" could not have implied a clearer condemnation of Germany's racial policy.

The feared bombshell exploded on March 11, when Hitler invaded Austria. Italy, because of her unsettled differences with England and France, as well as her military weakness due to the costly Ethiopian War, was no longer in a position to repeat her 1934 gesture of sending troops to the Brenner. France, the only power besides Russia which had a strong continental army, was in the throes of a cabinet crisis. Russia had her own internal differences and no common frontier with either Germany or Austria.

There is no question that Mussolini was caught completely unprepared. Hitler informed him of his move with a letter that was delivered to Mussolini by Prince Hessen Darmstadt, who had made a special trip by plane from Berlin to Rome, many hours after Nazi troops had already entered Austrian territory. Prince Hessen, who was King Victor Emmanuel's son-in-law by virtue of his marriage with Princess Mafalda of Savoy, had become a sort of confidential messenger for Hitler. Only the evening before, Guido Rocco, head of the government press bureau, had told me that the plebiscite which Schuschnigg had proclaimed with the obvious intention of showing world public opinion that Austria refused to be annexed "will lead to a clarification." And the following day, he admitted to the whole body of foreign correspondents that the "Italian Government considered the situation so grave that it did not feel it could make any statement at present."

While Mussolini was doing some fast thinking, the greatest confusion reigned in government circles which were awaiting instructions from him as to what attitude to take. The Italians with whom I talked did not mince their words in voicing their anger and bitterness at what they called Hitler's betrayal. The Führer's name was mud in those days. The thing they had dreaded—a common frontier with Germany—was a *fait accompli*.

Mussolini held a meeting of the Grand Council of Fascism the next day. The foreign correspondents and all the editors of Rome's newspapers were told to be at Palazzo Venezia that evening. We were ushered into the Sala delle Battaglie, which had been named after a series of mosaics set in the marble floor depicting Italy's victories in the first World War. The mosaics were a gift of Count Volpi di Misurata, leading industrialist and one of Italy's wealthiest men. Two "musketeers," Il Duce's special bodyguards, wearing dapper black uniforms with silver skull and crossbones pinned on the fez and epaulettes, guarded the door leading into the room where the Grand Council was in session. Sixteen others stood at attention in the corners of the large rectangular-shaped salon. We had been waiting only a few minutes when Dino Alfieri, at that time Minister of Popular Culture, emerged from the Grand Council room carrying a sheaf of papers. He stopped in the middle of the hall and read aloud a communique. The fact that a statement was being issued while the session was still on betrayed Mussolini's intention to show that he was absolute master and powerful enough to ignore the advice of his closest collaborators even on such an important question as Austria's future. The communique made it plain that Il Duce had not yet decided on a course of action. It was noncommittal and contained no reference to the Rome-Berlin Axis. Its very reticence indicated the distrust with which Mussolini regarded Hitler's move.

It was only on March 13, that the officially inspired Italian press began to explain to the people that the Austrian events were "logical and inevitable." It printed a telegram sent by Hitler saying "Mussolini, I shall never forget it," and Il Duce's reply, "My attitude is determined by the friendship between the two countries consecrated by the Axis."

The general opinion among the Italians, who felt that their leader had been tricked, was that the answer should have read, "Nor shall I."

After hesitating for three days, Mussolini decided to make the best of a bad job and announced to the Chamber of Deputies that Italo-German relations were not going to be affected by Hitler's annexation of Austria. That it was a bitter pill for him to swallow was evident. Il Duce had suffered his first political setback since the proud days of the Ethiopian War. His cockiness had gone. He read a lengthy speech, which for the most part was listened to in silence by the servile members of the Chamber. It was, for once, permeated with sober realism. Mussolini realized that he had to cope with somebody stronger and more ruthless than he. In a few passages, he resorted to the demagogic oratory with which he inevitably aroused the enthusiasm of the masses. Those passages were applauded with unusual warmth because they were anti-German.

"For us Fascisti," he thundered, "frontiers are sacred. They must not be discussed, but defended."

"What with?" a German correspondent sitting next to me in the press gallery whispered in my ear.

I thought it was just a quip since, in common with many other colleagues, I did not at that time suspect Italy's woeful military weakness.

If to the Italian dictator the fall of Austria meant the crumbling of a pillar of his foreign policy, which sought to maintain a buffer state between Italy and Germany; to the Vatican, it meant the disappearance of a one hundred per cent Catholic nation. The papal nuncio to Vienna was summoned to Rome for a report on the circumstances which had led to the anschluss. There was an atmosphere of dire pessimism in the Vatican. One of the first things the Nazis did was to arrest Monsignor Sigismund Waitz, Archbishop of Salzburg, and close the Central Seat as well as some of the branches of the Catholic Action Association, although that lay organization founded by Pius XI for collaboration of the laity with the apostolic mission of the Church, had been guaranteed by a concordat.

Monsignor Waitz was released after a few days and allowed to go to Vienna for an episcopal conference called by Cardinal Innitzer. As he stepped from the train, he was searched on the plea that he was suspected of carrying documents proving alleged relations between him and French, as well as German communists. This was but a small incident compared to many other Nazi outrages reported to the Vatican. Five priests of the archdiocese of Salzburg were imprisoned, and one of them, Canon Seinwender, was struck in the face. The Kilpinghaus, a home for young Catholic artisans, was confiscated and the priests, nuns, and youths obliged to leave. The convent of the Most Precious Blood also was searched and money there seized. Catholic women's and Catholic young women's organizations in the archdiocese of Salzburg were dissolved as well as women's organizations in the diocese of Linz. Again in Salzburg, the offices of the Catholic University were occupied and all practicing Catholics who held high posts dismissed. The Austrian Catholic press became Nazi overnight. All the principal collaborators were either discharged or imprisoned, while Reich commissioners were installed in the offices of every Catholic newspaper and publishing house.

A group of Nazis invaded the house of Monsignor Ferdinand Pawlikowski, Bishop of Graz, seized books and documents which they destroyed, and took the prelate to jail. He was released shortly afterwards with apologies by the police commissioner from Berlin who explained that the measure had been taken in order to protect the bishop from "threatened Communist aggression!"

Despite these instances of persecution, which were a clear proof that Hitler was determined to smash Catholicism in his newly acquired domain, the Austrian episcopate, after long deliberation, issued a declaration urging the faithful to vote for union with Germany in the plebiscite that was to be held on April 10. With that move, Hitler wanted to show the world that Austria was predominantly in favor of the anschluss and that, therefore, the charge that he had taken the country against the will of the majority of the people was unfounded.

In view of the circumstances, the attitude of the Austrian bishops was truly amazing. Their declaration praised the accomplishments of Nazism in the social and economic field, as well as its fight against atheism, and affirmed that it was a national duty for the bishops to profess themselves Germans and to support the German Reich.

Indignation in the Vatican was unbounded. Pius XI called Count Andrea dalla Torre, editor of *L'Osservatore Romano*, to his study and dictated to him an editorial published on April 1, which disavowed the declaration and strongly rebuked the Austrian bishops who, it said, had acted without the knowledge and consent of the Holy See. Moreover, with that statement Pius XI indicated to Hitler that there could be no compromise between them, and he rejected whatever political advantage the Church might have obtained by supporting the plebiscite. The same day, Father Filippo Soccorsi, head of the Vatican radio station, informed me that late in the evening there would be a special broadcast in German for the Austrian people. I was able to secure a copy of the text, which an anti-Nazi Austrian colleague gladly translated. It contained scathing criticism of Cardinal Innitzer, Archbishop of Vienna, who had promoted the episcopal conference. Austrian Catholics were told that they need not follow his advice, for Innitzer had "bowed down before the mighty and successful of the day." Instead of recognizing, as was his duty, the sheep in wolf's clothing, he had believed Hitler's promises despite the "sad experience" of others and the warnings of the Pope.

Both *L'Osservatore Romano* editorial and the broadcast were ignored by Innitzer who, in open defiance of papal wishes, ordered that all church bells be rung on April 9 during the last big rally to be staged by the Nazis in Vienna on the eve of the plebiscite. Perhaps a clue to his attitude might be found in the fact that the Austrian Cardinal was a native Sudeten German and former member of the Schober cabinet which had strong pan-German leanings.

Pius XI acted swiftly. He instructed Cardinal Pacelli, his Secretary of State, to telephone Vienna and summon Innitzer to Rome immediately. The Austrian, who had hardly time to pack his bag, reached the Italian capital the next evening. As an indication of papal displeasure, no representatives of the Holy See and of the Secretariat of State were at the station to welcome him. Innitzer went straight to the Vatican where he was promptly received by Pacelli.

That conversation lasted far into the night. The Secretary of State wanted to know the reasons that had prompted the leader of the Austrian episcopate to turn a complete political somersault on the question of the anschluss when only one month before he had publicly voiced his support of the Schuschnigg regime. Innitzer explained that Hitler, in a private meeting which had taken place soon after the seizure of Austria, had given him guarantees concerning the future of the Church, and that he had received similar assurances from Goering and from Joseph Buerckel, who was the organizer of the plebiscite.

Pacelli worked until very late to prepare the report which he handed to the Pope at eight o'clock the next morning. Two hours later, Innitzer was ushered into Pius XI's private study. It was a dramatic audience. Vatican circles said that Pius was prepared to remove the Austrian Cardinal from the Vienna See, on the ground that he had flouted papal warnings and condemnations of Nazism.

It was past noon when the medium-built, stoop-shouldered, white-haired prince of the Church descended the stairway which leads to the Courtyard of Saint Damasus, where I had been waiting for him. His meek, thin, tired face was flushed. He looked at no one as he waited for his limousine. In those few seconds, I approached him and asked if he could comment on the Austrian situation.

"No, no, I have nothing to say," he replied.

It did not take long to learn what had happened. The Pope had handed Innitzer a statement, which I understand had been prepared by Pacelli, and had made him sign it. As Head of the Church in Austria, and also in behalf of the whole Austrian episcopate, Innitzer signed and virtually retracted the declaration urging Catholics to vote for the anschluss. It said:

The solemn declaration of March 18, of the Austrian Episcopate was not intended to be, obviously, in approval of what was not and is not compatible with God's law and the Catholic Church's freedom and rights. That declaration, moreover, must not be interpreted by the State and party as an obligation of conscience, nor must it be exploited for purposes of propaganda.

For the future, the Austrian Bishops demand:

That no changes shall be made without previous agreement with the Holy See in all questions contemplated by the Austrian concordat.

That, in particular, the application of all regulations relative to schools and education as well as to the formation of youth shall correspond with the parents' natural rights and the religious and moral formation of Catholic youth in accordance with the principles of the Catholic faith; that propaganda contrary to the Church and to the Catholic religion shall be forbidden; that Catholics shall retain the rights to proclaim, defend, and practice their Catholic faith and Christian principles in all fields of human life and by all the means at the disposal of contemporary civilization.

Rome, April 6, 1938.

Theodore Cardinal Innitzer, also in the name of the whole Austrian Episcopate.

The Holy See had once more proved the compactness and discipline of the hierarchical organization of the Church, and had severely chastised churchmen whose loyalty had been temporarily swayed by Hitler's false promises. Vatican foresight and wisdom were confirmed two months later when Hitler extended to Austria the divorce and marriage laws already adopted in the Reich. Those measures substituted for the compulsory church wedding a compulsory civil wedding performed by a state official "in the name of the Reich," and abrogated the legal validity of the principle enforced by the Church on its followers—that a Catholic marriage cannot be divorced. Innitzer's hope that Hitler would respect the feelings of six million Catholics were shattered by that decree which spelled the end of the dominant position the Roman Catholic Church had enjoyed in Austria for eight hundred years.

While Hitler was consolidating his hold on Austria, Mussolini was completing negotiations for a pact with England and beginning conversations with France. His motives were clear. In reviving the threat of a Stresa front, he hoped to strengthen his position vis-à-vis his Axis partner, increase Italy's potential bargaining value, and thus counterbalance the already uncomfortable German pressure.

On April 16, Guido Rocco announced to the foreign correspondents that Count Ciano had invited them to witness the signature of the Anglo-Italian pact at six o'clock that afternoon. The Hall of Victory, named after a tapestry which overhung the ornamental fireplace next to Ciano's study in the Palazzo Chigi, was transformed into a diminutive moving picture studio by a dozen cameramen busily setting up klieg lights and tripods in order to record the event. Ciano had neglected nothing that would make the ceremony look impressive. He quickly learned the theatrical histrionics of his father-in-law. About twenty high government officials, diplomatists, and Fascist hierarchs, all formally dressed in morning coats, stood around a large table where clerks were placing silver inkstands and quill pens. A few minutes later, Ciano and Lord Perth, the British ambassador, walked into the square-shaped salon from which all furniture had been removed to make room for the guests.

While waiting for the Egyptian Minister to Rome, who was to sign one of the documents, Ciano, who appeared in excellent spirits and was thoroughly enjoying the show, shook hands with several of the diplomatists present. The ceremony of the signature lasted about ten minutes. The pact itself did not last even that long because it was for Mussolini a political expedient and not a pledge. I must say, however, that at that moment every observer in Rome really believed a new era had begun. Our feeling was certainly shared by the Italian people.

As we were filing out, I looked through a window that overlooked the small square called, Largo Chigi, and saw a solid mass of people jamming the sidewalks on either side of it in front of La Rinascente, Rome's largest department store, and of Galleria Colonna. They had heard of the signing of the pact and had waited to have a glimpse of the diplomatists and high officials. When the black limousine bearing Lord Perth issued from Palazzo Chigi, the people recognized it and cheered the smiling British Ambassador as he sped towards Via del Tritone. That was not a commandeered demonstration; as a matter of fact, I was told that Mussolini did not like it.

For a time, the daily attacks of the Italian press against England, which had kept everybody on tenterhooks for years, disappeared. The many problems originated by Italy's conquest of Ethiopia seemed to have been permanently settled. True, Virginio Gayda, official mouthpiece of the Fascist Government, was stating in Rome's *Giornale d'Italia* that the Rome-Berlin Axis remained the fundamental guiding principle of Italy's foreign policy, but his editorials were believed to reflect Mussolini's hopes to revive the four-power pact among England, France, Germany, and Italy, stillborn in 1933, mainly because of Little Entente opposition to it. Moreover, hadn't Il Duce instructed Ciano to tell Jules Blondel, French chargé d'affaires in the absence of the pro-Italian Count de Chambrun, who had been permanently recalled from Rome by the socialist Blum Government, that Italy was ready to negotiate an agreement along the lines of the Anglo-Italian accord?

The Vatican did not share the general rejoicing, however. While Chamberlain, in another manifestation of his chronic wishful thinking, was asserting in London that the Axis did not conflict with the Anglo-Italian pact, Pius XI announced that he would not stay in the same city with Hitler, who was to pay a return visit to Mussolini on May 3, and witness the festivities in honor of the arch foe of the Church. For weeks, the Pontiff had been engaged in feverish political activity with the Nazi Government to obtain guarantees for the Church in Austria and to halt the persecutions against the clergy and faithful. The negotiations had failed. The Vatican, which had hoped that Hitler, in view of Austria's absorption that had swelled the number of Catholics within greater Germany to more than twenty millions, would desist from pursuing his anti-religious policy, had no more illusions. "It is going to be a fight to the finish," a prelate connected with the Secretariat of State predicted. In fact, the possibility of a discussion between Pius and Hitler was wilfully eliminated by the Pontiff's voluntary withdrawal to his summer home. Any meeting, which some Vatican circles hoped might have brought the two leaders together, was futile since years of experience had already shown that no common basis for a discussion could be found.

Frederick T. Birchall, star correspondent of *The New York Times*, came to Rome to cover the Hitler-Mussolini show. Cortesi and I did most of the legwork as well as some of the writing which Birchall incorporated in his daily stories. For many days before the visit, plain-clothes men poured into Rome from all parts of Italy. Mussolini was taking no chances. He told Arturo Bocchini, chief of police, to adopt whatever measures he deemed necessary to ensure Hitler's safety. All foreign Jews were given the alternative of either leaving Rome or going to jail until the visit was over. Well-known anti-Fascists were rounded up and taken to *Regina Coeli*, which is Latin for Queen of Heaven—a very unusual name for Rome's Sing Sing. At police headquarters, we found that the local OVRA (secret police) numbering sixteen thousand, had been strengthened by an additional thirty thousand men brought in from other towns. Policemen armed with sub-machine guns were placed on roof tops and everyone of the people who lived in the houses along the route of the parade of welcome was investigated. Day and night, sewers and the bases of pillars bearing the Italian and German colors were inspected to make sure that they concealed no bombs.

On arrival at the new Ostiense Station, Hitler found a Rome resplendent in a blaze of lights. Our estimate was that three hundred thousand people, distinctly lukewarm in their demonstration of enthusiasm but obviously enjoying the stupendous spectacle, lined the itinerary from the station to the Quirinal Palace where the former paperhanger was the guest of the House of Savoy.

"No reigning monarch of these days or of the past was ever received in a foreign country with such a pageant as the Italian Duce put on tonight for his colleague, the German Fuhrer," Birchall wrote. "For Chancellor Adolf Hitler's arrival, a whole section of Rome, stretching across the city had been transformed. Along the three-mile route that he traveled from the new railroad station built for him to the King's palace, ruins of the past were floodlighted to enclose a modern phantasy of white pillars and gilded symbols of Fascism and Nazism. There were illuminated fountains, huge pylons spouting flames, and everywhere, flags without end—banners of Germany, of Italy, and of Rome."

The only dark spot in this phantasmagoric display of light and color was the tiny papal state across the Tiber. Before leaving for Castel Gandolfo, Pius gave orders to close the Vatican Museums which Hitler had planned to visit, and to refuse admittance into the city of all members of the German official party. The day after the arrival of the German Dictator, Pius remarked at a general audience that "sad things are happening, both far and near. Among these sad things is certainly the fact that it has not been considered both out of place and untimely to hoist in Rome the emblem of a cross that is not the cross of Christ."

With his clear reference to the swastika and to Hitler's visit, Pius not only restated Vatican opposition to the Axis but fired the first shot in the battle with Mussolini which lasted until the Pontiff's death in February, 1939. In a previous attempt to throw cold water over officially inspired enthusiasm, L'Osservatore Romano, a few days before Hitler's arrival, had joyfully printed extracts from German racial studies just out of the Nazi presses. These extracts extolled the superiority of the Nordic races over those of the Mediterranean, and one of them went so far as to say that the Italians would have no difficulty in colonizing Ethiopians, since "the racial difference between them and the Africans is not very great."

What the Italian dictator once called the "wailings of an old man" failed, however, to mar the Italo-German festivities. Mussolini spent twenty million lire—more than one million dollars at the official exchange rate of that year—to impress his colleague with Italy's military strength. He built a cardboard town outside Rome to give Hitler a realistic display of dive bombing, and Italian pilots who had for many months been attacking defenseless Spanish towns held by the Loyalists demonstrated their unchallenged skill. The most spectacular number in the elaborate program was the naval review held off the Bay of Naples. Mussolini especially wanted to show his partner, who had no navy to speak of, that Italy was a full-fledged naval power and superior to Germany at least in that field.

All the modern units of the Italian fleet were mobilized for a series of maneuvers which even sophisticated British naval experts admitted were carried out with striking efficiency. Two twenty-five-thousand-ton battleships—the Giulio Cesare and the Conte di Cavour—eighteen cruisers, nineteen flotilla leaders, six destroyers, twenty-six torpedo boats, twenty-four submarine chasers, four escort ships, eighty-five submarines and six auxiliary vessels participated in that display which, in point of the number of ships, was the largest ever held since the First World War. King Victor, Hitler, and Mussolini saw the show from the deck of the Cavour while Italian reporters and foreign correspondents had a ringside seat aboard the transatlantic liner, Rex.

As we were having lunch, Margherita Sarfatti-Grassini, Mussolini's erstwhile friend, caused a sensation when she announced "Cardinal Ascalesi is on board the Cavour!" About a dozen correspondents rushed to the rail and looked at the battleship silhouetted against the dark-blue mountains of Capri. Yes, someone dressed in purple was standing next to Hitler. Cortesi focused his glasses on the ship.

"Take it easy, gentlemen," he said after a few seconds. "That purple is the lining of a Nazi cloak."

After what the Pope had said, the presence of Ascalesi, Archbishop of Naples, would have been a truly sensational story. We felt somewhat cheated.

During the visit, Hitler went to work on Mussolini to convince him that he had nothing to fear from Germany. As a result, the distrust which the Italian dictator felt for his colleague was greatly allayed. In his toast at the end of the six-day pageant, the Führer stated that the frontier between Italy and Germany was "intangible." That, he declared was his "political testament to the German people."

All other potential points of friction were settled. As a price for Italian friendship and collaboration, Hitler renounced his claims on South Tyrol where about three hundred thousand Austrians under Italian domination had been made restless by events in Germany. He likewise reassured Mussolini in regard to the future of Trieste, the port which was once Austria's main outlet to the Adriatic. Hitler was after bigger game. If I can believe what an Italian foreign ministry official said, the real basis for Italo-German political, economic, and military collaboration was laid during that trip.

Feeling certain of Germany's support, Mussolini resumed his boisterous and arrogant ways. To five thousand Genoese he said a week later that Italy and Germany were ready to fight together to the end if the democracies were foolish enough to declare war on them. He rendered impossible the continuance of the well-advanced Italo-French conversations by the pointed remark that Paris and Rome were on the "opposite side of the barricade" in Spain. It was his way of saying that France was thwarting Italy's effort to secure a hold in that Mediterranean country through a Franco victory.

Although it could not be guessed at the time, subsequent events made it clear that the Italian and German dictators had agreed on a common policy to undermine France, which they thought to be the only first-class military power on the continent other than their own. Mussolini's idea was to keep friendly relations with England in order to ensure her neutrality until the time he felt ready to carry out, with Germany's help, his plan for a Mediterranean Empire.

EIGHTH CHAPTER

It was one of those dreaded summer afternoons in Rome, when Scirocco, the hot humid south wind, blowing all the way from Africa, saps one's strength, causes drowsiness, and makes one languidly long for a good-sized, snow-capped mountain. It was the kind of weather which transforms ambition into laziness, an active brain into a vacuum, a vigorous body into a stagnant piece of flesh.

A few unlucky correspondents who had not managed to go to Ostia, Rome's bathing place, fifteen miles away, were morosely sipping iced drinks, their sagging bodies resting on the comfortable, generously padded armchairs of the modernistic hotel lobby-like, brown-colored hall of the Foreign Press Club bar. There was only one wish in our minds—that Mussolini would take a day off and do nothing that would make a story, for even the most ambitious newspaperman felt that life was already unbearable enough without adding to it the physical and mental exertion involved in the reporting of news. It looked as though our wishes were to be fulfilled. The morning and afternoon newspapers were stating for the nth time Italy's reasons for intervening in Spain. Even Virginio Gayda, the prolific editor of the *Giornale d'Italia*, whose main task was to write officially inspired editorials for the almost exclusive benefit of the foreign press, had failed to produce his daily two thousand words.

Then the telephone on the first floor where the working rooms were located pierced the silence. Everyone secretly wished the call were not for him. It would take too much effort to abandon the feet-on-the-table position we all had adopted in our defense against the July climate. The call, we heard with dismay, was for all the correspondents. The two ushers on duty leaned over the circular balustrade carved into the ground floor ceiling and announced:

"The Ministry of Popular Culture has just phoned saying that an important communique will be sent here in thirty minutes."

We sighed and grunted. There was still hope, however. Despite the fact that it had been functioning for many years, the Government press office had a rather vague idea of what was news for foreign consumption. It sent dozens of communiques containing poorly written propaganda which inevitably ended in the wastepaper basket. We waited. Finally the messenger bearing the communiques arrived. We dragged ourselves away from the chairs and listlessly climbed the two flights of stairs to the first floor.

We were so astonished by what we read that we forgot to curse Mussolini, the Ministry of Popular Culture, and Italy in general. Fascism had inaugurated an anti-Semitic policy. A group of anonymous university professors had signed what the Ministry of Popular Culture called an "Aryan manifest," advocating a vigorous racial policy to prevent the "Aryan" Italians from being contaminated by "extra-European races." It was the most sensational story that had come out of Rome in many weeks. It confirmed sporadic measures already taken unofficially against the Jews in Italy, and at the same time, it proved the extent of German influence on Fascist policy as well as Mussolini's decision to cast his lot with Hitler against the democratic powers.

The manifesto was issued on July 14, 1938, and consisted of ten points. It asserted that the majority of the forty-four million Italians were the descendents of families emigrated to Italy a thousand years before; it scotched the "legend" that barbaric hordes had settled in Italy; it affirmed that the influx of non-Italian races had been negligible and that, therefore, the racial characteristics of the Italians had not been altered. One of the professors with whom I talked some time later confided, however, that the whole manifesto had been drawn to include the ninth point which stated that "Jews do not belong to the Italian race . . . Jews represent only the part of the population that has never been assimilated in Italy, because it is made up of non-European racial elements differing absolutely from the racial elements that have given origin to the Italians."

For many months the Italian Government had been quietly eliminating Jews from key positions. As soon as they reached the retirement age, they would not be allowed to stay, and their jobs would be taken by non-Jews. The manifesto, then, merely advocated the hastening of this process of elimination. Exactly two weeks before, I had had another confirmation of this unobtrusive anti-Semitism. For years I had been buying books in one of Rome's largest stores and had come to know many of the employees quite well. The last time I had been in the shop one of the clerks had drawn me aside and shown me a circular issued by the Ministry of Popular Culture. It forbade publishers to print translations of foreign books by Jewish authors. All existing copies of such books were to be returned by booksellers to the publishers who were permitted to sell them privately until the entire stock was exhausted. Publishers were allowed to print books by Italian Jews, but booksellers could not display them in show windows.

With the exception of Berlin, which hailed the issuance of the manifesto as a victory for Hitler's racial ideology, the first international reaction, and that of the Italian people as a whole, was that Mussolini had imitated his partner. Was there a racial problem in Italy? One could cite scores of statements, including the one Il Duce himself gave to Emil Ludwig—that there was no "anti-Semitism in Italy," and that "the Jews had fought bravely under the Italian tricolor in the First World War"—to prove it did not exist. Only three months before, Ciano had said that the ratio of Italian Jews was of about one per thousand. True, many German and Austrian Jews had taken shelter in Italy as a consequence of the Nazi pogroms, but the final total of the official census taken in August, 1938, showed that they amounted to a bare 57,145 as compared to 44,000,000 "Aryan" Italians! The figure accounted for both Italian and foreign Jews.

Italy, in modern times, had never proved a fertile field for the Jew because of her economic poverty, low standard of living, overpopulation, strong competition with the quick intuitive Italian mind and the traditional frugality and thriftiness of the lower and middle classes. Even in the prosperous period of the great Florentine bankers and of the powerful maritime republics of Venice and Genoa, which virtually monopolized European trade from the fourteenth to the seventeenth centuries, Jews did not attain a leading position in the economic and political fields. Most of the Jews in Italy had settled in the richer industrial regions of the north or in the commercial and maritime centers. South of Naples, one could almost count them on the fingers of one hand. To give an example, statistics published in the fall of 1938, showed that there were twenty-four in Calabria, ten in Lucania, and four in the whole of Sicily!

Great Jewish fortunes did not exist in Italy. There were certainly none that could compare with those of the Cianos, Alberto Pirelli, and Count Volpi. The press was exclusively in "Aryan" hands, as were the publishing houses. Politically, Jewish influence was nihil, owing to the overwhelming majority of Italians in the Chamber of Deputies and the Senate; industrially, the largest plants and combines were under absolutely Italian control; commercially, there were many large stores and wholesale houses which were reliable and had never been accused of shady dealings; educationally, the very few Jewish professors in the Italian universities and schools had devoted their activities exclusively to scientific and cultural fields, and their books had materially contributed to the national culture.

Therefore, no political or economic issue was connected with the Jewish question. As for the religious aspects of the problem, not even the most rabid, anti-Semitic Fascists such as Telesio Interlandi, editor of the extreme right-wing newspaper, Tevere, and Roberto Farinacci, editor of the Regime Fascista, had ever raised it. It was obvious that the Jewish religion could hardly find propitious conditions for its propagation in the country that was the cradle of Christianity.

This was not a situation that had been created by Fascism. Even in the liberal and socialist eras, Italian Jews never identified themselves with left-wing parties as, incidentally, Mussolini himself had done in the days before he organized the Fascist movement.

For all these reasons, Il Duce's anti-Semitic policy left the Italians cold. They could not understand it. Anne O'Hare McCormick, leading editorial writer on foreign affairs for The Times, arrived in Italy when the Jewish campaign was at its height in the winter of 1938–39. She found that it was "universally unpopular." Even one hundred per cent Fascists, she said, were critical and apologetic.

As a matter of fact, thinking Italians suddenly displayed great consideration for Jews and went out of their way to show them that they harbored no racial prejudices. A typical illustration of this reaction was what Trilussa, Italy's greatest living poet, told Princess Victoria Colonna, leader of Roman society.

Trilussa had a unique social position. His genius, natural wit, culture, perfect manners coupled with a profound liking for, and understanding of, the humbler folks made him one of the most popular figures not only in literary and aristocratic circles but in the middle and lower classes. He dined indifferently with princely families in their historical palaces or with bricklayers and taxicab drivers in the "osterie" of the Roman suburbs.

His satirical poems in the Roman dialect were as popular in the Italian capital as those of Walt Whitman in the United States during the last century. They always contained a good-humored but dangerously corroding criticism of Fascism. The popularity of his works was such that Mussolini had decided to censor them personally. Though he enjoyed them for their outstanding artistic quality and exquisite humor, Il Duce more often than not sent them back with a laconic "NO" written in red pencil on the margin of the manuscript. Not long before I left Italy, Trilussa showed me quite a number of these poems stored away in his desk.

Princess Colonna, whose salon he had been frequenting for about twenty-five years, telephoned him one morning and said that His Highness, the Duke of Spoleto, nephew of the King of Italy and future King of Croatia, was in town and had asked to hear the "latest ones from Trilussa." Could he come to dinner at her house that evening?

"I am very sorry, but I can't," the poet said. "I have been invited by the Foa family. I am sure His Highness will understand that if I canceled the invitation at the last minute I might hurt the feelings of old friends who, through no fault of their own, are now being discriminated against."

"Could you come after dinner?" the Princess asked.

At eleven in the evening the personal car of the Duke of Spoleto was in Via Pasquale Stanislao Mancini, where the Jewish Foa family still lives, to take Trilussa to the Colonna Palace.

The reasons that had driven Mussolini to create an artificial prob-

lem which had antagonized world public opinion and bred more
hatred than any other single Fascist measure up to that time were
purely political. Having decided to collaborate with Germany against
the democracies, the Italian Dictator felt that Italy's Jewish population would undoubtedly oppose an alliance with a power that had
made Jew-baiting one of the most spectacular manifestations of its
domestic policy. Il Duce feared that in the event of war, Italian Jews
in important positions would exert their influence to sabotage Italy's
war effort. His was a preventive measure, therefore. By eliminating
the Jews from key posts and by replacing them with men whom he
could trust, he hoped to strengthen his domestic front. His mistake,
as many Italians pointed out, was that he need not issue legislations
affecting all Jews to strike only at a score who, because of their positions, might have represented a potential threat. Moreover, these
men had never been politically active against Fascism, not even during the genesis of the Rome-Berlin Axis. Il Duce himself acknowledged their loyalty to the country and quietly found new jobs for
them. Edda, who was studying law at Rome University, reported
that one of her professors by the name of De Vecchi affected by the
anti-racial laws, was by Mussolini's express order given a post in the
International Institute for the Unification of Private Law, with headquarters in Rome.

Some of the Fascists of the "old guard," that is, men who had
played an important part in the creation of the Fascist regime, did
not hesitate to show their hostility to the measures. Their leader was
Italo Balbo, the "enfant terrible" of Fascism because of his strong
personality, intelligence, ruthlessness, and courage.

After two months of press campaign intended as psychological
preparation, the Grand Council of Fascism met on October 6 to endorse officially the "Aryan manifesto." Three weeks later, Balbo invited a group of foreign correspondents to witness the emigration of
eighteen thousand Italian farmers to Libya. The Fascist Government
commandeered a dozen merchantmen and shipped the emigrants to
many newly built villages on the fringes of the Sirt Desert and in
Cyrenaica. There they found a small-sized field, a three-room house
with an oven, a stable, a barn, and agricultural implements.

The correspondents were treated with a liberality typical of Balbo. Whenever we stopped at a hotel, the Air Marshal gave us not only rooms and food but the freedom of the bar as well. Don Minifie, of *The Herald Tribune*, and I were the only two American correspondents. Balbo's anti-German feelings were never more clearly shown than during that trip. Although a half-dozen Nazi newspapermen had been invited, he constantly avoided them. His attitude was so obvious, that on their return to Rome, the Germans signed a protest which they handed to the Ministry of Popular Culture.

At nearly every meal I was invited to sit next to Balbo. It was while we were dining in Misurata, a small town between Tripoli and Bengazi, that I asked him what he thought of the racial legislation.

"It won't mean a thing," he said in his blunt way. "Just between you and me, I fought it tooth and nail (*a spada tratta*, was the expression he used.) De Vecchi and de Bono did the same. So, when we saw that the Chief (Mussolini) was determined to carry through his plan we proposed that Jews whose loyalty to Italy and the Fascist regime could be proved, be exempted from the laws. The exceptions will mitigate the measures, for they affect the majority of Jewish families which almost all have a member to whom discrimination can be applied."

Balbo was not giving me a cock-and-bull story. The day after the Grand Council meeting he had flown from Rome to Ferrara, his home town. He made a point of visiting every one of the prominent Jews and went so far as to invite to lunch the Jewish-born *podestà*, or mayor, of Ferrara, who, of course, had sent his resignation to Rome the same morning. While the press bannered the anti-Jewish measures, hundreds of sympathetic Italians gaped at the daring exhibition of cordiality as Balbo walked into the most popular restaurant of the town arm-in-arm with his Jewish friend.

As was to be expected, Fascist spies reported the gesture of defiance to Rome. The story made the rounds of all government and social circles. It even reached the ears of handsome, dapper, melliferous Dino Alfieri, Minister of Popular Culture, and one of the most servile members in the Italian Cabinet. Alfieri was a political opportunist and a born courtier. He belonged to the Nationalist Party in the period prior to the March on Rome but hastened to change the blue shirt of that organization for the black shirt of the Fascists as soon as Mussolini seized power.

In the lobby of the Hotel Excelsior a few days later, he asked Balbo:

"Is it true that you shook hands with all the Jews in Ferrara?"

"Absolutely," Balbo confirmed. "And I want to assure you that I'll do the same with you when all the former 'Nationalists' will be banned from the Fascist Party."

Italy's racial legislation, when it was finally completed after a series of decrees over a period of many months, defined a Jew; first, he whose two parents are Jews; second, he who is born of a Jewish father and a foreign mother; third, he who though born of mixed marriage, professes the Jewish religion. It did not regard as Jew he who was born of a mixed marriage and professed a religion other than Jewish on October 1, 1938.

The laws prohibited marriage between Italians and persons belonging to the Semitic and other "non-Aryan" races. Jews, both teachers and students, were banned from government-supported schools, the army, the Fascist Party, the judiciary, and liberal professions. They were forbidden to open new shops or buy those belonging to "Aryans," and to own stores with more than one hundred employees. This last measure was not difficult to evade, however, as I discovered.

Tipped off by an influential Fascist, the owner of a wholesale and retail clothing store in Rome, discharged ten of his one hundred nine employees three days before the anti-Jewish decrees came out. Having cut their number to ninety-nine before the laws were published, he continued to operate his business unmolested.

An official communique issued at the beginning of November announced that three thousand five hundred twenty-two Jewish families out of fifteen thousand were to receive special treatment. These were: families of men who fell in the Fascist cause; families of men mutilated or invalided for the Fascist cause; families of men who joined the party before the March on Rome or during the second half of 1924, (the period when thousands of Fascists disgusted by the murder of the socialist deputy, Giacomo Matteotti, engineered by Mussolini's henchmen, resigned from the party); and families of Fiume legionaries, that is, of those volunteers who, led by Gabriele d'Annunzio, the Italian poet, occupied the Adriatic port which was being denied to Italy at the Paris Conference soon after the First World War.

There was considerable surprise in Rome at the announcement that only three thousand five hundred twenty-two families had not been discriminated against. One of the professors who had signed the Aryan manifesto explained that in reality those to whom exemptions would be applied amounted to about eight thousand. The reason for announcing the small figure was that, after all the hullabaloo sponsored by Mussolini to make the people conscious of the "Jewish peril" the Fascist Government felt that it would have looked ridiculous if it had to admit that the number of Jews against whom forty-four million Italians had to defend themselves consisted of a few thousands. Even on the basis of official figures, the Fascist Government still looked ridiculous. Out of the 57,145 Jews about 10,000 were foreign since the April 1931 census listed the number of Italian Jews at 47,825, or what at that time was 1.2 per 1,000 population. Allowing the conservative estimate of four members per each Jewish family, the 3,522 families officially exempted represented about 14,000 Jews who, added to the 10,000 foreigners, brought the total up to 24,000. In other words, when all was said and done, the racial laws affected slightly more than 30,000 Jews!

The tension between the Fascist Government and the Vatican which had been slowly developing as a result of the gradually closer Italo-German co-operation broke into an open, personal fight between Pius XI and Mussolini over the anti-Jewish campaign in the summer of 1938.

The day after the so-called Aryan manifesto was published, the Pope branded it a "true form of apostasy." He attacked "excessive nationalism" which he said was in direct contrast with the Catholic doctrine. As the enslaved Italian press obeyed Fascist Party instructions to vilify the Jews, Pius XI fought with truly amazing vigor. On July 21, he defied the Fascist Government by urging the members of the Catholic Action Associations to oppose the racial policy.

"The spirit of faith," he said, "must fight against the spirit of separatism and against the spirit of exaggerated nationalism which are detestable and which, just because they are not Christian, end by not being even Human."

The Catholic Action in Italy is a strong lay organization conceived and organized by Pius soon after his ascension to the papacy in 1922. Although official figures are lacking, its membership numbers many hundreds of thousands. There are associations in every diocese supervised by a bishop. The various diocesan branches are under the supreme control of a national committee which, during Pius XI's reign, was responsible to the Pope alone. The members of the organization are laymen who co-operate with the Church in the furthering of the Catholic doctrine. They also have the duty of promoting Christian education, charitable enterprises, parochial schools, Catholic press, and other activities.

The papal appeal contained in the July 21 speech was the signal for a campaign throughout Italy against the racial laws. By word of mouth and in their own press, Catholic Action members counteracted Fascist propaganda so effectively that Achille Starace, Secretary of the Party, issued confidential instructions to the heads of the Fascist clubs in every town of Italy telling them to take retaliatory measures. Boisterous black shirts, whose livelihood depended on their political jobs, invaded and smashed printing presses belonging to the Catholic Action in the provinces of Brescia, Bergamo, and Venezia where they sequestrated copies of parochial sheets, beat up people whom they found reading them and wrecked the seats of several Catholic Action clubs.

At the same time, Starace instructed the heads of the local *fasci* to expel the more prominent Catholic Action members from the party. To most of them, expulsion meant that they would also lose their jobs which depended upon their political membership. Bishops were alarmed. Many went to see the Pope personally while others sent detailed reports of Fascist pressures and violence.

However, Pius XI was ready to plunge Italy into a very grave domestic conflict rather than yield to Fascist measures that struck at one of the fundamental tenets of the Catholic faith. On July 29, he delivered an address in which he warned Mussolini that the Church was ready to defend with all the means in its possession the activities of the Catholic Action.

"*Qui mange du pape en meurt!* (He who strikes at the Pope dies,)" he thundered from his summer residence in Castel Gandolfo. This was an allusion to the saying in medieval times when the papacy was engaged in a formidable struggle with the Holy Roman Empire.

The Catholic doctrine, Pius stated, is universal. Humankind is a single, great, universal human race. All men are, above all, members of the same, great kind. Therefore, rascism is a barrier "between man and man, between people and people, and between nation and nation." He served notice to Mussolini that he would not withdraw his appeal to the Catholic Action to fight the racist theories, and that "since Catholic Action and the Catholic Church are inseparable," the battle was not between Fascism and an organization but between Fascism and the Papacy.

Mussolini retorted with equal intransigence. He had flown from Rome to Forli, on his way to his mountain retreat in Rocca delle Camminate in northern Italy, and had barely alighted from the plane when he told a group of Fascists gathered at the airport to welcome him, "I want you and everyone to know that in the race question as well we will go straight ahead." This was the same phrase with which he hurled defiance at the League of Nations during the Ethiopian campaign when sanctions were applied on Italy. However, the fight was one of words. The Italian dictator knew the power of the Church over the Catholic Italians.

With the Forli statement, which was in keeping with his blustering dictatorial ways, he merely wanted to save face. He gave up his planned period of rest and returned to Rome where, according to what I was told at the Vatican, he asked the help of Father Tacchi-Venturi, his Jesuit friend who had had an important part in the solution of the Roman question between Italy and the Holy See. He gave him a message for the Pope in which he promised that he would not molest Catholic Action if the latter abstained from its anti-racial campaign and confined itself to strictly spiritual fields.

In return, the Fascist Party would give guarantees that no retaliatory measures would be taken against party members who belonged to Catholic Action and that those who had been expelled would be reinstated.

Tacchi-Venturi reported to the Pope who, while agreeing to stop any active intervention on the part of the lay organization, made it clear that he would continue to condemn the racial laws as un-Christian. Mussolini bowed to the doctrinal intransigence of his adversary and attempted to limit the effect of papal utterances on the people by forbidding the Italian press to reprint Pius' speeches. An agreement was signed between Achille Starace, as Secretary of the Fascist Party, and Lamberto Vignoli, President of the Catholic Action in Italy.

Pius' sharp criticism of the racial laws was known only by the few thousand Italians who bought L'Osservatore Romano. The papal speeches were boycotted or their meaning distorted in such a manner that the Vatican newspaper printed a bitter editorial deploring the "imaginary, imperfect, confused and misleading version" given by the Fascist press. At the same time editorials led by Virginio Gayda claimed that the compromise on Catholic Action was a victory for Mussolini. It was another manifestation of face-saving. Had the Italian Dictator felt strong enough, he would have shown the same brand of Hitlerian intransigence that had made all agreements between the Catholic Church and National Socialism impossible. The mere fact that he had reinstated the Catholic Action members expelled from the party, and submitted to the persistent papal criticism of his racial policy was sufficient to show that he had not had his way.

Although nothing appeared on the surface at the time, both Pius and Mussolini were anxious to avoid a political conflict because war clouds were again gathering in the international sky. Hitler had started a violent press campaign against Czechoslovakia to pave the way for the annexation of the Sudeten Germans. Il Duce, who was aware of Italy's military weakness but was not quite sure how far his tricky partner would go, had no intention of weakening his domestic front by engaging in a struggle with the Church that would have incalculable consequences—just for a few thousand harmless Jews.

It is one of the ironies of modern history that Il Duce was hailed throughout Europe as the saviour of European peace at the four-power conference in Munich during which Chamberlain and the French Premier Edouard Daladier yielded once again to Hitler's aggressiveness. No doubt Mussolini was quite sincere in his efforts to prevent a clash between France and England on the one hand and Germany on the other since the last thing he desired at that moment was war. But his motives were far from humanitarian. He just did not have the necessary strength for strong-armed methods. Unlike his wary partner, he had used most of his military power in Ethiopia and in Spain, where Franco's victory, incidentally, was still a long way off. Obviously, the next best thing was to assume the noble role of peacemaker.

When on September 28, Lord Perth handed to Ciano a note from Chamberlain asking Mussolini's intervention to prevent Hitler from "using force to solve the Sudeten problem," the Italian dictator was all too willing. He telephoned Hitler and had very little difficulty in convincing him that the English Premier was, after all, offering him just what he wanted without the necessity of firing a shot.

As Il Duce was crossing the Italo-German border bound for Munich, Pius made a heart-rending broadcast. He repeatedly broke down and sobbed while he begged God to take his life if by this means the world could be spared the slaughter and ruin of war.

Once again, though for different reasons, Italian and Vatican policies coincided. The Munich agreement represented for Mussolini nothing more than a breathing spell; for the Vatican, the maintenance of peace—one of the basic aims of its mission.

At Munich, Mussolini satisfied himself of France's military unpreparedness and domestic disintegration. She had refused to pick up Hitler's challenge, and had been unable to honor her mutual assistance pace with Czechoslovakia, a death blow to her prestige in eastern Europe. There could be only one explanation for her attitude—weakness. According to a well-informed friend in the Italian Ministry of

Foreign Affairs, Mussolini's plan of demanding French territories and possessions—Tunis, Jibuti, Corsica, Nice, Savoy—was conceived at that conference. The Rome-Berlin Axis had London and Paris on the run. The Italian dictator decided to imitate his partner, who had been so successful at Munich, and attempt to obtain some chunks of the French Empire by the mere rattling of his saber.

He started on his plan the very day after his triumphal return from Munich. The Italian people were so happy over the fact that war had been averted, that they showed their gratitude with an enthusiastic manifestation in Piazza Venezia which almost equalled the one for the creation of the Empire.

Ciano summoned Gayda to his office and told him to soft-pedal the wave of joy that was sweeping the whole of Europe with the exception, of course, of mutilated Czechoslovakia. The result was an editorial in which the official mouthpiece of the Fascist Government bluntly stated that "Italy does not share the optimism" of the Western democracies, and that the only tangible result of the Munich crisis was the "confirmation of the vitality of the Rome-Berlin Axis." He followed this with attacks against France in the succeeding days for having refused to recognize the part that Mussolini had played in Munich. To the French press, which rightly pointed out that Il Duce had acted in that manner because of Italy's unpreparedness and his people's unwillingness to accept war, Gayda tartly replied that Rome would never forget those "supreme insults."

While the press was thus preparing the ground for the Fascist demands on France, Mussolini attempted to appease Chamberlain by submitting to a token withdrawal of Black shirts from Spain. This was one of the clauses of the Anglo-Italian agreement which had not yet been ratified by the British Parliament. The Italian dictator was eager to abstain from steps that might jeopardize Chamberlain's premiership since the fall of that statesman, who, despite the many handwritings on the wall, deluded himself into thinking that the Axis dictators had a sense of honor and would respect given pledges, meant a change in British foreign policy that could only be hostile to Italy. Relations with England were materially improved by the withdrawal of ten thousand legionaries from Franco's army, and on November 16, the Chamberlain Government formally recognized the Ethiopian Empire.

That was what Mussolini had been waiting for! He was now free to start his campaign against France.

On the morning of November 30, I went to the Credito Italiano, a bank in Corso Umberto, to cash a check. The teller, who had known me for years, was quite excited.

"I hear that there are going to be pretty big happenings today," he said.

"What do you mean?" I asked. "All I know is that Ciano is making his annual report on foreign policy to the Chamber of Deputies."

"That's it. A deputy, who is an old client of ours, just told me that at the end of Ciano's speech, he had been instructed to get up from his chair and shout: 'Tunis, Tunis!' It seems that we are going to ask France to give us Tunis."

I telephoned Cortesi and told him about it, then went to the Foreign Press Club, the news-exchange of all foreign correspondents. Andre Rabache, I found, had also heard the rumor and sent a story to Le Matin of Paris and to the Exchange Telegraph Agency of London, which he represented. He had told them to hold the story for release on a flash after the session.

At 3 P.M., Cortesi and I took our seats in the press gallery which was so packed that Guido Rocco, head of the Government Press Bureau, could find no room and had to crouch on the steps of the short aisle next to Luigi Barzini, Jr., who was covering the meeting for Il Corriere della Sera of Milan.

While Costanzo Ciano, President of the Chamber and father of Count Galeazzo, the Foreign Minister, was opening the session, Dino Alfieri, who was sitting on the ministerial bench, received a message from an usher. He glanced at it and immediately went over to the Foreign Minister. They talked for a few seconds, then Count Ciano showed a sheaf of papers and the message to Mussolini, who was in the Premier's chair, at his left. Mussolini read the message, perused the sheaf of papers, halted at one, took his pen, and scribbled a few words on it. He handed the papers back to Ciano. As this was going on, Costanzo Ciano was hurrying through the formalities. He finally announced that the Foreign Minister would speak.

Count Ciano read a lengthy exposition on the part which Italy had played in Munich and revealed that Mussolini had ordered partial mobilization before his departure for the four-power meeting. At the very end of the speech he concluded with the statement that the Fascist Government intended "to defend with inflexible firmness the Italian people's interests and national aspirations."

Then what we had been told really did happen. Roberto Farinacci, who was sitting in the front row bench directly facing that of the cabinet members, got up and shouted, "Tunisia" several times. Achille Starace and Dino Alfieri were galvanized into action. They too sprang to their feet and echoed the cry; Starace motioned to the deputies to follow his example. Costanzo Ciano, who was sitting in the upper dais, added his stentorian voice to the pandemonium that was unleashed by hundreds of deputies shouting at the top of their lungs, "Tunisia," "Jibuti," "Nice," "Corsica."

Officers in the gallery assigned to the representatives of the armed forces broke into a thunderous applause. I looked at Mussolini. He sat impassive, hands across his chest, chin stuck out, eyes staring vacantly into space—in a well-studied dictatorial pose. He made no effort to stop the show. On other occasions a mere gesture had been enough. Finally Costanzo Ciano decided that the point had been driven home, and he motioned for silence. Mussolini got up and left, without looking at anybody, as cheers broke out again.

François Poncet, French ambassador, stayed throughout the performance, as did Lord Perth, the English ambassador. His hands resting on the railing of the diplomatic gallery, Poncet stared curiously at the gesticulating deputies and took in every detail of the scene. He said afterwards that he never thought of leaving as a sign of protest, for he wanted to give an accurate description of the demonstration to his government.

Mussolini had taken elaborate precautions to make the shouts look spontaneous, but it so happens that Italians love to talk. Guido Rocco, who seldom knew what was going on in Italy, was apparently the only high government official who had not been informed of the plans. Ciano had neglected to tell him. As soon as the session was over, Rabache jumped from his seat and was rushing to the telephone when Rocco stopped him:

"Please, please," he wailed, "don't mention the shouts."

Rabache did not even answer him.

Our newspaper dead line was several hours away so we were not in a hurry. Cortesi tried to obtain the text of the speech but was told that it would take some time. We waited in the newspapermen's room of the Chamber for more than thirty minutes, and nothing happened. Finally, we saw one of the ushers attached to the presidency and asked him what was the matter. There were some changes made at the last minute by Mussolini, he said, so the original copies of the text had been annulled and others were being prepared.

What had happened was that Mussolini, who had timed the demonstration with the beginning of a general strike in France, had had to mitigate the tone of Ciano's speech when Alfieri received the news at the opening of the session that the Daladier Government had succeeded in breaking the strike in twenty-four hours. The success of the French Premier had not been foreseen by Mussolini, who thought that the general strike would be followed by a cabinet crisis. Had this happened, Ciano, according to what I heard, would have come out with a strong anti-French statement.

The new development in Fascist policy threatening peace came as a jolt to the Vatican. However, the Pope abstained from any pronouncement since at that moment his attention was monopolized by the consequences of the racial policies both in Germany and in Italy.

Dispatches sent by the Austrian clergy to the Vatican described in great detail the demonstrations in Vienna against Cardinal Innitzer who, having finally realized his mistake in supporting Germany's annexation of Austria, had bravely condemned in his sermons the anti-Catholic persecutions occurring with increasing frequence in the territory under his jurisdiction. One of the dispatches was published in L'Osservatore Romano and deserves to be quoted as a proof of Nazi excesses.

On Friday evening, October 7, a service for Catholic Youth was held in the Cathedral of St. Stephen. The Cardinal Archbishop addressed those present, encouraging them in their works. The youths, about six thousand strong, on issuing from the Cathedral acclaimed Cardinal Innitzer with filial affection.

These manifestations were greeted by whistling and singing amid shouts of "Our faith is Germany! Down with Innitzer!" on the part of groups of Hitler Youths and detachments of Storm Troopers which had taken up positions in the square.

The young Catholics, though greatly superior numerically, did not reply and dispersed quietly. Later, groups of Storm Troopers gathered before the Archbishop's residence and improvised threatening demonstrations, pounding on the door and shouting that the Cardinal should be taken to a concentration camp. The police, called by the secretary of the Archdiocese, intervened to protect the palace, and the rioters left the square at eleven o'clock but were still uttering threats.

The next day, at eight-fifteen in the evening, another hostile demonstration began against the Archbishop's residence on the side of the square but later spread to the other front of the building—on Rothenturmstrasse. The palace was soon struck from all sides by stones, and the glass broken in every window. Police intervention was asked immediately, and the request was repeated when the rioters attempted to break in the doors.

Various police stations gave assurance that they would take the necessary steps, but a quarter of an hour later, a heavy door was broken open by the rioters, who penetrated the palace smashing everything they found in the vestibule and on the stairs.

Household members ran to protect the chapel and the Archbishop. Fearing that the Holy Sacrament might be profaned, a priest consumed the holy particles, and it was later seen how timely was this action because the invaders, after striking the Archbishop's secretary on the head, causing him to fall to the ground unconscious, invaded the chapel smashing a statue.

Then they continued their vandalism, breaking into the Cardinal's study where they forced open his desk and destroyed a crucifix. The Cardinal's purple robes, pectoral cross, and ring were removed. Everywhere furniture was broken, paintings torn down, and art objects ruined.

In the square a bonfire was made of the Cardinal's purple robes and various objects of the Cardinal's personal wardrobe. In Viennese newspapers no word of this violence appeared.

Papal wrath for this and other incidents was not long in manifesting itself. For the first time, Pius XI attacked Hitler personally on October 21. He likened him to Julian the Apostate (Roman Emperor Flavius Claudius Julianus). The persecutions of the Christians under that ruler's reign, he said, were not, and were not intended to be, the most violent, most sanguinary in history, but certainly the most obstinate, most double-faced, and astute. They had now been revived, and not without disciples and apostles who tread the footsteps of Judas and were permeated with his spirit.

As was to be expected, Hitler forbade his press to reprint the speech and continued to encourage attacks against the clergy. Other incidents occurred in Munich where the archiepiscopal palace of Cardinal Faulhaber, a fearless opponent of Nazi racial laws, was stoned and the prelate himself insulted by a mob of youngsters who shouted, "Nach Dachau mit dem Schwein," ("Send the pig to the concentration camp") while the police abstained from interfering until the demonstration had been fully carried out.

In Italy, conditions were almost as bad. The Italian Cabinet had met on November 7, and had incorporated in a series of bills the "Aryan principles" set forth at the October meeting of the Grand Council. The measure that especially worried the Holy See was the one decreeing marriages between "Italians of the Aryan race" and members of other races illicit, and, therefore, null if they were celebrated. It was a flagrant breach of the Concordat between Italy and the Holy See signed in 1929. Article XXXIV of that agreement stipulated that "the Italian State, wishing to restore to the institution of marriage—basis of the family—a dignity in conformity with the Catholic tradition of its people, recognizes civil validity to the sacrament of marriage disciplined by canon law." In other words, the Vatican had obtained the condition that the Italian Government accept the decision of the Church in the question of marriage. Moreover, the parish priest was empowered "to draw up the marriage act, a copy of which he shall send to the municipality within five days so it may be transcribed in the register of civil marriages." This meant that the Italian Government had no say in the matter except the recording of the religious marriage.

Monsignor Borgongini Duca protested to Ciano against the breach of the Concordat two days after the promulgation of the decrees. The Italian Government merely acknowledged the step. The Pope made another effort to deter Mussolini from carrying out his anti-Semitic policy. He wrote two letters, one addressed to him and one to King Victor, in which he appealed to them to abstain from violating the concordat. The King was the only one to reply with assurances that his government would take into consideration the papal objections in order to reach a satisfactory solution of the two divergent viewpoints.

The Vatican did not insist because the breach was substantially juridical with scant practical consequences. Jews who married Catholics were very few and the measure would not affect the three hundred thousand religious marriages performed in Italy every year. Nevertheless, the hostility with which it was greeted among Catholic Action members brought a revival of Fascist persecutions. In his last Christmas Eve speech to the college of cardinals, the Pope disclosed that Catholic Action clubs had been invaded and devastated in many Italian cities including Milan, Turin, Bergamo, and Venice, and that Cardinal Schuster, Archbishop of Milan, who had deprecated the marriage law, had been the target of a hostile demonstration similar to those current in Germany.

Despite the provocations, Pius showed great restraint. He went so far as to praise both King Victor and Mussolini personally for having brought to a satisfactory conclusion the negotiations for the solution of the Roman question, whose tenth anniversary was seven weeks away.

Tired and ill—he had suffered a serious relapse which had forced him to bed for a short time only a few days before—the eighty-year-old Pope hoped that Mussolini would use the privileged position derived from his partnership with Hitler to bring about an understanding with England and France. He did not, therefore, wish to antagonize the Italian dictator with a resurgence of domestic hostilities at a moment when Germany seemed to be satisfied with her new acquisition of the Sudeten Germans and had sent von Ribbentrop to Paris for the signing of a "good neighbor" treaty at the beginning of December. Moreover, Chamberlain was expected in Rome early in January.

During that period, secret negotiations were being carried out between the papal Secretariat of State and the Italian Ministry of Foreign Affairs to find a modus vivendi that would conciliate the doctrinal view of the Church with the Fascist racial policy. An agreement, according to what I was told, was eventually reached although no mention of it has ever been made.

Mussolini did not intend to lift a finger to help the Jews, however. He made this clear in a conversation he had with William Phillips, United States Ambassador to Rome, on January 3, a few days after the latter's return from Washington. He turned down flatly a proposal by President Roosevelt to throw Ethiopia open to Jewish immigrants from Italy and other European countries. The President was encouraged to make the appeal by the fact that on October 6, the Grand Council approved a resolution to the effect that "it does not exclude the possibility of permitting controlled emigration of European Jews into some parts of Ethiopia, in order, among other things, to divert Jewish emigration from Palestine."

A friend showed me what he said were the minutes of that meeting dictated by Ciano who was present at the conversation. Mussolini smilingly replied to Phillips that there were other countries where Jews could settle more easily than Ethiopia. He said that Russia was one of those countries, and that to his knowledge, the Soviet Government had never officially declared itself opposed to immigration of foreign Jews and capital. Another country, he added, was Brazil with vast expanses of unexploited land. The best place of all, however, he humorously concluded, was the United States. "If that country were to increase its density of population from the present forty-one per square mile to the Italian level of three hundred forty-five, it could accommodate about one billion more people," he said. The Italian dictator also declined the suggestion that he should forward the President's plan to Hitler. He explained that it would be futile since, "Italy and Germany have a perfect identity of views on the Jewish question."

The visit of Neville Chamberlain and Lord Halifax, who was at that time Foreign Secretary, to Rome on January 11, was a complete fiasco. The submissive manner in which the Western democracies had accepted Hitler's annexation of the Sudeten Germans in Czechoslovakia, and their obvious military unpreparedness had emboldened the Axis. No agreement was reached on any of the problems on the agenda—the Anglo-Italian relations in the Mediterranean and the Red Sea, French-Italian relations, the Spanish Civil War, and the Jewish question.

At a reception which he gave in honor of the English visitors in Palazzo Venezia, Mussolini displayed a marked indifference that approached boredom. He abstained from addressing his two guests all the time I was there, and, when the moment came for Chamberlain and Halifax to leave, he perfunctorily walked at their side, escorted by Ciano with whom he talked as far as the door. While Chamberlain was putting on his coat and grasping his umbrella, Mussolini turned his shoulders and engaged in conversation with a woman who happened to be standing near. The English Premier waited until Mussolini finally shook hands with him and Lord Halifax.

Pius granted a private audience to the two English statesmen who reported to him the failure of their conversations with the Italian dictator. The Pontiff spoke English badly, but he had his own interpreter, Monsignor Joseph Patrick Hurley, American prelate of the Secretariat of State. The results of that conversation were not disclosed, but after Pius XI's death less than a month later, I was given a general indication of the subjects discussed. The Pope explained to Chamberlain his views on the totalitarian regimes, and on the duties of the democracies, expressed the sorrow with which he had seen the inauguration of anti-Semitic policies both in Italy and in Germany, and spoke of the necessity of giving aid to the refugees who had fled from those two countries.

"The problems were more numerous and difficult in past centuries," Pius concluded, "but you know better than I the strength of the English race."

With these words, the Pontiff indicated that he expected England to halt the dictators, although he still felt reasonably sure that it was possible to maintain peace.

NINTH CHAPTER

In the twilight of his pontificate, Pius XI suffered many a bitter disillusion and died just in time to be spared a series of blows that would have shattered the last scant hopes he entertained for an understanding between England and France on the one hand and Berlin and Rome on the other. During the seventeen years of his reign he had by signing agreements with thirteen nations obtained state collaboration for the spiritual mission of the Church, but this grandiose political structure was tottering when Eugenio Pacelli succeeded him.

In the years that followed the First World War, Pius XI's policy had been generally successful because the Roman Catholic Church had the advantage of its doctrinal and organizing strength over the weakness and instability of lay governments and their unconstructive policies. In other words, the Church appeared as a shining spiritual beacon to the embittered, discouraged, tired peoples who were longing for a social and moral restoration of human values swept away by the war storm. The desire of individuals for religious practice had made Pius' task easier and had given the Church greater strength as a social force. This was especially due to the fact that the ruling classes in general were composed of anti-clerical elements which were blamed by the people for the economic and spiritual crises that were the aftermath of the war.

Vatican policy had been successful until leaders presented to the masses, programs of materialistic conquests which, because of the tangible results they promised, replaced the moral program of the Church with its less understandable and concrete aims. The Christian creed, advocating peace and good will among men, was scorned by governments that believed only in the doctrine of force and were glorifying it as the principal means for the attainment of materialistic welfare. The new leaders resolved to brook no interference from a moral power such as that of the Church, which was opposing not only their doctrine but their methods of developing the programs on which the success of their policies depended.

Political conditions in 1939, were no longer the same as in the previous two decades and a new policy, therefore, was necessary to cope with them. When Pacelli chose the name of Pius XII, it was generally thought that he would follow his predecessor's footsteps. His pontificate has shown, however, that he has taken from Pius XI only the methods that had proved constructive. He realized, for instance, that strong pronouncements had not deterred the dictators from pursuing their policies of aggressiveness; therefore, he based his official criticisms and censures on doctrinal grounds, thus avoiding the personal fights that had characterized the last stage of Pius XI's pontificate.

At a time when Europe was a powder barrel, the main concern of the Vatican was the preservation of peace. All other problems were relegated to a secondary place by the threat of the tremendous disaster that would result from a European conflagration.

In the period between his election and coronation, Pius XII tried to achieve a compromise with Hitler on the situation of the Church in Germany. He held a three-hour conference with the four German cardinals—Michael Faulhaber, Adolph Bertram, Karl Joseph Schulte, and Theodore Innitzer—who had come to Rome for the conclave. They made a detailed exposition of Catholic life and examined the possibilities for a *modus vivendi*, which might spare the Church the persecution it was suffering at the hand of the Nazis. Two days after that meeting, the Pope received Diego von Bergen, German Ambassador to the Holy See, but, like his predecessor, Pius XII saw that no conciliation was possible between the Vatican and Nazism. The news of his negotiations, which were intended to be secret, leaked out. One of our tipsters happened to be in the Courtyard of St. Damasus, when the German Cardinals arrived one after the other. His curiosity aroused, he went to the second floor just in time to see them enter the papal study.

The news of the conference broke in the press, and the Pope was disturbed. He gave orders to the Secretariat of State that all newspapermen, Italian and foreign, be excluded from the Vatican grounds. Even Monsignor Enrico Pucci, head of a semi-official agency for the dissemination of Vatican news, was evicted from his cubby-hole office in the Courtyard of St. Damasus. Nevertheless, correspond-ents had many employees of the Holy See on their pay roll, and we continued to be informed of all diplomatic activity. The papal order was strictly enforced for some weeks, and, finally, allowed to lapse.

In his first speech, made the day after the election, Pius XII, who had chosen *Opus Justitiae Pax* (peace is the work of justice) as his motto, appealed to all the peoples in the world to forget their quarrels and enjoy the "sublime gift of peace." Again, the day after the coronation ceremony, he told the college of cardinals that his intention was to dedicate his pontificate to the achievement of peace—"the boon that humanity desires above all others."

But the triple tiara had barely been placed on his brow when Hitler invaded Czechoslovakia.

As the swastika was raised over the Castle of Hradzin, the Prague residence of Dr. Eduard Benes, President of the Republic, Pius XII, who had been minutely informed of every development of the crisis by the Vatican representative in Prague, and by Cardinal Carlo Kaspar, Primate of Czechoslovakia, was reported to have stated, "This is the beginning of the end."

The Vatican was dismayed not only because six million more Cath-olics had been placed under the Nazi yoke and were going to suffer the same fate as the persecuted Austrians, but also because the chances of mediation between the democracies and the totalitarian states seemed to have been dashed as a result of Hitler's cold-blooded gesture. Indeed, the political consequences were regarded with such grave concern by members of the papal Secretariat of State that they eclipsed the purely religious issue.

The end of Czechoslovakia marked the end of Chamberlain's appeasement policy. Hitler, who had promised at Munich to respect the territorial integrity of that country if he were allowed to incorpo-rate the Sudeten Germans, had thrown away the mask. His oft-repeated contention that the Reich only wanted to unite the Ger-mans outside her territory had proved to be a ruse for a clear-cut policy of aggression. With Europe on the brink of war—Chamberlain in a speech made in Birmingham had branded the German coup an "arbitrary and ruthless gesture"; Edouard Daladier, French Prime Minister, had asked Parliament for full powers—the Vatican remained silent. It did not wish at that moment to aggravate with an official condemnation the supercharged international atmosphere. Pius privately discussed the various aspects of the crisis with Galeazzo Ciano, Italy's Foreign Minister, in an audience granted on March 18. Ciano was stated to have assured the Pope that the Fascist Government had no intention of precipitating war and would show moderation in regard to the Italian demands on France, which were currently agitated in the press.

The disappearance overnight of Czechoslovakia took the Italian people by surprise. While the Rome radio was blaring forth a blow-by-blow account of the occupation, I made the rounds of many of the shopkeepers in Via Margutta to learn the popular reaction.

"They have even stood that," was a sample of the comment I heard —"they" meaning Britain and France, and "that" the latest development in Nazi policy.

"He has gobbled up Czechoslovakia, too!" was another comment.

The official reaction was distinctly warm. To the Fascist Government, the new German step meant a further weakening of France, and it hastened the process of knocking from under Paris the props that still supported her prestige in central and eastern Europe. Beneath all this, however, there was the feeling that Mussolini had once more been tricked by his partner. In September 1938, Il Duce had written in his own newspaper, Il Popolo d'Italia, that "whenever three and a half million Czechs are to be offered to Hitler, he would decline such a gift. He is concerned and worried about three and a half million Germans, and about them alone."

Ministry of Foreign Affairs officials described to me how Hitler broke to Il Duce the news of his decision to take Czechoslovakia. At 4 A.M. on March 15, Bernardo Attòlico, Italian Ambassador in Berlin, telephoned Mussolini at Villa Torlonia. He told the half-awake dictator, who had been roused from sound sleep, that Hitler had personally informed him a few minutes before of the documents signed by Dr. Emil Hacha, Czech Premier, and Frantisek Chvalkovsky, Czech Foreign Minister, which placed Prague under "the Reich's protection." Nazi troops, he said, were about to march into Czech Territory. At 6 A.M., that same day, Prince Philippe of Hesse, acting as Hitler's personal envoy, left Berlin by special plane and landed in Rome at 1 P.M. He went straight to Palazzo Venezia where he handed Mussolini a letter in which Hitler explained the reasons that had prompted him to decree the Nazi protectorate over Czechoslovakia.

That afternoon, Edda went to see Milos Czermak, Czech Minister to Rome, whom she had known when he was his country's representative in Tirana, Albania. While she was talking to him, three members of the German Embassy arrived to take possession of the Legation. One of them was a Viennese who, exactly one year before, had stood by as a similar visit was paid to the Austrian Legation, soon after the Nazi occupation of that country. Czermak's face seemed to be made of stone. The Germans took inventory of the furniture and documents; they sealed every room with tape and swastika. The Minister escorted the usurpers from room to room like an automaton, mechanically answering questions. When they left, Mrs. Czermak broke down and cried.

To cope with the English and French rage, Italy went through the motions of preparing for war. The newspapers advised the people to buy gas masks, which, incidentally, could not be obtained anywhere for the simple reason that no store was supplied with them. Electrical crews replaced white globes with blue in all streets. Questionnaires were sent to the head of every family with the request that he notify the authorities how many persons in his household would have to be evacuated in case of air raids and how many held a driving license.

The Fascist Grand Council met on March 22, and came out with a braggadocio resolution warning the democracies that "the password of Fascism remains today, as always, 'to believe, to obey, to fight,'" and reasserted "particularly at this moment, its full adhesion to the Rome-Berlin Axis."

As subsequent events showed, it was, of course, pure bluff to intimidate the democracies. The war of nerves was on. The Italian people were jittery and would never understand a war fought over Czechoslovakia. Italy was as militarily weak as ever. It was soon clear, however, that Chamberlain and Daladier had no intention of fighting the Axis. Mussolini, emboldened by the powerlessness of the democracies, thought that the moment had come to name officially his demands for French territories and possessions.

"The Italo-French problems," he told fifty thousand Fascists in Rome's stadium on March 26, "consist of Tunisia, Jibuti, and the Suez Canal." But the Italian dictator was cautious. He merely enumerated the problems, and carefully underlined that they were only of a "colonial" nature. Nice and Savoy were momentarily forgotten. Moreover, he abstained from threatening France with war or other dire results if he failed to reach an understanding with her. In substance he stressed that if differences between Italy and France were not solved, they would continue to exist and eventually become chronic.

It was a disappointing speech for many rabid Fascists and a mildly reassuring one for the overwhelming majority of the Italian people, who had been afraid of finding themselves in a situation where the only recourse was to fight. The speech was in keeping with the imperialist policy Mussolini had initiated in 1935. He wanted to induce France to grant him concessions in Tunisia where the prolific Italians would eventually obtain political control by sheer weight of numbers; he wanted a share in the management of the Suez Canal, which was financially controlled by the French, in order to build Ethiopia into a fortress and a permanent threat to England's African possessions, without having to pay the expensive tolls that were a heavy drain on Italy's scant gold reserve; and, finally, he wanted Jibuti to convert that harbor into a very valuable base for economic penetration in the Red Sea countries.

Many of the correspondents in Rome attributed Mussolini's meekness to his knowledge of the people's adversion to war, and to Hitler's suggestions which Hans-Georg Viktor von Mackensen, German Ambassador to Rome, had conveyed to Ciano that, in view of the strong reaction against the Axis existing in England and France as a result of the Czech coup, it was not the right moment to deliver ultimatums. No doubt, these considerations influenced to a certain extent Mussolini's attitude. But Cortesi, who knew Italy and Fascist ways thoroughly, was the first to perceive that Il Duce had something else up his sleeve. "When Mussolini makes a speech like that," he said, "he has a plan. He obviously does not want a war with France now, but it is inconceivable that he would start such a violent press campaign, climax it with a speech officially approving it, and then decide that he is going 'to wait'!"

What Mussolini had in mind, the world saw ten days later.

He invaded Albania.

A semi-feudal state and the least advanced of all European countries, Albania has been called the Italian Belgium. Her geographic position has made her a coveted prize for Yugoslavia, Greece, and Italy. Directly facing the Southern Italian province of Apulia, across the sea, this tiny Balkan state is of great strategic importance for the control of the Adriatic. A power which has naval and air bases in Albania can bottle up that stretch of sea from the Straits of Otranto to Susak, the small port on the Italo-Yugoslav border.

In the First World War, Italy occupied Valona, an Albanian harbor, and its surrounding territory. As a result of this move, the powerful Austrian fleet never did operate in the Mediterranean and was forced to remain virtually idle in the Yugoslav harbors which were, at that time, part of the Austro-Hungarian Empire.

Its ruler, King Ahmed Zog, came from a family of chieftains who held sway in the savage, almost inaccessible region of Mati, composed of rugged, isolated mountains where no road was built until 1934. He was born about 1896, the exact date not being known since Albania was at that time under Turkish domination and no registration of births existed. The Turks were chased from the country in 1913, at the end of the first Balkan war, after having ruled in Albania for four hundred years.

Zog's father held a position in the court of the Sultan in Constantinople. He was the curator of the Sultan's birds, that is, he supervised their rearing. Zog went to the Military Academy in Constantinople and came out of it a trained cadet. When the First World War broke out, and Austria occupied northern Albania, he

suggested that Vienna arm and clothe five hundred of his mountaineers to keep peace in the Mati region. His suggestion was accepted
and he was given the rank of colonel in the Imperial Army. However,
the Austrian commander in charge of the forces of occupation soon
discovered that the ambitious Albanian leader was trying to feather his
own nest rather than serve the cause of the Empire. Zog was invited
to visit Vienna and, once there, he was never allowed to return to
Albania until after the end of the war.

Back in his home grounds in 1919, the young chieftain—his father
had died and he had inherited the leadership of his bands—organized the first national Albanian congress, composed of all the chieftains, with the intention of securing Albania's independence. Zog
became successively under-secretary, minister of the interior, and
prime minister. In 1924, the intellectuals and liberals, who feared his
dictatorial ways, ousted him. Zog fled to Yugoslavia. Fan Noli, a
Greek orthodox bishop who had led the revolt, became premier.
However, he made the mistake of refusing Italy's, Greece's, and
Yugoslavia's help, and turned to Russia instead. Moscow promised
financial aid to the bankrupt government, but in December of the
same year after nine months of exile, Zog was back in Tirana, with
the support of Yugoslav troops. Italy and Greece did not interfere
because the fall of Fan Noli prevented Soviet Russia from securing
a hold in Albania which she might have turned into a center of
Bolshevist propaganda aimed at all the Balkan countries.

Zog proclaimed himself president of the republic and immediately
began the work of consolidating his regime. Italy was the strongest
neighbor, so he asked her for a loan without which he could not
hope to carry out the program he had planned. The result of his
policy of collaboration with Italy was a treaty of alliance and friendship, which gave Rome the right to intervene at any time Albania's
territorial integrity was threatened. Both Yugoslavia and Greece were
ever ready to slice Albania among themselves, and by securing Italian
support, the King hoped to stave off permanently the threat of
foreign invasion.

In the first years of his rule, Zog accomplished a great deal for his
country and a great deal against his enemies, whom he eliminated or

neutralized in less than two years. He built hospitals and roads with money obtained from Rome, but in so doing, he handed the country over to Mussolini. At his suggestion, Parliament offered him the crown of Albania, which he accepted in September 1928, taking the name of Zog I—Zog being the Albanian word for "bird," a fitting tribute to the position his father had held in the Turkish court.

In 1932, he felt sufficiently strong domestically to refuse the renewal of the Italo-Albanian treaty of alliance. He sought to rid himself of Italian economic domination and appealed to the League of Nations for a loan which was refused. For two years, Zog proceeded to stamp out every vestige of foreign encroachment. He discharged military and technical advisors and closed schools most of which were directed by Catholic or Greek Orthodox priests. Unable to live on its own resources, Albania was bankrupt by 1934. The army—fifteen thousand men trained by Italian officers—the state employees, and even the members of the diplomatic corps had not been paid their salaries for six months. Forced by necessity, he renewed the Italo-Albanian treaty and maintained normal relations with Rome, although he steadfastly resisted all attempts by Mussolini to set up Fascist organizations in the country.

Tall, handsome, and gifted with courage, shrewdness, and cunning, Zog, in the early part of his career, was by far the ablest Albanian leader, but at the end of the political turmoil, he became absolute ruler and degenerated into a despot. Many factors contributed to this change. He led for fifteen years a very unhealthy life. From 1924, until 1931, he literally never left the small eight-room villa in the heart of Tirana, which was called the Royal Palace. He lived behind its six-foot-high walls protected by a bodyguard of three hundred of his faithful mountaineers, who were quartered in the spacious courtyard. From 1931, until the time he was forced to flee the country in April 1939, he spent three months every summer in a wooden barracks built outside of Durazzo, in a desert spot near the sea, while his bodyguard watched all approaches to it, day and night. The reason for this was that many influential Albanians, who had lost power and wealth through Zog's policy of ruthless suppression of all political opponents, were constantly plotting to assassinate him.

Then there was his family. His mother was the strongest influence in his life. She was Turkish-educated, backward in the western sense, and shortsighted politically. His six sisters and one brother had not been properly educated and, though possessing natural intelligence, were incapable of co-operating with their brother in the enormous task of lifting the country from the pitiful state in which it had lived throughout the centuries of Turkish exploitation. Three of his younger sisters, Rujie, Mexhide, and Mexhemie, visited the United States in 1938, with the secret hope of finding an American husband.

The seclusion in which Zog lived warped his judgment. He drank and smoked a great deal. He lost the sense of proportion necessary to understand the needs and problems of the people and to direct foreign policy. He became selfish, greedy, and mentally lazy. He surrounded himself with advisors who were elderly yes-men of Turkish mentality and education. The exponents of the younger generation he ignored or obstructed whenever they proposed wise reforms. In the very last years of his rule, he was hated by his own people.

Through Edda, who had lived for many years in Albania, and was in 1939, Rome correspondent of *Drita*, the official Tirana newspaper, I was able to unfold the complete story of the invasion. She knew Albanians in the pro-Zog and anti-Zog camps. And when Italy annexed the country, she put me in touch with many men who later became prominent figures in Albanian political life, and with exiles who closely collaborated with Zog in England. She, of course, lost her job the same day the Italians entered Tirana and suppressed the newspaper.

The duplicity shown by Mussolini in his dealings with Zog would make Machiavelli, if he were alive, discard Cesare Borgia and take the Italian dictator as the prototype of his prince. The Albanian coup had been prepared by Il Duce two years before. It was the first example I know of fifth columnist work outside of Spain, and it set the pattern which Hitler so successfully used in his invasion of the low countries.

There were two reasons for Mussolini's move: one, psychological, and less important; the other, political, which outweighed every other consideration. Hitler had been scoring success after success.

He had taken Austria, the Sudeten Germans, and finally, Czecho-slovakia. Mussolini had nothing to show on the credit side of the Rome-Berlin Axis. The Italians were beginning to ask what the advantages were of a partnership that seemed to work only in one direction—Berlin. Unarmed, primitive Albania was an easy booty, and its conquest, with the proper propaganda build-up, could be magnified into a useful political argument to answer the popular question.

The main reason, however, was that control of the small Balkan state represented an element of vital importance in Mussolini's plan to dominate the Mediterranean. Albania would, in time, be de-veloped into an invaluable jumping-off point for the Fascist armies, which could easily attack Yugoslavia, hemmed in by Germany on the north and Italy on the south, as well as Greece, whose traditional pro-British policy was a potential obstacle to Fascist expansion.

While signing treaties of friendship with Zog, the Italian dictator kept on his pay roll a group of about twenty Albanian political refugees headed by Mustafa Kruja—appointed Albanian Premier in December, 1941—who had fled the country when Zog returned from his forced exile in Yugoslavia. They would be useful when the time came to overthrow Zog.

Mussolini began to weave the threads of his conspiracy in 1936, as he embarked on a policy of collaboration with Germany. Toward the end of that year, Achille Starace, Secretary of the Fascist Party, sent Giovanni Giro, one of Italy's ablest Fascist organizers, to Albania with instructions and full powers to obtain Zog's permission to create an Albanian Lictor's Youth movement and a "Work Through Joy" organization. For several months, negotiations went on between the King and Giro without results. Since Zog was supported in his opposition to the Italian plans by the members of his government, Rome thought the best way to make Albania Fascist was to bring about a cabinet shake-up and place in power younger men of pro-Italian leanings. The King refused to accept this suggestion.

His efforts having failed, Giro returned to Rome in May, 1938, and submitted a report to his Fascist superiors in which he suggested the deposition of Zog who, in his opinion, was guilty of not wanting to Fascistize Albania. No decision was taken at the time, however. The Italian Government apparently preferred to drop its Albanian plans rather than start an open conflict with the King.

In September, when the Czech-German crisis seemed to lead to war, word reached Italian ears that Zog had made overtures to powers hostile to Italy, and offered to denounce the Italo-Albanian pact so as to deprive Italy of the use of Albanian ports and territory for military purposes in the event of conflict in the Mediterranean. In other words, the King sought new allies in the democratic camp.

The Italian plan elaborated at the time was to undermine Zog from within by encouraging elements hostile to his regime, and, if possible, to assassinate him. Giro was again chosen for this task. He left at the end of September for Tirana, where he began an intense propaganda campaign against the King. Chiefs of clans known to be hostile to Zog and influential "nationalists" whom the King had steadfastly excluded from participation in the government were approached.

Giro found a fertile field. Zog could not, by any stretch of the imagination be called a popular ruler. It was whispered all over Albania that he had personally squandered a very large amount of public funds which were to have improved the low standard of living of his people. It was an open secret that Italian loans granted for the execution of public works and other improvements had found their way into the King's private coffers and those of his "key men."

Albanian public opinion favored the overthrow of the regime provided, of course, that Italy would be content with placing in the saddle a government friendly to her without depriving the country of her independence. Giro, who was amply supplied with funds, toured every region of Albania and had secret meetings with chieftains whose support he bought.

The preparatory work was in full swing, and a revolt was about to break out when, on February 20, 1939, the Italian plan struck a snag. Zog learned of its existence.

One of the King's enemies was Murat Haxhi, the chieftain of Dibra, Albania's most savage region. Haxhi had been able to defy with impunity the Albanian ruler. He was the leader of about ten thousand mountaineers who could repulse a force ten times greater since no roads connected the lowlands of the central region with his domain. There was a weekly air service, however, from Tirana to Dibra. In the middle of February, Giro took a plane and visited the chieftain. He offered him two thousand gold napoleons (ten thousand dollars) for Zog's head. Haxhi accepted.

After the pleased Giro left, the chieftain did some fast thinking. Although he had constantly opposed Zog, relations were more or less regulated by a tacit, *modus vivendi*. The King did not interfere with him in Dibra, and he did not interfere with Zog in Tirana. But suppose Zog were killed? What would be the consequences? The *jambanxhi* (foreigners) would take his place. And foreigners were more powerful; they had strong weapons and many, many men. He might lose his power.

Haxhi took the plane for Tirana, with three of his bodyguard. Twenty-five others reached the capital on muleback and on foot. He stopped at the Hotel International. Three of his men slept in front of the door of his room; the others, in quarters on the ground floor. The Chieftain sent an emissary to Zog asking for a meeting. There was some hesitation caused by distrust, and Haxhi had to wait a full week before the audience was granted.

Escorted by all his men, he walked into the Royal Palace, handed Zog the two thousand napoleons and told him of his deal with Giro. Things began to happen. The King summoned the Italian Minister, Francesco Jacomoni, to his presence and laid before him the proofs of the conspiracy. He ordered Jacomoni to repatriate Giro immediately, otherwise, he would not be answerable for his life. Needless to say, the Italian Minister disclaimed all responsibility for Giro's activities and said that his Government had not sanctioned them. Giro left by special plane for Rome, on February 22, and on the same day, four Albanians charged with participating in anti-Zog propaganda were arrested.

While the police, acting on the King's instructions, were preparing to make further arrests, Mussolini, through Jacomoni, demanded the immediate release of the four Italophile Albanians and warned that if others known to be Italophile were seized Italy would denounce the

1927 treaty of alliance. Faced with this ultimatum, the King yielded.

Zog's next step was to inform Britain of the tenseness of his relations with Italy, which endangered his throne, and inquire whether,
in case of a crisis, Albania could count on English help. The British
Minister in Tirana saw the King several times in March, but Zog,
having failed to receive a definite reply from London, opened negotiations with the Italian Government hoping for a compromise. He sent
Zef Sereggi, his aide-de-camp and closest friend, as minister to Rome
in place of Dimitri Berati.

It was too late. Mussolini was determined to oust Zog, despite
the fact that the Albanian ruler was ready to grant every Italian demand including the right to build naval bases and strategic roads;
the free passage of Italian troops, and facilities for their quartering.
On Good Friday, the First Italian Naval Squadron disembarked thousands of soldiers in the Albanian harbors of Santi Quaranta, Valona,
Durazzo, and San Giovanni di Medua.

Zog became popular overnight. In the days immediately preceding
the invasion, students led by Mehdi Frasheri, ex-premier and a true
patriot who still today commands the respect of all his countrymen,
held demonstrations in the streets of Tirana and in front of the royal
residence demanding arms with which to fight the Italians. Even
some of the men who had accepted Giro's money rallied to Zog's
side. Patriotic, proud, and with an indomitable love for independence
which four hundred years of Turkish rule had not been able to
extinguish, the Albanian people showed an impressive solidarity with
their ruler. The hatred which had been accumulating for fifteen
years was forgotten the moment their country was in danger. They
preferred a leader, no matter how inept, of their own blood to the
hated *jambanxhi*.

But they had no weapons. A few heroic Albanians opposed the
landing at Durazzo, and were quickly overwhelmed. Had the population been supplied with arms, there is no doubt that it would have
fought the Fascist invaders every inch of the ground and would have
carried guerrilla warfare into the impervious mountains as they did
later.

Zog, his Hungarian wife, Geraldine Apponyi, whose mother was

American, and their son, born only two days before the invasion, fled to Greece. The year before, when the marriage took place, King Victor and Mussolini had sent precious gifts which were delivered personally by the Duke of Bergamo, cousin of the Italian monarch, and by Count Ciano, who represented Il Duce at the various ceremonies.

Mussolini set up a puppet government headed by Shefket Verlaci, the wealthiest man in Albania and an irreconcilable enemy of Zog. The feud between the two men dated back to the time when Zog, after being crowned King, broke his engagement to Verlaci's daughter. A parliament, hand-picked by the Italians, dutifully offered the crown of Albania to King Victor, a few days after the total occupation of the country. Thus Mussolini betrayed not only Zog, but the Albanian nationalists who had believed his promises to respect Albania's independence.

The Italian troops had barely entered Tirana on April 9, before Pius XII deplored the lawlessness of the dictators and their brutal suppression of Czechoslovakia and Albania.

"How is peace possible," he said in his Easter sermon, "if pacts solemnly sanctioned and the plighted word have lost that security and value which are the indispensable bases of reciprocal confidence and without which ardently desired disarmament, both material and moral, becomes each passing day less possible of realization?"

The Vatican attitude was all the more impressive since the Italian occupation of Albania would be distinctly advantageous for the Catholic Church. The one million Albanians who had become Italian subjects were 68 per cent Mohammedan, 20 per cent Greek-Orthodox, and 12 per cent Roman Catholic. During his reign, Zog had adopted a policy which fomented antagonism among the faithful of the three religions, and placed the Catholics in a position of political inferiority —so much so, that the League of Nations had recognized them as a religious minority. In 1938, Zog, who was Mohammedan, had asked the Holy See to grant him dispensation in view of the fact that he was to marry a Catholic woman, but the Holy See had curtly refused because of the King's unwillingness to have his children reared as Catholics. From the political point of view, therefore, the seizure of the country by a Catholic power would, no doubt, improve the condition of the Church and aid the Vatican in achieving the unification of the orthodox churches with the Roman Catholic, which had been under way in Albania since the years before the First World War.

The papal reproach was balanced by an appeal to the "have" nations—England and France. He urged that "those goods and riches which God showered upon the world for the benefit of His children should be conveniently distributed." Formally, then, the Pope remained in a very lofty moral and religious plane. He did not allow the fight waged by the Nazi regime against the Catholic Church to push him into any strong attack against the totalitarian regimes. The sermon showed his chief concern was to maintain peace—and that he was determined to use all possible means of bringing about an understanding between the democracies and the Axis.

Pius was preparing the ground for a peace move that would, in his opinion, save Europe from chaos and ruin. He abstained from taking sides on political questions because he wished to convince both governments and people of his absolute impartiality—first prerequisite of a potential mediator—although his vast diplomatic experience told him that the chances of success were dismally few.

TENTH CHAPTER

European chancelleries were still echoing with the anguished cries of the Czech people mourning the death of their independence when Hitler, towards the end of March, sent a note to the Polish Government demanding the return of Danzig to the Reich and the right to build a road through the Polish corridor separating Prussia from Danzig itself. Having finally become convinced that dictators' pledges were as ephemeral as snow flakes, Chamberlain suddenly changed his policy of noncommittal appeasement into one that clearly showed England's strong determination to halt the aggressiveness of the Axis. He concluded a pact of mutual assistance with Joseph Beck, Polish Premier, thus serving notice to the German dictator that an attack against Warsaw would mean war with England as well as with France, which had associated herself with the English decision.

It was clear, however, that, so far as Italy was concerned, the British Government had hopes of weakening the Axis by attempting to separate the two partners. Moreover, the German pressure on Poland counseled moderation in regard to Italy. Chamberlain made a statement in the House of Commons on April 13, in which he tacitly accepted Italy's annexation of Albania. Despite the insistence of the opposition parties, he refused to denounce the Anglo-Italian agreement of April, 1938. He told his critics that the status quo in the Mediterranean—one of the fundamental clauses of the agreement—had not, in his opinion, been violated by the annexation of a country whose shores were on the Adriatic Sea! True, the British Premier gave to Mussolini the same kind of warning he had given Hitler by extending to many European nations, including Yugoslavia and Greece, which bordered on Albania, unilateral guarantees to intervene in case their independence were threatened. France, uneasy over the truculence of the officially inspired Fascist newspaper which continued to clamor for Tunisia, Jibuti, and Suez, limited herself to press polemics and official support of Chamberlain's policy.

Hitler, in a blistering speech delivered on April 28, not only repeated his demands on Poland, but denounced three treaties: the German-Polish non-aggression pact of 1934; the Anglo-German naval agreement of 1935; and the Anglo-German consultative pact concluded with Chamberlain at Munich, in September, 1938. At the same time, both he and his Italian colleague rejected with caustic sarcasm a peace offer Roosevelt made on April 15. In his appeal, the American President had asked the two dictators to give assurances that they would not jeopardize for at least ten years, the independence of a number of nations in Europe, the Near East, and Africa. As a compensation for this guarantee he offered to promote a world conference which would insure for all countries, free access to raw materials and other products.

Alarmed by the Nazi demands, Warsaw began to concentrate troops on the German-Polish border. The British Parliament voted compulsory military training in May, and pushed negotiations for a pact with Russia. On May 12, Chamberlain announced the signing of a mutual assistance pact with Turkey to cope with possible Fascist aggression in the Mediterranean and the Balkans. The Axis' reply to the British initiatives was the conclusion of an Italo-German military pact on May 21.

As these decisions were taken, other European nations displayed a diplomatic activity which was in itself a proof of the gravity of the moment.

Gregory Gafencu, Rumanian foreign minister, left Bucharest on April 18, for a series of meetings in Berlin, London, Brussels, Paris, and Rome. Paul Teleki and Stephen Csaki, Hungarian premier and foreign minister respectively, saw Mussolini and Ciano the same day in Rome, and arrived a week later in Berlin where they had meetings with Hitler, Ribbentrop, Goering, and Hess. Alexander Cincar-Markovitch, Yugoslav foreign minister, came close on their heels for a parley with Ciano on April 22, in Venice. Worried over the tension among the big powers, the statesmen of these three nations were strenuously attempting to maintain their neutrality in the event of war.

Ernest Urdareano, the closest advisor of King Carol of Rumania, whom I met in Mexico in 1943, told me that the purpose of Gafencu's trip was to sound out England and France as to what military support Bucharest would be given if she joined the democratic camp. The visits to Rome and Berlin, he said, were merely a diplomatic screen to cover the real purpose of the trip. Had Gafencu visited only London and Paris, he would have antagonized and aroused the suspicion of Rome and Berlin. The Rumanian Foreign Minister satisfied himself that England could not, at that moment, give effective aid, and Rumania, therefore, based her foreign policy on that established fact. Urdareano explained that Carol had no recourse other than to submit to Nazi pressure, in view of the fact that Rumania, hemmed in between Germany and Russia, was in a hopeless position.

On May 3, Viacheslav Molotoff, Chairman of the Council of People's Commissars, was appointed Commissar of Foreign Affairs of the U.S.S.R. in place of Maxim Litvinoff, who was regarded as the exponent of a policy of collaboration with the democracies. Immediately afterwards, Vladimir Potemkin, Assistant Commissar for Foreign Affairs, started on a round of official visits to Sofia, Bucharest, and Warsaw. Only very few people at the time guessed that the replacement of Litvinoff marked the beginning of a new phase in Russian foreign relations which was to culminate in the signing of the German-Soviet pact of August 1939.

Through its diplomatic representatives and influential clergymen abroad, the Vatican was kept informed in detail of all these meetings. Scores of telegrams and many international telephone calls were received daily at the Secretariat of State. They all contained the same fateful prediction: Germany intended to annex Danzig, and Poland was determined to resist; the result would be war.

At 8 A.M., on the second day of May, Cardinal Maglione, Papal Secretary of State, entered Pius XII's private study on the second floor of the Apostolic Palace. It was the customary visit which he paid to his sovereign every morning. Maglione found the Pontiff walking nervously back and forth in the spacious room, sometimes pausing to glance at St. Peter's Square where water spouts from the two twin fountains formed a rainbow against the rays of the bright Roman sun. On the Pontiff's desk was a dispatch from Monsignor Cesare

Orsenigo, papal nuncio in Berlin, which reviewed the political situation in Germany, and especially commented on Hitler's abrogation of the 1934 German-Polish treaty. Orsenigo had very little hope that a clash between Berlin and Warsaw could be averted. Also on the desk was another dispatch from Monsignor Filippo Cortesi, papal nuncio to Warsaw. It explained that the Polish Government, having in mind the fate which had befallen Czechoslovakia after the compromise at Munich, was adamant in its refusal to consider Hitler's demands.

Maglione had, of course, seen the two telegrams sent to him in a special code two days before. Since their arrival, Pius XII had spent most of the time in profound meditation. The Secretary waited for a few seconds until the Pope went over to his desk and sat down. In crisp, lucid sentences, he explained his decision.

Instructions must be sent to the papal representatives in Berlin, Warsaw, Paris, London, and Rome, to see the political leaders in the countries where they were accredited and convey Pius' personal appeal to abstain from rash decisions that might lead to war. The Vatican felt impelled to make this move because one of its basic aims was the maintenance of peace. Moreover it had no political or territorial interests to foster. The papal representatives must impress upon the lay leaders that the current problems, unless solved by common agreement, would inevitably lead to war. In the past few weeks the Vatican had seen the gap widening between the great powers. The intensification of military preparedness was all the more ominous because of the lack of any diplomatic or political initiative that might bring about an understanding. Distrust was dominant in international relations. This feeling precluded the success of peaceful gestures any government might be inclined to make. Tension had become so marked that the Vatican, which hitherto had not interested itself in political quarrels except in so far as they had affected peace, felt that it should make an attempt to place European peace on a firmer foundation. The Pontiff was convinced that negotiations conducted in a spirit of mutual comprehension and loyalty could not fail to avert war. The Holy See placed itself at the disposal of all the great powers. It was to be made clear, however, that the Vatican had no intention of participating personally in any meeting. Its aim was merely that of fostering contacts among the various countries. There its intervention ended. The political aspects of the problems and their solutions were left to the chosen representatives of the interested parties.

Maglione returned to his office and drafted the dispatches which were substantially similar; those addressed to Orsenigo and to Cortesi stressed more forcibly the hope that an understanding would be reached on the Danzig issue. Within two hours the Secretary of State was back in the Pope's study for the final approval and, after a few slight modifications, the messages were sent.

This scene was described to me many weeks later by a Vatican prelate who, because of his position, was cognizant of many facts generally not known by even close collaborators of the Pope. He was not, at that moment, betraying any secret since Pius XII himself had, in the meantime, publicly admitted his peace initiative.

The appeal was, of necessity, vague, inasmuch as the Vatican was bound by Article XXIV of the Lateran Treaty with Italy not to intervene in temporal conflicts unless specifically asked. This article said: "The Holy See, in relation to the sovereignty which belongs to it in the international field, declares that it desires to remain and will remain apart from temporal conflicts of other states, as well as from international congresses promoted for such purpose, unless the parties in conflict make a joint appeal to its mission of peace. It does, however, reserve to itself the right of making its moral and spiritual power recognized."

Next day the papal appeal had been delivered. By May 9, the Vatican was in possession of the replies. The five governments unanimously stressed that none of them wanted war.

Encouraged by the expressions of good will, Pius sent new instructions to his representatives. They were to consult the various governments and obtain their point of view on the problems that needed an immediate solution in order to proceed with preliminary soundings. The Pope was especially eager to bring about an understanding between Germany and Poland, and messages in this sense were sent to the nuncios of those two countries. At the same time, the Secretariat of State telephoned Monsignor Valerio Valeri, papal nuncio in Paris, and asked him to sound out Georges Bonnet, French foreign minister, as to what the possibilities were for a rapprochement with Italy. The same question, Monsignor Borgongini Duca submitted to Ciano in regard to France.

At this point, the papal overtures met with difficulties. Bonnet told Valeri in no uncertain terms that Paris would refuse to participate in any diplomatic move that would involve a discussion of the Italian claims over French territories. Warsaw persisted in its refusal to discuss the Danzig question, and referred the Vatican to Beck's speech of May 5, which asserted that any suggestions for a settlement would be accepted on condition that Poland's special rights in Danzig be recognized and that no attempts would be made to infringe upon Poland's sovereignty over her own territory. London explained that after the experience of Munich, it had lost faith in Hitler. It did not see, therefore, what advantage could be gained from a meeting with a leader who had consistently broken all the pledges he had given. Nevertheless, the British Government made clear that it favored any initiative that might alleviate the current tension. Berlin's attitude was negative. Hitler bluntly replied that he was preparing "his own solution" of the Danzig question. Italy's answer, instead, was distinctly favorable. The reason for this attitude was obvious. She was one of the powers that were clamoring for territorial concessions. Any peace conference with the participation of France and Poland would automatically imply a sacrifice on the part of these two countries, and Rome would have everything to gain and nothing to lose from an international conference.

A crop of fantastic reports followed the Vatican steps. Dispatches from Paris, London, and other European capitals went so far as to state that the Pontiff had suggested the holding of a five-power conference in Vatican City, and that Cardinal Maglione was planning to make a trip to Berlin, Paris, and London.

At the Secretariat of State, the reports were described as pure fantasy. It was pointed out that in no way had the Vatican concerned itself with specific considerations or appraisals of specific problems.

Its task had been to urge a general meeting of the interested powers or bilateral negotiations confined to the countries interested in the settlement of specific questions.

The Pope himself, on June 2, gave an explanation of his diplomatic activity. He disclosed that "at the beginning of May, after mature deliberation, We thought it timely to make known to some statesmen of the great European nations the anxiety the situation was causing Us at that moment and Our fear lest international dissensions become aggravated to a point of degenerating into a sanguinary conflict." His step, the Pontiff said, had "met in general with the sympathy of the governments and, after it had come to public attention through no encouragement on Our part, it met with the gratitude of the people. As a result of this step, we received assurances of good will and determination to maintain peace which was so much desired by the people."

It was soon apparent that his efforts had failed to produce concrete results, however. While assuring the Holy See of their intention to avoid war, the great powers were feverishly intensifying their military preparedness. Despite the disheartening outlook, Pius persisted in his efforts. He told the Vatican representatives to inquire as to the terms on which each nation would be ready to come to an understanding and to explain that such a step would be merely advisory since the Vatican wished only to assist diplomatically in the solution of the crisis in the supreme interest of world peace.

The same suggestion was made to Francis d'Arcy Godolphin Osborne, British minister to the Holy See, Reverend Pietro Tacchi-Venturi, Mussolini's intimate friend and advisor, a representative of the French Embassy, and an influential British prelate, in private audiences the Pope granted on a Sunday—a proof of his anxiety since visitors on that day of the week are received only for very important reasons. The mere fact that Tacchi-Venturi had been at the Vatican indicated that the Pope was attempting to enlist the support of the Italian dictator for his peace moves. But, in addition to the very serious tension between Germany and Poland, Pius was concerned over the possibility of an Anglo-Franco-Soviet pact being negotiated in Moscow. At that time, the Holy See feared that the planned alliance with the two Western democracies would enable the Soviet to play an important part in European diplomacy. This attitude was easily understandable in view of the fact that the Church is an irreconcilable enemy of Bolshevism, which had systematically attempted to stamp out every form of religion in the U.S.S.R.

On June 13, President Ignaz Moscicki of Poland, received Monsignor Cortesi, who handed him a papal message. Pius, according to what I was told at the Vatican, had asked that the Polish press halt its attacks against Germany, so as to create an atmosphere more conducive to discussion. Poland was merely refuting the atrocity stories which Joseph Goebbels, Nazi minister of propaganda, was manufacturing daily for the consumption of the German public and to pave the way for Hitler's declaration of war. Cortesi also urged the Polish President to undertake direct negotiations with Hitler. Pius, he explained, was ready to act as intermediary with Germany, if it were so desired. The reply was the same as on previous occasions: Poland refused to submit to German pressure.

Monsignor Cortesi was in Rome, three days later, and gave to both the Pope and Maglione a pessimistic report on his diplomatic efforts.

At the end of June, the Vatican knew that it was fighting a losing battle.

This, at least, was the feeling of prelates who had been following the papal activity. The results had been purely formal. None of the five governments had given concrete replies or offered definite proposals. They praised the papal efforts, admitted that all questions could be solved, and recalled specific statements made by their leaders on the problems with which each nation was specifically concerned. But, and this was the diplomatic way of rejecting the Pope's offers, they stressed that they could not give up what they called their "vital rights and national interests," and that, unless those rights and interests which their policies protected were recognized in advance, they could not consider proposals for any form of international meeting.

The Italian people, as well as Catholics from the other European countries, had been following the papal diplomatic offensive with undisguised interest. Letters received at the Vatican from all parts of Italy showed the deep anxiety felt over the possibility of a clash between the Axis and the Western democracies. Parish priests wrote to their bishops that the earnest wish of their flocks was to spare Italy from war. It was to this feeling that the Pope had referred in his statement of June 2. Even Fascists in official position, who had applauded Mussolini's Albanian coup, began to sober up when they saw that England had decided to go to war rather than submit to further Axis aggressiveness. The army, conscious of Italy's state of unpreparedness, was another conservative force.

Moreover, there was a very strong popular feeling against Mussolini's policy. Despite a steady barrage of propaganda, the Italians found the link with Germany highly unpalatable. The greatest resistance was encountered among elderly Italians who had fought the Huns during the First World War and who had been taught to regard them as the traditional enemies of their country. Their generation had grown up in a period when French culture dominated Europe and was admired and absorbed by Italians of the middle and upper classes. On the other hand, with the danger of war drawing nearer every day, the Italian alliance with Germany and its implied military support assumed an importance which it never had before, when, for instance, the problem of Italian claims against France had not yet darkened the international horizon and when the Anglo-Italian agreement seemed to have composed the quarrel originated by Italy's conquest of Ethiopia.

Mussolini knew full well the degree of Italian nervousness and antagonism his policy had generated. He had a very accurate information service which reported the slightest trend in public opinion. Commendatore Arturo Bocchini, chief of police, was to Il Duce what Fouché was to Napoleon, and, like his French counterpart, the best-informed Italian. Agents telegraphed to headquarters from every town in Italy, whenever they thought there was news of a political character that Rome should know. They mingled with the people in food markets, cafés, restaurants; they traveled on buses, trolley cars, and trains; they engaged people in conversation to learn their reaction to current political events of domestic and international character.

Next to Bocchini's office, at Palazzo Viminale, a score of alert young men made digests of the telegrams and compiled a summary which they handed to their chief every morning at eight-thirty. One hour later, Bocchini was received by Mussolini in Palazzo Venezia. Another man who saw Il Duce every morning was the commander in chief of the Carabineers, or military police. The Carabineers also had their own information system, very similar to that of the police. Finally, there was the Minister of Press and Propaganda. He was received not once, but twice a day. In the morning, he brought to the Italian dictator a digest of the dispatches and editorials printed in the foreign press, which were transmitted by the press attachés in the Italian embassies and legations abroad. In many cases, the attachés were also correspondents for Stefani, Italy's official news agency. A great deal of this information never appeared in the Italian newspapers. It was for Mussolini's private knowledge and that of his ministers. In the afternoon, the Minister of Press and Propaganda again reported to Il Duce who gave him instructions concerning the treatment of foreign and Italian events in the Fascist newspapers. The instructions were very detailed. Typewritten copies of them were sent to the Associazione della Stampa Italiana, in Piazza San Silvestro, for relay by the local correspondents to the out-of-town dailies. Other copies were sent to the Roman editors personally.

Mussolini went to the extent of giving the "points" which should be commented upon in the editorials. The Ministry of Press and Propaganda usually wrote a pattern editorial based on these points and released it with additional instructions. The smaller newspapers sometimes did not even trouble to rewrite the official comment with the result that newspapers in northern Italy and in Sicily, at the two ends of the peninsula, would publish an identical editorial. The instructions were extremely useful to foreign correspondents, and for a few hundred lire a month, I was able to obtain them daily from an Italian newspaperman, who, incidentally, was risking a very stiff jail sentence every time he met me. But, as most Italian intellectuals, he was anti-Fascist and very glad to contribute to the exposé of the

inner workings that kept in motion one facet of the Fascist dictatorship.

Bocchini's reports had shown Mussolini that Italy's northern
regions were especially worried over the possibility of war. In the
middle of May, Il Duce decided to make a tour of some of the cities
in Piedmont, one of the provinces bordering France. In view of the
tension caused by the Fascist claims on French territories, the Pied-
montese felt that they would be the first to suffer from the impact
of war. Mussolini again appeared in the role of a moderator. His
speech in Turin, on May 15, was an attempt to reassure the anxious
populations that he was not planning to plunge Italy into a European conflict.

"A cold, objective examination of the situation shows that there
are not at present in Europe problems big or acute enough to justify a
war that would, by logical development, become universal," he said.

On May 16, after a brief inspection of the Italian defenses along
the French border, the Italian dictator disappeared. Not a word
concerning his whereabouts was published in the press. Finally, on
May 18, he resumed his tour and spoke in the town of Aosta. During
those forty-eight hours the rumor spread throughout Italy that Il
Duce was ill. The truth was that Mussolini, already three times a
grandfather, had once more become a father. A woman with whom
he had been in love for some years, gave birth to a son in a quiet
villa on the Adriatic. Soon after his Turin speech, the Italian
dictator had received news from his mistress' mother of the im-
pending birth and had decided to interrupt his political tour.

All the Italians knew of this illicit love affair and never really
cared. To their Latin minds, it was nobody's business what Mussolini did in his private life. It must be added in all fairness to the
ladylove that she, as far as I know, never used whatever influence
she might have had to play a role in Italian policy. She did, of course,
take care of the members of her immediate family including her
father, who wrote boring articles for a Roman newspaper whose
editor had been "invited" by Palazzo Venezia to accept his literary
contributions.

The story of how she met Mussolini was given me by a woman

friend of hers. According to this version, it happened in 1936. The young lady, whose name I prefer not to mention, had been separated for some time from her husband, an officer in the Italian air force, who was a member of a mission which had been sent to China for the purpose of negotiating with the Chiang Kai-shek Government the sale of Italian airplanes. She, as many women at the time, was an ardent admirer of the twentieth-century Bismarck who had created an Empire for Fascist Italy. She had vainly asked for an audience at Palazzo Venezia. Mussolini's intimates regarded her as a pest and, of course, spiked all her efforts.

In the summer of 1936, Mussolini usually left his office for a few hours in the afternoon and went bathing. He had a private beach at Castel Fusano, eighteen miles from Rome. Just before entering the town of Ostia, there was a sharp detour leading to Castel Fusano. One day Il Duce, who was driving a motorcycle, had slowed down in order to take the curve, when suddenly a blonde, tall, good-looking, somewhat plump young woman threw herself in his path. Mussolini swerved just in time. There was a screeching of brakes as two automobiles filled with plain-clothes men following at a short distance, halted almost instantly. The excited agents thought it was an attempt at Mussolini's life and pounced on the blonde. The Italian dictator handed the motorcycle to one of the men and walked over to the woman who was screaming and crying hysterically.

Her voice broken by sobs, the enamored female explained that she had wanted to meet Il Duce, oh, for such a long time, but never could. What she had just done was the only means she could think of to make herself noticed.

Mussolini was amused. He turned to a secretary, told him to arrange an appointment for the girl on the morrow, and shoved off. It looked like a nice adventure, one of the many which dotted the dictator's private life. But the blonde was there to stay—Mussolini really fell in love.

Late in the summer, the rumblings of war were beginning to be heard and the closer collaboration between Italy and Germany was a logical sequence to the intensified Anglo-French activity. The military pact signed in Berlin, as a description of subsequent events will show, was at that moment a political expedient with which the dictators hoped to intimidate the democracies. It had, instead, exactly the opposite effect—it made England and France more determined than ever to build an antiwar front.

Mussolini had no intention of declaring war on London and Paris, but he did not know whether the democracies would respect his neutrality once Hitler attacked Poland. He, therefore, took certain precautions.

On June 19, Marshal Pietro Badoglio, chief of general staff, went to Tirana. His visit was announced a few days after the Italian Government had appropriated 1,200,000,000 lire for Albania's economic improvement and 800,000,000 lire ($100,000,000 in all) for the creation of a network of strategic roads that were tantamount to a huge military spearhead from Italy to the heart of the Balkans. Badoglio's task was to make a complete survey of Albania's strategic possibilities before the beginning of the public works program, decide where to build accommodation for eighty thousand troops, and transform five airfields, hitherto used only by the Italian civil aviation, into military airports. At the same time, preparations began for the holding of military maneuvers in Piedmont, the following August. The problem to solve was whether the "French Army" could successfully invade Italy; it could not, the press proudly announced after the maneuvers were held. Mussolini also recalled a number of specialists of many classes, held meetings with the general staff officers, strengthened the defenses on the French border, and sent troops to Libya.

Despite these discouraging signs in Italy, and similar war measures in England, France, Germany, and Poland, Pius XII marshaled all the spiritual and diplomatic resources of the Vatican as well as the prestige and influence of the Roman Catholic Church to forestall the dreaded avalanche of blood and steel. During July and August, the Pontiff set aside every other problem to concentrate exclusively on diplomatic activity. He never, until the last day, desisted from his efforts. His work to save Europe and the world from the ravages of war, although it was not successful, will undoubtedly remain as one of the outstanding contributions to peace given by a single man in our century. His great intelligence and profound diplomatic experience was coupled with a truly amazing sense of balance, knowledge of problems and a realism that were unmatched by any of the European statesmen. The approach of the latter to the problems was dictated by nationalist considerations which, though quite human and understandable, warped their judgment and consequently impaired their efforts.

The manner in which Pius conducted the negotiations and the humanitarian motives that inspired him have been recognized even by governments ideologically hostile to the Vatican. Benedict XV, who found himself in a similar situation during the World War I, was often attacked by both the Central Powers and the Allies. Pius XII, throughout the whole period of his intervention, was never accused by responsible leaders of favoring this or that group of belligerents—an eloquent testimonial to the loftiness of his motives and the unselfishness of his aims.

Pius XII's work was in keeping with a tradition set by many of his predecessors. Although by signing the Lateran Treaty in 1929, the Vatican had agreed to forego all forms of purely political activity such as those which characterized the reigns of Gregory VII, Innocent III, Boniface VIII, and Pius IX, yet throughout its history from the Middle Ages to the present day, the papacy had constantly worked in behalf of peace and intervened in disputes between lay powers.

In the period between 1870 and 1929, when the Pope was in voluntary confinement in the Vatican, Leo XIII and Pius X had welcomed appeals for mediations in international quarrels. In 1885, for instance, Leo had intervened between Germany and Spain in a dispute involving the ownership of the Caroline Islands. Ten years later, he had performed the same role between Haiti and Santo Domingo, when they could not agree on the delimitation of their borders. In 1898, Spain had appealed to the Vatican for a settlement of her quarrel with the United States. The Pope accepted the appeal, but Washington refused to consider mediation.

During the First World War, Benedict XV had to cope with Italian objections to Vatican interference with international issues. An article of the secret Treaty of London, signed in 1915, tied the hands of the papacy as far as its direct participation in any peace conferences was concerned: England, France, and Russia agreed "to support such opposition as Italy may wish to make to any proposal aimed at allowing a representative of the Holy See in any peace negotiations for the settlement of problems arising from the present war." Italy's attitude was partly due to the feeling that the Vatican was attempting at the time to reacquire the temporal power lost when Italian troops occupied Rome in 1870. Up to 1929, the Holy See still formally claimed what had been known as the papal states. By renouncing all of its territorial aspirations and by accepting only a few acres of ground as a final settlement for her temporal losses, the Vatican obtained recognition as a sovereign state. Moreover, its prestige increased inasmuch as it permanently divorced itself from a policy, common to all lay powers, which fostered temporal gains.

During July and August, many of the Vatican representatives accredited to the big powers held conferences with the Pope. Monsignor Amleto Cicognani, the able and experienced Apostolic Delegate in Washington, and Monsignor Paolo Marella, his colleague in Tokyo, had arrived in Rome. No announcement was made in regard to these and other meetings which the Pontiff had in those two crucial months. The publicity given to the earlier peace efforts made the Vatican extremely reserved. The collation and drafting of dispatches, the subjects discussed in conversations, and the decisions taken were known only to a handful of prelates. However, the names and position of the people received by Pius were in themselves an indication of the general trend of Vatican diplomacy.

Cicognani, from what I heard, had had meetings with high American officials in Washington, who had discussed with him President Roosevelt's decision to send a personal representative to the Vatican. In view of this important development in the relations between the Holy See and the United States, and the influence which Washington could exert in behalf of peace, the Pope had summoned his Apostolic Delegate to Rome.

The first week in July, the Pontiff saw the Norwegian and Swedish Ministers twice, and the Belgian Ambassador once. From this it was surmised that he was seeking to enlist the support of the smaller powers for his peace offensive. At the same time, he dispatched Monsignor Cortesi back to Poland with other proposals for a settlement of Danzig, and cabled similar instructions to Orsenigo. Hitler's attitude, however, precluded all possibilities of negotiations. After having publicly stated that he wanted to annex Danzig outright, the German dictator steadily rejected every offer of a compromise. If somebody had to give in, it would be Warsaw, and not Germany, which relied on her formidable military strength.

Borgongini Duca saw Ciano to whom he relayed a papal appeal for Mussolini to intercede with Hitler. On August 10, the Italian Foreign Minister left for Salzburg where he had a two-day meeting with Hitler and Ribbentrop. He was back in Rome on the afternoon of August 13, and went directly to Villa Torlonia, Mussolini's residence. He remained closeted with Il Duce for two hours. He then telephoned friends and told them that he needed some relaxation. These friends, Marquis d'Ajetta and his wife, had been invited to dine at Villa Aldobrandini, in Frascati, which is a small town, near Rome, famous for its excellent wine. Ciano, who knew Prince Clemente Aldobrandini, the host, said he would like to come along and escape the summer heat in the city.

It was a most interesting dinner. The Italian Foreign Minister, who was usually very discreet, appeared to be beside himself. He was asked the question uppermost in Italian minds. Will there be war?

"We don't want war," he said. "And we told them [the Germans] so when we signed the military pact last May. The Chief [Mussolini] hopes to convince Hitler yet. *Glie l'ho cantata a Ribbentrop su tutti i toni, ma e' una testa dura.* [I argued with Ribbentrop until I was blue in the face, but he is stubborn.] I told him that our information indicated without doubt that England would march to help Poland, but Ribbentrop says he has different reports. He says that England will yield this time too."

Everybody held their breath; Ciano fingered a glass of wine, took a sip, and continued:

"After the official conversations ended, I never addressed a single word to him. *Ho fatto il maleducato anche con la figlia.* [I was bad mannered even with his daughter.] At the dinner they gave me on

the Wofgansee (a lake near Salzburg) they put her on my right.
I turned my shoulders to her and looked at the panorama through
the window during the whole meal."

That was all he said about his trip, but it made the party a very
merry one for the relieved guests.

At the Italian Foreign Office, I was told that there had been an
intense exchange of views between the two Axis partners. At Salzburg, Ciano, acting on Mussolini's instructions, laid the cards on the
table. He gave Hitler a complete picture of Italy's lack of resources
and military strength to show that, in the event of war, Rome could
not join her ally for a long time. He invoked the secret clause of the
May 21 Italo-German military pact which stipulated that it would
become operative in 1945, and stressed that the political and military
disadvantages of Italy's intervention at that moment would by far
offset the advantages. Rome's entrance in the war, he said, would
result in the loss of Libya, badly defended and open to the attack
of French and English forces. Thus, the control of the central
Mediterranean would pass into the hands of the democracies, a fact
that could not but influence the attitude of Greece and Turkey,
already potentially hostile to Italy. On the mainland, the lack of
armaments would force Italy to remain on the defensive. Her position, in regard to France, was strategically unfavorable. The Italian
people were psychologically unprepared for war. They regarded
Danzig as a purely German-Polish problem.

Hitler's reply, as related to me by Italian officials, was that the
negotiations for a Soviet-German economic pact were virtually concluded. This would leave Germany free to deal with Poland, which
could be liquidated in a few weeks. Hitler did not think that London
and Paris would go to war over Poland, especially in view of the
fact that they would lack the support of Russia. Therefore, Italy's
aid was not necessary.

Mussolini did not share the views of his colleague. Count Dino
Grandi, Italian ambassador in London, and without any question the
ablest diplomat produced by the Fascist regime, had reported that
Chamberlain would honor the pledge given to Poland. Raffaele
Guariglia, Italian ambassador to Paris, was certain that France would

support any English decision, including a declaration of war. The two ambassadors were not quite sure but that England would wage war on Italy for the very same reasons that counseled Mussolini to be cautious, despite the fact that England's policy had up to then tended to separate Rome from Berlin. They stated that Anglo-French decisions would be largely determined by Italy's attitude.

On his return from Salzburg, Ciano was literally besieged by diplomatists. François Poncet, French ambassador, Sir Percy Lorraine, British ambassador, General Boleslaw Wieniawa Dlugoszowski, Polish ambassador, and William Phillips, United States ambassador, had conversations with the Foreign Minister. They all wanted to know the results of the Salzburg meeting. Ciano's reply was an assurance that Italy was trying in every way she could to settle the quarrel between Berlin and Warsaw, and that she had no intention of going to war. He told Dlugoszowski that the Nazi frame of mind was one of "determination," and that the only chance of averting war was to yield to Germany.

James A. Farley, at that time United States Postmaster General, arrived in Rome for a short visit in August. I had known him at the time he was Chairman of the New York State Athletic Commission, and I was earning my living by writing sports news for a New York daily. The Pope, who had met Farley several times during the trip to the United States in 1936, granted him a private audience. It lasted more than thirty minutes, an unusually long time for a visitor who had no official matter to discuss with him. Farley held an "off the record" press conference at Ambassador Phillips' residence after his meeting with Pius. All he said, however, was that "His Holiness will do everything in his power to aid the maintenance of peace among nations."

Farley's discretion was a disappointment in a period when we were working very hard to gain a picture of the intense diplomatic activity in which both Rome and the Vatican were engaged. I did some investigating, and with the help of my Vatican friends was able to obtain in a few days a general idea of the nature of the conversation.

By the middle of August, Pius, I was told, had lost all hopes of averting war. His diplomatic representatives had already informed him that Germany and Russia were about to conclude a nonaggression pact. When he saw Farley, the Pope spoke to him quite frankly. He outlined his peace efforts and the discouraging results, then asked whether Roosevelt would run for a third term. Farley, who had seen the American President the day before sailing for Europe, said he had Roosevelt's word that he did not want to be re-elected, and that, at any rate, he would not break a tradition established by George Washington, who had refused to be nominated for a third term. The Pope interrupted him to point out smilingly that his own election had broken a much older tradition! In other words, the Pontiff was sure that Roosevelt would run, just another proof of the excellence and accuracy of Vatican information on foreign affairs.

A few days later, the fears of the Holy See were confirmed by the signing of the Soviet-German pact. The bewildered Italian people read enthusiastic press accounts of how the Axis had put one over on the democracies and had halted what it called "Chamberlain's encirclement policy." Newspapers which for seventeen years had played up the Bolshevist bogey, dished to their readers harrowing stories of Soviet atrocities and depicted Stalin as nothing short of a monster, threw the usual political somersault. They proudly asserted, as did *Il Resto del Carlino*, an official Fascist Party newspaper published in Bologna, that the pact was "doubtless made on Italian advice—it is pure Machiavellianism from the viewpoint of political philosophy."

For several days, the Vatican paused in its negotiations. There was nothing else to do. All efforts had been shattered by Hitler's intransigence, bolstered by the success of his Russian negotiations with which Germany had eliminated the threat of a two-front war. Italian officials, after the shock of the Soviet-German alliance abated, felt, paradoxically enough, relieved. They were certain that the democracies, deprived of Soviet support, would back down.

The Pope realized fully, the consequences of the pact. His personal appeals to the heads of governments having failed, he decided to make what was to be his last public address to the peoples of Europe and their leaders before the outbreak of hostilities. He summoned to Castel Gandolfo, where he was spending the summer, Count

Giuseppe dalla Torre, editor of *L'Osservatore Romano*, and told him to announce a broadcast for seven o'clock the next evening, August 24. Father Soccorsi, director of the Vatican radio station, arrived at the papal villa, to make the necessary technical arrangements. At the same time, the Pontiff instructed Monsignor Domenico Tardini, one of the most intelligent prelates of Curia, who was Secretary of the Congregation of Extraordinary Ecclesiastical Affairs, to arrange appointments with the British, French, Polish, and Italian Ambassadors to the Holy See for the morrow, and to recall to Rome Cardinal Maglione who was spending a few days of rest in Casoria, his native town, near Naples. Finally, Pius gave orders not to be disturbed except for very urgent reasons and worked far into the night to prepare the address he was to broadcast. The next morning he handed to each diplomatist the text of his speech and asked them to convey it to their respective governments.

With guns cocked all over Europe, the Pope walked into the study of his villa at five minutes to seven. Prelates who stood next to him as he spoke reported that he was hardly able to control his emotion. The speech, with its loftiness of thought and stirring exhortation to the world gave a clear measure of the Pontiff's intellectual stature and deep love for mankind which overshadowed every other consideration.

A grave hour sounds anew for the great human family, an hour of tremendous deliberation in which the spiritual authority, whose task it is to induce souls to return to the way of justice and peace, cannot remain disinterested.

And it is so with all you who bear so much responsibility. May you hear through Our voice, the voice of that Christ from whom the world received the school of life in which millions of souls place their confidence in time of peril and Whose Word can dominate all the uproar of the earth.

And so here We are with you, leaders of peoples, men of politics and arms, writers and orators on the radio and the tribune, and all others who influence the thought and action of their brethren and have responsibility for their fate. We are armed by nothing more than the word of truth and, above the contests and the clash of factions, We speak in the name of God.

Today, while notwithstanding our repeated exhortations and the special interest We have taken, international conflicts are becoming more worrisome; today, when the tension between spirits seems to have reached such a point as to cause concern lest the tremendous turbine of war be set in motion, We address more fervently with paternal soul anew all governments and peoples. We urge that the former try to solve their present divergencies by the only suitable means: that is, with common and loyal understandings, while foregoing accusations, threats, and causes of reciprocal diffidence; We urge that the latter may encourage by determination, calmness, and serenity, the peaceful efforts of their governments: it is with the force of reason and not force of arms that justice advances. Empires not founded on justice are not blessed by God.

Dangers are imminent, but there is still time; nothing is lost through peace, everything may be lost through war. Let men again understand each other, let them resume negotiations: by negotiating with good will and with respect for reciprocal rights, it will be shown that honorable success is never precluded peaceful and purposeful negotiation.

May the omnipotent cause which is pleaded by the voice of this Father of the Christian family, of this servant of servants whom Jesus Christ sends unworthily but truly among men have a ready and willing hearing both in minds and hearts. May the strong hear Us, may the powerful hear Us, and may they act in such a way that their power may not mean destruction for peoples but the guardianship of their tranquillity, of their order, and their labor.

We plead for this in the name of the Blood of Christ, and as We plead, We feel and We know that We have with Us all men of good heart, all those who hunger and search for justice, all those who suffer every grief from the ills of life.

We have with Us the hearts of mothers which beat with ours; mothers who would have to abandon their families; the humble who work and know not; the innocent on whom weighs the tremendous menace; the young generous knights of the pure and most noble ideals.

And with Us is that Christ Who made fraternal love His fundamental and solemn commandment and the substance of His religion—the promise for the well-being of individuals and nations. Fully mindful that human work is worth nothing without divine aid, We invite all to raise their eyes to Heaven and by fervent prayers to the Lord seek that His Christian Mercy may descend abundantly on this upset world, placating hates and making the dawn of a more serene future shine.

In this expectation and with this hope, We impart on all our fraternal blessing, which comes from the heart.

The only solace for Pius was the fact that Borgongini Duca had already received assurances that Italy would not enter the war unless she were attacked. An indication of this attitude was that King Victor Emmanuel had not interrupted his vacation at the royal country estate in Sant'Anna di Valdieri, a few miles from the French border. Had there been a real danger of war, the Italian sovereign would certainly have chosen a safer place to spend his holidays. The same day of the Pope's speech, he received Ambassador Phillips who delivered to him a message from Roosevelt which urged the king to use his influence for peace on the Continent. The sovereign asked Phillips "to thank the President cordially for his message" and promised to convey it immediately to Mussolini.

Lord Halifax, British foreign minister, Georges Bonnet, and King Leopold of Belgium telegraphed to the Pope their appreciation for his "moving and dignified" peace appeal. Hitler, Moscicki, and Mussolini ignored it.

The last week in August, the Vatican representative sent almost a blow-by-blow account of political developments. Scores of telegrams warned of the imminence of war and recorded the unsuccessful efforts to halt Hitler. What the Pontiff had attempted for three months— to induce Berlin and Poland to start direct negotiations—was now being pursued by England, France, and Italy. The Vatican watched hourly the feverish diplomatic activity of those powers. English, French, German, Italian, and Polish prelates were asked to listen in on broadcasts issuing from the capitals of the big European powers. Clerks of the Secretariat of State took recordings of all political news to the Pope, regardless of the hour in which they came. When Hitler, in reply to the British and French proposals, asked as the price of his collaboration that his claims on Poland be satisfied first, the Vatican knew that no human effort could prevent the catastrophe. Nevertheless, Pius launched an eleventh-hour desperate appeal of a personal and confidential nature. The appeal contained concrete suggestions for a political solution.

As dawn broke on August 31 over the Roman campagna, the Pope entered his study. From the desk he could gaze at the fields still yellow with the stubs of the harvested wheat, where bare-chested farmers were preparing the soil for the next sowing. Secular oaks and elms threw a mantle of green velvet over the hills which encased the light-blue waters of the tiny Castel Gandolfo lake, quivering under the rays of the nascent sun. It was a scene of bucolic tranquillity such as those Virgil had described two thousand years before. It required a painful mental effort to revert one's thoughts to the imminence of war.

The Pope had just finished a message addressed to Germany, Poland, England, France, and Italy, when Maglione arrived. He instructed the Secretary of State to summon the ambassadors of those countries and hand them the document.

"The Holy Father," read the message, "does not want to abandon the hope that the present negotiations may culminate in the just and peaceful solution for which the whole world is praying. Therefore, His Holiness implores in the name of God, the Governments of Germany and Poland to do what they can to avoid incidents and to abstain from taking any measures likely to aggravate the present tension. He asks the Governments of England, France, and Italy to support his request."

The rest of the message, containing the papal proposal, was kept confidential. It suggested to Germany and Poland a fifteen-day truce, during which those two nations would pledge themselves to do nothing that would feed the warlike atmosphere fomented by the press campaigns and the various military measures. That period, in the Pope's judgment, would permit the holding of an international conference among the five governments directly concerned and to which representatives from Belgium, Switzerland, Holland, the United States, and Vatican could be invited. Purpose of the conference was to study a peaceful revision of the Versailles Treaty preliminary to the conclusion of a collective, nonaggression pact which would place European peace on a permanent basis.

Hitler and Beck received the document before noon. The same day, Halifax instructed Nevile Henderson to see Ribbentrop and explain that "His Majesty's Government wishes to support the papal appeal with all the seriousness at its command." A similar step was made by Sir Howard Kennard, British ambassador in Warsaw.

But the German war machine was already in motion. At 6 A.M. of September 1, Orsenigo in Berlin, telephoned directly to Maglione in the Vatican, to tell him that Nazi troops had invaded Poland from four points, fifteen minutes before. Maglione, in turn, telephoned the Pope at Castel Gandolfo. Members of the papal household saw the Pontiff go to his private chapel and kneel in prayer.

Tears streamed from his eyes, and his body was shaken by sobs.

ELEVENTH CHAPTER

A few weeks before the outbreak of the European conflict, Mussolini, like Pius, exerted pressure on Germany and Poland for a compromise solution. His efforts were supported and encouraged by the Vatican. As in former instances, however, humanitarian considerations did not prompt the Italian dictator to remain neutral and to pursue a policy in behalf of peace. There were several political factors that obliged him to stand aside as his partner was beginning the conquest of Europe. Most important of them was Italy's domestic and colonial vulnerability. Mussolini was not going to risk an invasion by France. Poorly armed Italy could not have halted her at a moment when Germany was engaged in Poland and, therefore, not eager to divert any of her military strength to help her ally. Another reason was the uneasiness he felt about the Soviet-German pact. Despite the favorable attitude officially adopted by the Fascist Government in regard to it, Mussolini did not welcome the direct participation of the U.S.S.R. in European politics. He looked upon the Nazi-Bolshevist marriage as a dangerous expedient that might give Moscow an opportunity to intensify her communist propaganda in the Balkans and eastern Europe. Those countries were uncomfortably near Italy, and the Soviet would likely find a fertile field in the anti-German and anti-Fascist Italians whose numbers would be swelled by the adverse reaction due to an unpopular war. Further, by remaining neutral, Il Duce hoped to limit the practical consequences of the conflict to Germany and Poland, and after the rapid liquidation of the Polish "episode," to bring about an understanding between Hitler and the two Western democracies. An accord of this kind would give him time to prepare adequately for the war which he planned to wage later.

The Vatican had no illusions about Mussolini's peace efforts. Yet, it approved of them because, in view of the circumstances, it was the ultimate aim that mattered. At the same time, the Holy See had interests of its own to defend. Although they might be called political, they were subordinated to the all-important task of preserving peace. Some of these interests coincided with those of Italy's. Like the latter, the Vatican feared the spread of Bolshevism in Europe, and at that moment, the danger was greater than ever because of the Soviet alliance with Nazism, the other arch foe of the Church. Faced with the coalition of its two bitterest enemies, the Holy See undoubtedly found comfort in the fact that Catholic Italy had not become their ally. As long as Rome remained neutral, there was the hope of reaching an understanding with England and France that might permanently detach Mussolini from his partner. And again, the Vatican, like Italy, was interested in circumscribing the conflict since its spreading, apart from humanitarian reasons, obviously represented a grave threat to the existence of the Church in Europe.

Another question in which the papacy was vitally concerned was Poland's fate, however. The Holy See had always regarded that country as an extremely valuable and important Catholic bulwark against the Lutheran and schismatic nations in northeastern Europe. Its relations with Warsaw had been, on the whole, very cordial. When the Polish State was dismembered in the eighteenth century, and after the short-lived Grand Duchy created by Napoleon, the papacy had favored the autonomist agitations of the Poles, who had been annexed by Prussia and Russia. Soon after the end of the First World War, the Vatican sent Monsignor Achille Ratti, who later became Pius XI, as apostolic visitor to Poland. When the Republic was formed, Ratti was elevated to the rank of nuncio. The end of Czechoslovakia, which marked the beginning of Hitler's march towards the East, resulted in an intensification of Warsaw's relations with the Vatican, since the latter was one of the powers opposed to Nazism.

The difference in the motives that prompted the Italian and Vatican attitudes had a clear manifestation in the way the Fascist press and *L'Osservatore Romano* presented war developments. Italian newspapers were full of stories glorifying the German Army. Although they carefully abstained from commenting editorially and gave a certain amount of space to British and French news, their coverage of the war had a definite pro-German slant. When Berlin claimed the fall of Warsaw on September 7, the Italian dispatches bore the optimistic date line of the Polish capital. The denial issued by the Polish Embassy in Rome, the same day was ignored. L'Osservatore Romano was the only one that printed it with a balanced picture of events with news from the various capitals.

An even sharper contrast was afforded by the strong criticism in L'Osservatore Romano of anti-Catholic measures taken in the Reich coincident with the beginning of the war. Stefani, the official news agency, released a statement to the Italian press explaining the German viewpoint. According to its version, a certain number of churches had been closed by the Nazi authorities on the pretext that, in case of air raids, the buildings were too far from habitations to be used as shelters, and people would not be able to reach them in time. It also announced that the large number of Catholic reviews and periodicals in Germany had been reduced to five because of the scarcity of paper. L'Osservatore Romano bluntly pointed out that isolated churches would not be targets for bombs and therefore, not dangerous enough to be permanently closed, and that, so far as the periodicals were concerned, the reduction could not be justified since there were thirty million Catholics in Germany whose needs should be considered. The Vatican statement, of course, was not reproduced in the Italian press.

As soon as the war began, the Pope appealed to all belligerents to conform to international agreements for the humanization of the war. When the new Belgian Ambassador, Adrian Nieuwenhuys, was received at Castel Gandolfo on September 14, Pius XII urged that "the life, property, honor, and religious feelings of the inhabitants of the conquered territories should be respected, that prisoners of war should be treated humanely and receive the comforts of religion, and that no use should be made of poison or asphyxiating gases." The Pontiff admitted that hope for peace seemed barred by the "booming of guns" but promised that he would strive to shorten the conflict, and, if that could not be achieved, do his utmost to prevent it from becoming a universal conflagration.

The Soviet invasion of Poland less than three weeks after the outbreak of the war was regarded by the Vatican as the most serious blow dealt the Church in Europe since Lenin's advent to power. A large territory inhabited by Catholics was now at the mercy of a State which had abolished religion in all forms. The situation was all the more serious because the Vatican had no diplomatic relations with Moscow. Resentment against Germany, whose attack on Poland had made the Soviet invasion possible, was very bitter indeed. The Vatican view was that Soviet intervention had dashed all hopes of localizing the conflict. *L'Osservatore Romano* termed it "a cowardly act on a false pretext" and warned that it was only the beginning of an offensive that would transcend from the military and political fields to ideological, moral, and social conquests. A radio broadcast from Moscow, it said, had already announced that the aim of the invasion was "to open the way for Communism into the Western World."

The so-called "peace offensive" launched after the fall of Poland, by Hitler and Mussolini was followed with considerable interest in Vatican circles. Speaking in Danzig, on September 19, Hitler inferentially held aloft the olive branch by stating that "the British statesmen do not have to worry about world conquest ideas on the part of Germany." At the same time, von Mackensen, German ambassador to Rome, delivered to Mussolini a note from Hitler in which it was suggested that the Italian dictator make a more open statement to induce England and France to accept a compromise. The Fuehrer, Italians explained, could not have gone any further without creating the impression that he was worried over the continuation of the war. Mussolini did as he was told and spoke on September 23, to a group of Fascist hierarchs in the Hall of Battles at Palazzo Venezia.

"With Poland liquidated, Europe is not yet actually at war," he said. "The masses of armies have not yet clashed. The clash can be avoided by recognizing that it is a vain illusion to try to maintain, or worse still, to reconstitute, positions which history and the natural dynamism of peoples have condemned."

In the period between Hitler's and Mussolini's speeches, *Il Popolo d'Italia*, which was owned by Mussolini, printed a series of editorials explaining the proposal which Il Duce finally launched. At the same time, Ciano received Borgongini Duca at Palazzo Chigi, and asked him to convey to the Pope, Mussolini's plea that the Vatican use its influence on London and Paris in behalf of the peace plan. A proof that the Holy See was seconding the efforts of the Italian dictator was seen in the fact that on September 22, *L'Osservatore Romano* reproduced one of *Il Popolo d'Italia* articles urging England and France to accept a compromise peace on the basis of a new Poland, with smaller territory, and without German, Ukrainian, and Lithuanian minorities. What chiefly mattered to the Holy See was to end the war, save twenty million Catholic Poles from extermination, and halt the dreaded Nazi and Soviet war machines before they invaded the Central European and Balkan countries.

After several meetings with Borgongini Duca, who was entrusted with the negotiations, Maglione conveyed to Monsignor Valeri, papal nuncio to Paris, and Monsignor William Godfrey, apostolic delegate in London, a papal message addressed to the heads of the two governments. From what I was told at the time, the Pontiff limited himself to expressing his desire to see peace re-established in Europe and counseled Britain and France to seize any opportunity that might achieve that objective and spare the world much graver ills.

London and Paris, which had promptly rejected Hitler's indirect offer the same day it was made on September 19, replied that their agreement with Poland was to negotiate no separate peace, and that, therefore, they could not break their word. Pius received Borgongini Duca in a private audience and ordered him to inform Mussolini of the Anglo-French refusal.

The Pontiff had abstained from condemning the invasion of Poland for many days after the end of the Nazi campaign because he hoped for an accord that would create a buffer state between Germany and the U.S.S.R. When efforts toward that objective failed, he made clear to the members of the Polish colony in Rome, on September 30, that the Vatican would fight for the resurrection of their country, as it had done in the past.

"We do not say to you 'dry your tears,'" he stated, thus indicating that the Poles should not abandon hope. "Poland does not intend to die. Like the flowers of your country, which under a thick blanket of winter snow wait for the warm breezes of spring, so you will know how to wait, confident in prayer, for the hour of heavenly consolation."

A realist, notwithstanding the fact that he is a spiritual leader, Pius betrayed anxiety for what he termed the "too well-known plans of the enemies of God," an unmistakable reference to Berlin and Moscow, which, he said, were bent on destroying Catholic life.

The fall of Poland left in its wake a number of very pressing problems to solve. The Polish Cardinal, Auguste Hlond, arrived in Rome just as the Germans and the Soviets were dividing the country between themselves. Hlond had an audience with Pius that lasted nearly an hour. He gave a full report of the devastation, the suffering of the population, and the destruction of churches caused by bombing. The Vatican instructed Monsignor Orsenigo to ask Hitler's permission to visit the part of Poland controlled by the Nazis, but the request was refused. Monsignor Carlo Colli, counselor of the nunciature, was later permitted to make a trip only to certain zones, and he reported that the nunciature in Warsaw had been completely wrecked by bombs.

Monsignor Cortesi, who had left Warsaw at the invitation of the Polish Government, took shelter in Rumania, and established a relief organization in Bucharest for spiritual as well as material assistance to the Polish refugees. Scores of thousands of people had poured into Bucovina, through the only frontier still open. They had fled for hundreds of miles under the constant threat of being captured by the invading armies and of being killed by bombs dropped not only on military objectives, but in cities and villages far removed from the theaters of operation. The Pope dispatched a considerable sum to Cortesi who, with the help of Monsignor Andrea Cassulo, nuncio in Rumania, supplied the refugees with food, lodging, and clothes. At the same time, Pius ordered the creation of a relief bureau, which, at the beginning, was attached to the Secretariat of State, and which answered the requests of families lacking news of their relatives caught in Poland during the war.

In Bucharest, Cortesi received a certain amount of information from both Nazi- and Soviet-occupied Poland. His reports kept the Vatican posted on what was happening in some of the Polish regions.

Bishops who had remained in their dioceses also managed to send news to Hlond, who was the Primate.

From this information, whose authenticity could not be doubted because of the painstaking documentation and lack of refutation on the part of Germany, Hlond compiled a memorandum which he submitted to the Pope and later released for publication on January 28. It contained horrifying details of mass shootings, man hunts by German Gestapo agents, plundering and persecutions conducted with a cold-blooded brutality and ferocity unequalled since the times of the Roman Emperors, Nero and Caligula.

The Nazi authorities, it appeared from the reports, were determined to exterminate the Polish people, and to eradicate the Catholic faith as well as all its organizations. Soon after dark, Gestapo agents began a hunt for Poles. Every night five hundred to fifteen hundred were taken away. The terrorized people remained in their dark rooms near the windows dreading their turn. They put on their warmest clothes as a protection against the bitter cold of the concentration camp, since they were given only a few minutes to pack a minimum of belongings and were not permitted to take any additional wearing apparel. Herded into the streets, these groups of people awaited the buses that carried them to the camps. Their wait sometimes lasted for hours, in a temperature of fifteen degrees below zero. In one case, several hundred Poles were placed in a camp at Glowno, where they slept on a cement floor without any mattresses. They found only some vermin-ridden, stinking straw that had been used for weeks. There were no hygienic facilities. In great, bleak rooms these people were left for days without doctors and medicines, despite the fact that sickness was rampant. During one period at Glowno, the strong, healthy men were torn from their families and sent under military escort to work in Germany. They were never heard from. Young men, as well as girls—and especially the pretty ones—from the age of fourteen up were deported to Germany to be subjected to Nazi education. After weeks of untold suffering, those who remained—women, children, old and sick people, were shipped in cattle trains to the Polish Gouvernement General, a zone where the Nazis were gradually concentrating Poles from the conquered regions. The trains were never opened during the entire journey, not even for food, drink, or natural needs. In that way, the Nazi victims traveled in freezing temperatures from two to four days. Upon arriving, there were invariably some people dead while the majority were seriously ill. Their destination in the first weeks of the Nazi occupation was Radom or Kielce. Later, however, they were dropped anywhere within the *Gouvernement General* area, and abandoned to their fate. At first, they were permitted to bring luggage, which was seized when they were on the train, however. The conquerors also allowed the people to take two hundred zlotys with them, but, as soon as they crossed the border of the *Gouvernement General*, all their money, except a few zlotys, was stolen. Women were submitted to indecent gynecological examinations under the pretext that they might be hiding valuables.

Besides their systematic breaking up of families, the Nazis jailed scores of thousands and executed countless numbers. Horrible things happened in the jails. At Bydgeszcz, prisoners had to lie down on their faces on a frozen cement floor. They were beaten into unconsciousness and constantly threatened with execution.

The persecution of priests was even worse, and religious communities were totally suppressed. To give an example: in September, 1939, five thousand men were locked in a stable where there was not even room to sit down. A corner of the stable was adapted for their bodily urges. A priest by the name of Casimir Stepcznski, and a Jew were forced to carry away with their hands human excrement, all day long! Scores of priests were shot outright in the first days of occupation. Dozens of others were humiliated, beaten, and tortured. Imprisonment occurred so suddenly that priests could not save the holy sacraments which were subsequently profaned. The Church of the Lazarist Fathers in Bydgeszcz was used for orgies organized by the Gestapo with young Polish girls who were forced to choose between death and submission to the lust of their masters.

Churches, archbishoprics, convents were sacked, the members of religious orders either imprisoned or exiled. In cases where the celebration of mass was permitted on Sunday, priests were obliged to say publicly a prayer for Hitler! Sermons were allowed only in German. Religious marriages were forbidden. Crosses, sacred images, and other objects of any value were taken away from altars. The Church, as such, entered the catacombs. Confessions were heard and the sacraments distributed secretly.

Hlond, in an interview he gave to Herbert L. Matthews, of The New York Times, soon after the publication of the memorandum which covered the period from September to December 31, 1939, said he had received additional details showing that the situation in Nazi-occupied Poland had become worse in January, 1940.

"Hitler is carrying out what he said about Poland in Mein Kampf," the Primate stated. "The Gouvernement General is now a vision of famine and death. The poor, deported people already total a million, and by April, the numbers may well reach three or four million, for the rate is steadily increasing. It is a tragedy without comparison, a transmigration such as never before occurred, a dark, apocalyptic disaster in the light of twentieth century progress.

"Since the reports were written, I have heard from an unimpeachable source of one train that reached its destination with more than one hundred persons dead from cold, hunger, and weakness. Another train that I know of had about forty dead bodies when it arrived. In my archdiocese alone, I have verified the fact that eighteen priests were shot, but I fear that the number is really much higher. Germany is proceeding barbarously toward a genuine extermination."

According to Hlond, the Soviet had not been guilty of the excesses of brutality performed by the Germans. True, they were sending thousands of Poles to Russia, but there were no indications that they were pursuing a policy of deliberate extermination such as the one taking place in the regions conquered by the Nazis. The Soviet were mainly concerned with stamping out class differences.

The memorandum climaxed a series of anti-German pronouncements issued by the Holy See during the last week in January. For several days the Vatican radio station, acting on instructions from the Secretariat of State, had been broadcasting excerpts from the reports in English. It had warned that stark hunger stared Poland's population in the face as her reserves of foodstuffs and tools were shipped to Germany to replenish the granaries of the conquerors. Jews and Poles, the Vatican said, were being herded into separate ghettos, hermetically sealed and pitifully inadequate for the economic subsistence of the millions destined to live there. Moreover, no less than four hundred thousand Polish families had already been transferred from their homes in German-occupied Poland to the *Gouvernement General* zone.

The feeling of horror caused by the exposé throughout Europe, including Italy, prompted Hitler to send a sharply worded protest to the Pope. Diego von Bergen delivered it to Maglione. Pius' reply was to order the publication of all the reports describing the Nazi atrocities. Von Mackensen also urged Ciano to intervene, but the Italian Government explained that the Vatican was a sovereign state, and that Italy could not meddle in questions that affected relations between other powers.

On October 27, word came from the Secretariat of State that the first encyclical of Pius XII's pontificate would be issued at twelve thirty. Many of the correspondents went to the Vatican well ahead of the time and were told to wait in the Scala Regia, built in the reign of Paul III by Antonio da Sangallo and used for reception of ambassadors. Prelates with whom I talked told me that Pius had revised the encyclical three times, in view of the whirlwind of international events that had culminated in the war. He had worked on it as late as the day before, despite the fact that the document was dated as of October 20. Printers of the Vatican Polyglot Press had been working for twenty-four solid hours to make copies of it, and were still at it. Papal gendarmes had been stationed around the building where the press was to prevent strangers from obtaining copies beforehand. The text had been translated into eight languages: Latin, English, French, Italian, German, Polish, Spanish, and Dutch. The English version had been done by Monsignor Joseph Patrick Hurley, attached to the Secretariat of State.

Contrary to tradition, which had established that the first encyclical of a Pope would contain the program of his Pontificate, Pius XII had postponed to a later date the aims he intended to achieve during his reign. The document was meant as guidance for the clergy and Catholics all over the world concerning the attitude they should take in regard to the war. It placed the Church squarely against the totalitarian form of government, racialism, and the forces that were attempting to abolish religion. It was a direct reply to those who had criticized the Vatican for not having taken a firmer stand against Germany and Russia, and showed that there could be no compromise between the doctrinal principles of the Church and those of Nazism and Bolshevism. It sharply criticized Hitler's policies, both domestic and foreign, and openly supported the restoration of the Polish State. Here are some of the passages:

The indispensable presupposition, without doubt, of all peaceful intercourse between nations and the very soul of the juridicial relations in force among them is mutual trust; the expectation and conviction that each party will respect the plighted word; the certainty that both sides are convinced that "wisdom is better than weapons of war" and are ready to enter into discussion and to avoid recourse to force or to threats of force in case of delays, hindrances, changes, or disputes, since all these things can be the result, not of bad will, but of changed circumstances and of opposition to genuine interests.

But, on the other hand, to tear the law of nations from its anchor in divine law, to base it on the autonomous will of states is to dethrone that very law and deprive it of its noblest and strongest qualities . . . to regard treaties as ephemeral and to assume the authority of rescinding them unilaterally, when they are no longer to one's advantage, would be to abolish all mutual trust among states. In this way, natural order would be destroyed between different peoples and nations, there would be dug trenches of division impossible to refill. . . . To consider the State as something ultimate to which everything else should be subordinated and directed cannot fail to harm the true and lasting prosperity of nations. This can happen either when unrestricted dominion comes to be conferred on the State as having a mandate from the nation, the people, or even a social class, or when the State arrogates such dominion to itself as absolute master, despotically, without any mandate whatsoever. . . . Among the many errors which are derived from the poisoned source of religious and moral agnosticism . . . is the forgetfulness of that law of human solidarity and charity which is dictated and imposed by our common origin and by the equality of rational nature in all men, to whatever people they belong. . . .

The idea which credits the State with unlimited authority is not simply an error harmful to the internal life of nations, to their prosperity, and to the larger, and well-ordered increase in their well-being, but, likewise, an injury to the relations between peoples, for it breaks the unity of the supranatural society, robs the law of nations of its foundation and vigor, leads to violation of others' rights, and impedes agreement and peaceful intercourse. . . . The charge laid by God on parents to provide for the material and spiritual good of their offspring and to procure for them a suitable training saturated with the true spirit of religion cannot be wrested from them without grave violation of their rights. . . . Now, what scandal is more permanently harmful to generation after generation than the formation of a youth misdirected toward a goal that alienates itself from Christ . . . and leads to open or hidden apostasy of Christ? . . . The blood of countless human beings, even noncombatants, raises a piteous dirge over a nation such as our dear Poland, which, for its fidelity to the Church, for its services in the defense of Christian civilization, written in indelible characters in the annals of history, has a right to the generous and brotherly sympathy of the whole world, while it awaits . . . the hour of resurrection in harmony with the principles of justice and true peace.

Stripped of its religious references, the encyclical was tantamount to a declaration of war on Germany and Russia. By condemning their policies and theories, the Pontiff substantially served notice that he would continue to fight, as Pius XI had done, those manifestations of the totalitarian regimes that injured religion and the carrying out of the Church's spiritual mission. Italy's case, he inferred, was different since "fortunately, false principles do not always exercise full influence, especially when age-old Christian traditions on which the people have been nurtured, still remain deeply, even if unconsciously, rooted in their hearts." In this passage the Pontiff, though condemning the principles of Fascist absolutism, acknowledged the fact that, in practice, Italy had compromised with the Church.

As a further clarification of his stand, Pius followed his slashing attack against totalitarianism with an appeal two days later to all Christians to unite themselves with the Catholic Church in its struggle to make the principles of Christian life respected. Nations which do not combat religion, he said, do not know what tyranny is, and the individual citizen enjoys many benefits which are denied in the anti-Christian countries.

Because of the distinction the Pope made between Fascism and Nazism, the Italian press printed a fairly good summary of the encyclical. Germany, however, issued through the Deutsches Nachrichten Bureau a version so distorted that it elicited a protest from the Vatican. Monsignor Orsenigo complained to Baron Ernst von Weisszacker, Undersecretary of Foreign Affairs, that the Reich's Ministry of Interior had forbidden publication of the papal document in any manner or form. This, he pointed out, was another violation of the concordat which provided for the full and unhampered transmission of papal directives and documents. Moreover, several priests, who attempted to read the encyclical in their churches, were arrested. The protest, of course, left things as they were. Weisszacker replied that the Ministry of Interior's order was a war measure and that the Government itself had grounds for a protest, since the papal references to Poland were regarded as hostile to the Reich.

The improvement of relations between the Vatican and Fascism, which began with Pius XII's election, reached its apex that winter. Harmony between the two powers was due in part to the tacit understanding reached on the racial question, and to Mussolini's determination not to pursue an anti-clerical policy that would create internal dissension and weaken the domestic front at a moment when national solidarity was needed more than ever. This policy was facilitated by the fact that, although the Pontiff had condemned the principle of racial discrimination in his encyclical, he, unlike his predecessors, had steadfastly abstained since the beginning of his pontificate from attacking Fascism directly.

But, as already stated, the basic bond of unity was the Bolshevist danger. Italian diplomacy was very active in Central Europe and in the Balkans, which it regarded as a valuable dam against the feared political penetration of the Soviet now pressing at Rumania's borders. Rome knew full well, for instance, Bulgaria's pro-Russian sympathies and Yugoslavia's pan-Slavic feelings; and the latter was Albania's neighbor. Mussolini's nightmare was that a Soviet move in southeastern Europe might end with the conquest of Albania which would bring Bolshevism to the shores of the Adriatic. The Church, irreconcilable enemy of Moscow, was a precious ally.

Consequently, orders went out from Palazzo Venezia to start an anti-Bolshevist campaign.

The first shot was fired, as usual, by Virginio Gayda, editor of *Il Giornale d'Italia* and a veteran polemicist who had risen to international notoriety during the Italo-Ethiopian crisis when he presented Italy's "case" before world public opinion with arguments supplied to him by Mussolini. On November 7, Ciano called Gayda to his office in Palazzo Chigi and gave him the theme for an editorial. The point to emphasize was that Italy's policy was "to preserve peace in the Balkans now threatened by new and growing dangers created by Soviet pressure."

Gayda's arguments were picked up by the rest of the press the next day. Italian editors made a field day of it. The *Corriere Padano* of Ferrara, Balbo's personal newspaper, was in the forefront of the campaign. Italy seemed to have forgotten that Moscow was the ally of her German partner. The press not only did not mention the Rome-Berlin Axis, but pointedly stated that Italian foreign policy, to quote Gayda, would be "dictated only by national interests," regardless of any ties with other nations! Moscow was warned that "Italy will never permit the further advance of Bolshevist Russia beyond the Carpathians, in the Danube Valley, in the Balkans, or toward the Mediterranean."

There was a feeling of great satisfaction in the Vatican over the Fascist stand. Only a few days before, *Il Popolo d'Italia* had attacked *L'Osservatore Romano* for an anti-Bolshevist editorial written by Professor Guido Gonella, the ablest expert on Vatican affairs in Italy. Now, the Fascist press was following the papal lead.

The Italo-Vatican front against Bolshevism was bolstered soon afterwards by the Finnish-Soviet War. *L'Osservatore Romano's* attacks became more and more violent, while the Fascist press, which during years of polemics against the democracies had developed a knack for invective that was almost an art, hurled insult after insult on Stalin. Further, many hostile demonstrations were held in front of the Russian Embassy. On December 2, 1939, hundreds of enraged young men in Fascist uniforms hissed, booed, and jeered the Russian leader, called the Soviets "cowards" and "buffoons," and afterward went to the Finnish legation where their enthusiastic cheers were mingled with cries of "Long Live Finland!" and "Resist the Invaders!" With tears in his eyes, the Finnish Minister, Eero Jaerngelt, appeared in the door of the Legation to thank the crowd. There was no question but what the Fascist Party had sent out word for the demonstration. Incidents like that did not happen in Italy, without Government instigation. Not even when Hitler seized Austria and anti-German feeling ran very high did demonstrations take place, for the simple reason that the Government refused to allow them. Other anti-Russian incidents occurred the following days in Rome and Milan. Gayda remarked that, "the Soviet aggression was unprovoked" and asked that the League of Nations impose sanctions on the U.S.S.R.

When Russia attacked Finland on November 30, the Pope was deeply shocked, but Mussolini was quite happy. In fact, if for the Vatican it meant the threatened subjugation of another country by an anti-Christian power, for the Italian dictator it was a fairly certain proof that Moscow would not invade the Balkans for the time being. Italy's interest, therefore, was that the Finnish-Soviet War should last indefinitely, for so long as the Soviet was engaged in the north, it would not be likely to start a war in the south.

Mussolini began making preparations to help Finland and did succeed in sending a small number of planes to Helsinki. On December 5, the Italian press joyfully announced that a first batch of twenty-five planes with Italian crews had reached the Finnish capital. But Il Duce's plan was soon scotched by Hitler. Another consignment of aircraft, which had been shipped through Germany, was held up. Berlin informed Rome that to allow the planes free transit would be a breach of her treaty with Russia. The planes were returned to Italy. At the same time, the Finnish Legation in Rome was besieged by Italian young men who volunteered in the war against the Soviet. After the German warning, however, the Italian Government forbade their departure by refusing to issue passports. Angered by the press attacks and the hostile demonstrations, Soviet Russia withdrew her ambassador, Nikolai Gorelchin, from Rome on December 11. It was not an open breach, and both Stalin and Mussolini tried to minimize the gesture. Gorelchin, who had just replaced Boris Stein, as Soviet ambassador, had not yet had time to present his credentials to Ciano. No official communique was issued in Rome regarding Gorelchin's departure, nor was any announcement made that Augusto Rosso, Italian ambassador to Moscow, had left Russia. As a matter of fact, relations between Fascism and Bolshevism had been excellent for many years, despite the attacks that appeared very often in the press. The two countries had found it mutually profitable to foster commercial exchanges. Stein, whom I once asked whether he did not take exception to the slanderous lies hurled at Stalin—the Italian press had in the winter of 1938, bannered the news that the Soviet leader had poisoned his mother—shrugged his shoulders and said: "We gave up protesting a long time ago. It's only for internal consumption." A few months later Gorelchin returned to Rome.

The expulsion of the U.S.S.R. from the League elicited the prize comment of the month from *L'Osservatore Romano*, which praised the decision as the only one to take in order "to eliminate from the circle of civilized nations the representative of a regime that not only practices, but even defends the policy of the jungle." Maxim Litvinoff, who was sent to Geneva as Soviet delegate, was branded by the Vatican newspaper "an authentic thief already placed on trial in France and charged with being a member of a gang specializing in swindling banks."

The Pope himself on December 24 denounced Russia's invasion of Finland as a "premeditated aggression against a small, industrious, and peaceful people on the pretext of a threat that neither exists nor is desired, nor is possible." Moreover, the Vatican openly intervened in behalf of Helsinki, by announcing two days later that the Pope had sent a "substantial" sum of money to Monsignor William Robben, Apostolic Vicar in Finland, for distribution among needy Finnish Catholics.

The parallelism of Vatican and Fascist policies, and the Italian people's wholehearted endorsement of Italy's neutrality created a unity never attained in the history of Fascism. Although the Italians hated the Fascist regime as much as ever, they were happy, however, to have been spared from the war. When on September 2, Mussolini announced that Rome would stay outside the conflict and take "no military initiatives whatsoever," the relief of the people in all walks of life was unbounded. Industrialists, merchants, financiers, even the small artisans—all had dreams of becoming prosperous by trading with the belligerent nations. French and English orders for military equipment virtually flooded the big plants in the north. The two democracies agreed to supply the raw materials if Italy would produce the weapons. Some contracts were made, but very little material was delivered, for Italy's neutrality lasted only nine months. The shipping companies did a capacity business. Their luxurious liners plied to and from the United States, as well as the South American countries with all available passenger space booked, despite the fact that fares had almost doubled.

The nervousness so visible in the weeks that preceded the war disappeared. Italy was preparing to enjoy the benefit of relative security after many years of such strong international tension that the people had acquired the habit of thinking in terms of day to day in view of the fact that the future was so uncertain. The Government did its utmost to encourage this feeling of security. In the middle of September, Mussolini received the Commissioner for the Universal Exhibition that was scheduled to be held in 1942, and told him to go ahead with the plans. He instructed Alfieri, who was Minister of Press and Propaganda, to give wide publicity to the program of operas that were to be performed in all major lyric theatres in the winter season. On December 15, Ciano delivered in the Chamber of Deputies a speech that contained some bitter comments about Germany, and removed whatever doubts there might have been as to Italy's desire to stay neutral. He complained that Hitler had once more tricked Mussolini, and accused him of having broken the pledge given at the time the military pact was signed in May, 1939. The agreement, he explained, was made on the understanding that it would not become operative until 1942, as far as Italy was concerned, and that Germany would not go to war until 1943 or 1944. "The Reich," he pointedly remarked, "agreed with us not to raise any question likely to originate new crises before this lapse of time." Moreover, he made the surprising disclosure that Berlin had informed Rome of the Soviet-German pact only thirty-six hours before it was signed, and that its terms were quite different from the ones Hitler had outlined to him at the Salzburg meeting on August 11.

True, Ciano supported the German viewpoint in regard to the reasons leading to the war with Poland and to the pact with Russia. But these statements were discounted as merely formal manifestations of solidarity with a power that, after all, was still an ally. Editorial comment made clear that Germany, by breaking her pledge when she went to war, had freed Italy of all her obligations. Hitler was bluntly accused of "untimeliness in view of the reciprocal undertaking assumed by Italy and Germany", as *La Tribuna*, a Rome newspaper, stated. It was clear that Italy was angry with her partner, and that she wanted peace. She had proved this desire by encouraging mediation between Germany and Poland, by seconding the Pope's efforts, and by her hostility to Russia. Not only that, but she had gone out of her way to dispel the profound diffidence that her seizure of Albania had caused in the Balkans.

On September 30, 1939, an exchange of notes between Greece and Italy had stressed the "friendly relations between the two countries which would contribute to the upkeep of peace in this sector of Europe." This proof of good will had been preceded by the withdrawal of both Italian and Greek troops from the Greek-Albanian border on September 20. Again, on October 31, Mussolini had fired many of his ministers who were thought to be pro-German. At the same time, Vatican officials had disclosed that he had resisted strong German pressure to prevent the distribution of *L'Osservatore Romano* in Italy because of its anti-German leanings. For weeks the German press had been carrying on a violent campaign against the Vatican newspaper, which, prelates said, was officially inspired. The *Frankfurter Zeitung* and the *Westdeutscher Beobachter* had distinguished themselves for the bitterness of their attacks. They had charged that the Vatican organ distorted the Pope's pronouncements by emphasizing their anti-German character! *L'Osservatore Romano*, they complained, prominently displayed British versions of the war and ignored the achievements of the German submarines! Moreover, it had unduly stressed the celebration of the fiftieth anniversary of the late Father Vladimir Ledochowski, general of the Jesuits, merely because he happened to be a Pole. All editorials demanded to know how long the Fascist regime was going to allow the distribution in Italy of a newspaper that did not express the Pope's thoughts and was hostile to the policy of the Axis!

The Nazi press soon learned that it was mistaken in differentiating between L'Osservatore Romano and the Vatican, for in the same speech of December 24, which had condemned Soviet aggression of Finland, Pius again referred to the German-Polish war and branded the Nazi "atrocities and illegal use of means of destruction even against noncombatants, refugees, old persons, women, and children, with a complete disregard for human dignity, liberty, and human life —acts that cry for the vengeance of God." The Pontiff could not have been more explicit. He also placed on Hitler the responsibility for the war by stating that "men in whose hands power was and whose shoulders bore the grave responsibility to abstain from armed conflict and so save the world from inestimable disaster" had refused to be persuaded, despite the fact that he had used every means "up to the last to avoid the worst."

Italy's official approval of the Vatican stand came in the form of a visit the Italian sovereigns paid to Pius on December 21. Exactly one week later, the Pope took the unprecedented step of returning it personally. Not even Pius XI, after the signing of the Lateran Treaty, had rendered such homage to the rulers of the nation which in 1870, had forcibly annexed the Papal States. It was a move dictated not only by the Pope's particular affection for the country to which he had belonged, but also by political considerations. He wished to show with a concrete gesture that the Vatican was fully supporting Rome's policy of neutrality and anti-Bolshevist stand. Italy was the oasis of peace in war-torn Europe, and the Holy See was sparing no efforts to keep it from being engulfed in the European conflict.

Now that there was no longer any hope for peace, the Pontiff's main concern was to prevent the spreading of the war by marshaling the support of countries having the same objective in view. The United States, as the only big power besides Italy still working in behalf of peace, officially recognized the importance and value of

papal efforts by resuming diplomatic relations with the Holy See for
the first time since 1868, when Rufus King of Wisconsin, American
Minister to the Vatican, left Rome because Congress under President
Johnson decided to abolish that post.

The American decision was announced in a letter which President
Roosevelt sent to Pius on December 23. He explained that he had
named Myron C. Taylor, former chairman of United States Steel, his
personal envoy "in order that our parallel endeavors for peace and
the alleviation of suffering may be assisted." In his Christmas Eve
speech to the College of Cardinals, the Pope expressed his "joy" for
Roosevelt's step, which, he said, was especially gratifying since it
would bring a valid contribution not only to the efforts for peace, but
also for the victims of war.

At the end of February, Taylor arrived in Naples. On board the
same liner was Sumner Welles, who was touring Europe, for a series
of conversations with Mussolini, Hitler, Daladier, and Chamberlain.
The simultaneous arrival of two prominent visitors raised a delicate
question of protocol. Taylor did not wish to ride in the same special
train which was to take Welles to Rome. The Italian Government
had prepared an official welcome for the American Under Secretary of
State, and Taylor had no intention of interfering with it. The problem was solved with the hiring of a black limousine, in which Taylor,
Mrs. Taylor, and Monsignor Hurley, who welcomed them in behalf
of the Pope, drove to Rome.

A special ceremonial was devised for Taylor's audience with Pius.
Instead of being received in the Hall of the Throne, as all ambassadors are, the Pontiff welcomed him in the Hall of the Little Throne,
which is used for distinguished visitors. At the same time, in order
not to antagonize the members of the other faiths in America, who
had already voiced their preoccupation over the appointment of a
presidential envoy to the Vatican, Roosevelt had taken pains to make
the whole thing look as personal as possible. He wrote a letter to
Taylor in which he appointed him his personal representative, and
a letter to the Pontiff, whom he addressed as "My Old and Very
Good Friend," in which he explained that Taylor had been sent as
"the channel of communication for any views you and I may wish to

exchange in the interest of concord among the peoples of the world."

The papal reception was of marked cordiality. Taylor was received with all the honors due to an ambassador and conversed with the Pope for forty minutes. During that meeting the basis was laid by the Vatican and the United States for a policy which aimed first of all at keeping Italy out of the war. Welles' visit had the same fundamental motive as far as that country was concerned. He saw Mussolini, to whom he delivered a personal message from Roosevelt. Its contents were not published, but I was told at the Ministry of Foreign Affairs that it expressed the President's willingness to improve Italo-American relations. The American Under Secretary of State had instructions to investigate the problems which stood in the way of peace. Roosevelt, as Pius had done in August, was attempting to effect a compromise among the belligerents.

The results of Welles' tour of the four European capitals were not disclosed, but, as subsequent events showed, Roosevelt's peace efforts bore no fruits. Welles had barely arrived in London, when Von Ribbentrop flew to Rome. He had conversations with Mussolini, Ciano, and the Pope. The main purpose of his trip was to prepare the ground for a meeting between the Axis dictators, and at the same time, to placate the Vatican, which was promoting a very strong anti-Nazi propaganda by means of its radio station and confidential instructions to the German clergy. As was to be expected, the reception he received was remarkably frigid. The Holy See went out of its way to give emphasis to it. The Secretariat of State issued an official communique pointedly announcing that Germany had asked for the audience through the German Ambassador to the Vatican—a statement that would have been tactless, to say the least, had it not been made deliberately. Pius wanted to emphasize that he had had no desire to see the Nazi Foreign Minister. This in itself was an indication that relations with Germany were as bad as ever, if not worse.

Although there had been a slight improvement between Church and State in the Reich, due to the patriotic feeling of the German episcopate and clergy because of the war, the fundamental issues were still unsolved, indeed, they were farther away from solution than

ever. Ribbentrop had an audience with the Pope that lasted one hour
and five minutes, an unusually long time, and soon afterwards, a forty-
five minutes' conversation with Maglione. In other words, he spent
nearly two hours in the Vatican on the morning of March 11, 1940.
For days, after the meeting, every correspondent in Rome was trying
to find out what the subject of the talks was. Finally, one of our
tipsters, who enjoyed the confidence of a high prelate in the Secretariat of State, gave us what he said was an accurate outline of the
reasons that had prompted Ribbentrop's "going to Canossa."

In the private mailbox at my house the tipster left a sealed en-
velope containing the story. He, like most Italians, had to use caution
in his contacts with foreigners, and especially Americans. Matthews
wrote the dispatch.

Briefly, Ribbentrop submitted to the Pope a peace offer which
consisted of eleven points.

1. General, simultaneous, and immediate disarmament on land,
sea, and in the air.

2. A return to the four-power pact, which would take the form of
a new European "directory" and serve as a sort of substitute for the
League of Nations. The four states would divide the zones of influence in Europe and would inaugurate an anti-Bolshevist policy with
the idea of "liberating" Russia, by arms if necessary, from Communism.

3. Recognition of absolute religious freedom, but first, Germany
would force all her Jews to emigrate under the direction of Britain
(to Palestine), Italy (to Ethiopia), and France (to Madagascar).

4. The status quo in the Balkans to be guaranteed.

5. The restitution within twenty years of German colonies or equal
colonial compensation or, at least, the protection of German emigration in determined areas of Africa.

6. Reconstruction of an independent Poland, composed primarily
of the central zone of Polish territory, with about ten million inhabitants. Gdynia to be a Polish free port; free trade for the Poles through
Danzig, and a general facilitating of Polish communications to the
sea. The Polish frontiers to be determined on the basis of a plebiscite

controlled by international commissions. Minority problems in Poland and the whole Danube basin to be solved by a vast transmigration of peoples, after which minorities would disappear.

7. Czechs, Slovaks, and Magyars to constitute a tripartite state allied to the Reich. For twenty-five years, the Reich would enjoy certain privileges regarding industries and communications in those territories.

8. Austria to remain in the Reich.

9. Creation of a Danubian federation as a sort of customs union to equalize the interests of large and small states in the Danube basin. In this federation, two great powers (Germany and Italy), two Balkan powers (Yugoslavia and Rumania), and three smaller powers (Bohemia, Slovakia and Hungary) would participate.

10. Absolute freedom of trade and access to raw materials; close contacts with the United States for economic co-operation; the facilitation of German and Italian emigration.

11. Free customs transit for Italian goods through Jibuti, French Somaliland; free passage through the Suez Canal on expiration of the present Suez convention in 1945; a new stature for Italians in Tunis.

The peace offer was immediately denied by Berlin as a propaganda maneuver engineered by the democracies; it was coldly rejected by London, which saw it as another manifestation of Germany's "war of nerves." The Vatican, however, did not debunk the proposals. It merely stated that it was not supporting that or any other plan of mediation.

The opinion in Vatican circles was that the acceptance of such terms would make Germany the strongest power in Europe. She would have her hands free to attack Russia, without having to worry about a second front in the West. She could hope to obtain very little by a conquest of France, as compared to the immense riches of the Soviet. Once she had Russia, Germany would be able to impose her own policy everywhere in Europe; she would be able to develop the enormous resources of her eastern neighbor and snap her fingers at any coalition of powers. The Pope saw through the plan, and was reported to have received it with such obvious coldness that Ribbentrop, just as he was about to take leave stated flatly that, the alternative was war to the finish. Germany, he haughtily warned, had the means to win before the end of the year.

Ribbentrop also discussed the proposal in detail with Maglione, who, after drafting a report of the conversation, went to see the Pontiff. At the end of this audience, Pius said, "I have spoken to him [Ribbentrop] out of the depth of my heart. Let's hope that God may open his eyes."

"Let's hope that He may close them!" exclaimed the quick-witted Neapolitan Cardinal.

the quiet little station which was once Austrian territory. Hitler had asked for Italy's support. His last peace move, presented by Ribbentrop to the Pope, had failed. He had to fight France and England before he could tackle Russia. England did not worry him then because she had no army and a weak air force. France, according to the information gathered by Nazi espionage, was not so strong as Germany.

"Even granting that conditions are equal and that one German is killed for every Frenchman, there will still be thirty-five million Germans left, since France has forty million people and Germany seventy-five million," Hitler was reported to have told Mussolini.

Axis collaboration was necessary because, by becoming aggressively anti-French, Italy would nail a large French army on her border and force the British to concentrate a part of their fleet in the Mediterranean. In the meantime, she could improve her relations with Russia. Once France was liquidated, England would certainly come to terms, and the Axis leaders would be the masters of Europe. Peace with England meant that the United States would not enter the war. So, the field would be clear for the campaign against Russia.

Mussolini agreed since it seemed to him that he had nothing to lose. He did not have to go to war until Germany had broken the French military power.

This was what I gathered at the Italian Foreign Office, and it coincided with information that reached the Vatican.

The Brenner meeting occurred the same day that Welles was received by the Pope, who informed him of Hitler's peace terms. At the same time, the Vatican was keenly interested in knowing the results of the American Under Secretary's mission. Welles was quite right in stating, just before he left, that he was taking no peace proposals with him. There weren't any. The Pope and he agreed that the Anglo-French and German viewpoints could not be reconciled. Italy, however, was a different question. The Vatican up to that moment still hoped that she would stay out of the war.

During the time of Welles' European tour, the Italian press had kept a noncommittal attitude. Indeed, on the whole, there had been an undercurrent of cordiality and of hopeful expectancy. Washington, after all, was pursuing a policy similar to Italy's at that moment. But, when the Under Secretary of State left Rome, after his second visit, the situation had drastically changed as a result of the Brenner meeting.

"Enough of the olive branch," wrote Gayda in the *Giornale d'Italia* on March 19. "There is a war, and it threatens to be long, arduous, and complicated. There is nothing for the belligerents to do today but to fight it out with whatever means they choose, and for other nations to face it with austere spirit."

"The task of Fascist Italy," wrote *La Tribuna*, another Rome newspaper, "is not that of a perpetual mediator, but of an absolute and determined protagonist."

With methodic deliberation the Italian dictator set about his twofold task: to create a feeling of nervousness in England and France by ostensibly drawing nearer to Germany, and to effect an improvement of relations with Russia, which would in itself cause apprehension in the democratic camp. Stronger criticism of the Allies appeared daily in the press. A pro-Soviet editorial of the *Frankfurter Zeitung* stating that there was "no contrast between Italo-German and Italo-Russian policies" was allowed to be displayed prominently in every newspaper. The suggestion that Rome intended to let bygones be bygones and establish friendly relations with Moscow filtered through dispatches from European capitals. The reason given to the people was that the Allies were attempting to foment trouble in the Balkans in order to open up a battlefield on which their armies could fight Hitler. By courting Russia's political support, so ran the Fascist argument, Italy was helping to prevent the spread of the war, because with Moscow's co-operation assured, the menace of both a Russian invasion and an Allied invasion of the Balkans would disappear. Not even Soviet Premier Molotov's speech early in April 1940, openly criticizing Italy's annexation of Albania the year before, altered this policy. As a matter of fact, a summary of it published at the time glossed over the unpleasant passages and stressed, instead, the attacks against England and France. Any pretext was seized upon to fan anti-democratic feeling. For instance, at the beginning of April, the

French magazine *L'Illustration* published on its front page cover a photograph of Welles and Reynaud in the latter's office. In the background there was a map of Europe which showed that Istria, an Italian region, had been taken from Italy. Fascist newspapers promptly reproduced the obviously retouched photo, and accused France of wanting to dismember Italy. Reynaud's official denial and personal assurance to the Italian Ambassador in Paris that such a map did not exist and that no redrawing of frontiers had been discussed with Welles, made not the slightest difference.

Mussolini, himself, took a hand in the campaign. The Italian Cabinet met on April 2, and approved measures for "civil mobilization in time of war" which affected every Italian citizen from the age of thirteen up. It allotted funds for the strengthening of the Maritime Artillery Militia, the measure being necessary, as Gayda tried to explain, by the "insistent and impudent attitude of French and British newspapers which advocate naval attacks against the Italian coasts!" A few days later, Il Duce bluntly warned that Italy must be ready for "whatever events this tardy spring may bring."

The invasion of Norway and Denmark on April 9, by Germany, and the inability of London and Paris to prevent it, strengthened the Italian dictator's conviction that he was backing the right horse. The Fascist press gave full support to the German official reasons for the invasion, and gloated over the blow struck at British prestige by Germany's success. It spoke of the "end of the Allied mastery of the seas" and told the Italians that Hitler had once more stolen the march on the democracies who had been planning to take Norway themselves. Hitler's contention, as stated in the German White Book, that four months before the end of Czechoslovakia's independence, Britain and France had planned a "preventive" war against Germany to be followed by a war against Italy, was exploited to bolster the anti-democratic drive.

The campaign gathered momentum with a broadcast by Giovanni Ansaldo, editor of Leghorn's *Telegrafo*, the newspaper owned by the Ciano family, that the "bugles will sound soon" and that those who thought that Italy would stay out of the war indefinitely were mistaken. The Allies were pictured as losing, and the pro-German atti-

tude became bolder. To impress the democracies, wide publicity was
given to the arrival of a German military mission to Italy, an official
communique explaining tartly that experts of the various branches of
the armed forces would exchange views and maintain "constant contacts" between the two countries.

The evening following the Brenner meeting, Edda and I went to
Alfredo's. Although I personally resented the fact that Alfredo treated
everybody like a pink-cheeked tourist, a meal at his post-card *trattoria*
was an experience that never failed to bolster one's morale. Many
restaurants in Rome had tried to rival him, but it seemed as though
he had the magic touch—at least as far as *fettuccine doppio burro*,
filet of turkey, and *omelette a la confiture* were concerned. Those
three dishes were the classic Alfredo dinner and we usually dropped
in once a month. I had just disposed of a generous butter-coated portion of *fettuccine* and was sipping a glass of *Orvieto soave* when An-
ton Germano Rossi, a well-known journalist and widely read humorist
author who had good political connections, came in with some friends.
As he went by my table, I stopped him.

"What's new, Tonio?"

"Did you read Gayda's editorial today?"

"Yes."

"Well, the ball has started rolling."

I must explain at this point that the press was the most powerful
means Mussolini had with which to mould public opinion. By
analyzing editorials, observers would obtain a fairly accurate idea of
which way the wind was blowing. Diplomatists took Gayda, Ansaldo,
and the anonymous editorials of *Il Popolo d'Italia*, Mussolini's personal newspaper, as seriously as Foreign Office statements. Sometimes
the problem was to find out why certain editorials appeared. Being
strictly controlled—although the Government always officially denied
it—the Italian press voiced views that could not be ignored by foreign
observers. Its main task was to prepare the atmosphere for Mussolini's decisions in the fields of both domestic and foreign policies.

Mussolini gave official support to the anti-democratic campaign by
telling a crowd gathered in Piazza Venezia, on April 21, Rome's
birthday, that the password for all Italians "from the mountains to

the sea is 'Work and Arm' "; and by stating a few minutes later to a group of hierarchs gathered in one of the halls of his palace that Italy's word was "sacred," and would be kept. This meant that Rome would join Berlin. With his approval, Francesco Giunta, a deputy and former secretary of the Fascist party, said at a meeting of the Chamber of Deputies on April 25, that "France has always been Italy's enemy from the remotest times until today," and that the traditional British friendship for the Italians was a "trite expression belied by history." The next day, Guido Buffarini-Guidi, Under Secretary of the Interior, announced that Italy did not "want to mortify herself by abstaining voluntarily from the war." Dino Grandi, former ambassador to London, who had been appointed President of the Chamber of Deputies, followed this up on April 27 with a strong anti-British speech.

The campaign, as such, was a success. French Premier Reynaud saw the handwriting on the wall and, before Mussolini committed himself more definitely, attempted to halt him by reiterating to the Senate Foreign Relations Committee France's desire to seek a settlement of her differences with Italy. He explained that these overtures, made "before and after September 1, 1930 [when war broke out], have remained until now without reply." François Poncet saw Ciano on April 22 to learn whether Italy were disposed to negotiations, but the reply was that it was not "the right moment." Mussolini was stalling while awaiting Germany's next and, in his opinion, decisive move—the attack on France.

The Vatican noticed the change immediately, of course, and, through L'Osservatore Romano, fought a strenuous battle to stem the interventionist tide. It logically pointed out that since Italy was a "nonbelligerent" she had nothing to fear from the Allies and that any deviation from her current policy was unjustified. In contrast with the Italian attitude, the Secretariat of State branded the Nazi invasion of Norway on April 9, 1940 as a gesture that had made that country "not only the victim of aggression, but the victim of falsehood." The Pope, I was told, had ordered his representatives to communicate directly by telephone to the Secretariat of State all the important developments of the war in the Scandinavian theater.

Cable messages and telegrams, which were normally used, arrived too late because of the rapid sequence of events. Theodore Suhr, Apostolic Vicar to Denmark, was able to reach the Vatican by telephone from Copenhagen and give a full report of the German occupation there. Vatican pronouncements spiked the German contention, to which Italy agreed wholeheartedly, that England and France intended to seize Norway. It was pointed out that neither Oslo nor Copenhagen had asked for German "protection." Further the Holy See praised the resistance of the Norwegian people and encouraged them to oppose the invaders.

"The way in which two neutral and unarmed nations, one of which [Poland] had been guaranteed by a ten-year nonaggression pact, have been involved in the war," wrote Professor Guido Gonella in L'Osservatore Romano the day after the invasion of Norway, "is enough to show the tremendous gravity of yesterday's events which throw a somber shadow on the trend of the conflict."

At that time, too, a witty prelate recounted a joke that made the rounds of the Vatican and of diplomatic circles in Rome.

Angered by Vatican hostility, so runs the story, Hitler sent Hermann Goering to Rome. Two days later Goering, whose fondness for decorations and uniforms is well known, wired to the German leader:

"Have placed the Holy See under German protection. All prelates in concentration camp. Pope has fled. Vatican in flames. Cardinal's robe suits me beautifully."

Once more, after a brief idyl, the Vatican and Fascism were pitted one against the other. Their attitude in regard to the war was irreconcilable, and the open clash inevitable. This was the more so since Italy's growing solidarity with Germany contrasted with the anti-Nazi stand of the Holy See, which had grown stronger, if anything, after the Ribbentrop meeting. The Vatican radio, in fact, had again launched a series of broadcasts, to make the world conscious of the persecutions that the Church was suffering in Germany. In one of them, on April 3, the speaker stated flatly that the hopes entertained at the time of the visit paid to the Pope by the Nazi Foreign Minister had failed to materialize. Reports from Germany disclosed that the Anti-Catholic propaganda had shown no signs of abating. The same situation existed in Austria. From the time that country was annexed until April, 1940, in Innsbruck and in North and South Tyrol, five churches and twenty-four chapels were closed, three priests sent to a concentration camp, fifty-five arrested, forty-eight forbidden to visit the schools, one hundred refused permission to teach religion to children, and ninety-three deprived of State subsidy. Moreover, fifty-two Catholic schools were suppressed, as well as 170 other educational institutions of various kinds; seven convents and other church possessions were seized and adapted to non-Catholic uses, such as military hospitals and city administration offices, while a large number of Catholic circles and associations were disbanded and their buildings seized by the Gestapo. What was happening in the Tyrol was typical of conditions prevailing everywhere in Austria.

However, what irked Mussolini most was the fact that the Italians seemed to be unconvinced by the official views ladled out to them every day, and were believing the Vatican reports instead. When the people saw that their press was giving them a biased picture of the international events, they turned to L'Osservatore Romano, which had an extremely accurate foreign service. The circulation of that paper had jumped from about 20,00 in the pre-war days to nearly 150,000 by the middle of April. The demand was so great and the popular interest so obvious that Gayda made some sarcastic references to the rapidity with which editions of the Vatican organ were sold out. Since there were not enough copies to satisfy the great demand, people usually waited at newsstands to snatch the newspaper as soon as it was delivered. Those who did not succeed in obtaining it, borrowed it from their friends.

The obvious fairness and authenticity of the Vatican coverage of the war and of its anti-Axis attitude represented such an effective spoke in the wheels of Fascist propaganda that it could not be tolerated by a ruling class determined to prepare the people for intervention. The most violent attacks against L'Osservatore Romano, and its editor, Count Giuseppe dalla Torre, came, as it was to be expected, from Roberto Farinacci, the extreme right wing editor of the *Regime Fascista*, who charged that since September, 1939, *L'Osservatore Romano*, and "therefore the Holy See have joined the cause of the Allies." He asked that the newspaper be put out of circulation on the ground that it was a tool for the enemies of Italy and "the evident mouthpiece of the Jews."

These charges heralded a new Fascist policy towards the Vatican which Mussolini was preparing to inaugurate. Up to that moment, however, relations were still officially good. Despite the diversity of views the Italian dictator was reluctant to antagonize the Holy See, inasmuch as he was still waiting to see whether Hitler's attack on France would be successful. The Fascist campaign was not so much anti-Ally, as pro-German. As far as its domestic implications were concerned, it was being waged in order to prepare the people psychologically for intervention. He strove to convince them that Hitler was winning and that Italy's interests coincided with those of Germany. During that first stage the emphasis was more on Berlin's strength and Allied weakness, than on anti-Allied slander aimed at fostering the necessary hatred for the decisive move.

The best propaganda in wartime has always been military success. And Germany had won the first round in Norway. A man of unbounded ambition such as Mussolini could not be swayed by any amount of pressure in behalf of peace. President Roosevelt and Pius again joined efforts to keep Italy outside the conflict. United States Ambassador Phillips delivered to Mussolini an appeal from the American President. At the same time Roosevelt asked Taylor to enlist the collaboration of the Vatican, and pressure on Mussolini came also from that quarter. A summary of the presidential message and of Mussolini's reply were published in January, 1943, by the State Department in a book called, *Peace and War*.

On April 24, said the official document, President Roosevelt sent a message to Mussolini stating that a further extension of the area of hostilities would necessarily have far-reaching and unforeseeable consequences not only in Europe, but also in the Near East and the Far East, in Africa and in the three Americas. The President said that no one could predict with assurance, should such a further extension take place, what the ultimate result might be, or foretell what nations might eventually find it imperative to enter the war in their own defense. The President said further that because of the geographic position of the United States, we had a panoramic view of the existing hostilities in Europe; that he saw no reason to anticipate that any one nation, or any one combination of nations, could successfully undertake to dominate either the continent of Europe or much less a greater part of the world. The President concluded his appeal with an expression of the hope that the powerful influence of Italy and of the United States might yet be exercised, when the appropriate opportunity was presented, "in behalf of the negotiation of a just and stable peace permitting of the reconstruction of a gravely stricken world."

The United States Ambassador to Italy, William Phillips, read the President's message to Mussolini during a conversation on May 1. Mussolini replied orally to the following effect: Peace in Europe could not be considered without a recognition of the conditions which had come about as a consequence of the war; Germany could not be beaten; Poland had been defeated by Germany and the latter would permit the creation of a new independent Polish state; Germany was also willing that a new Czechoslovak state be re-established; he hoped that the necessity of a "new geography" would be foreseen by the President; since a new map of Europe must come into being. Mussolini went on to say that the political problems which then made a peaceful Europe impossible must be liquidated; that this must be done before the economic problems could be disposed of. He also referred generally to Italy's aspirations in a reconstituted Europe and said that Italy's position as a "prisoner within the Mediterranean" was intolerable.

A direct reply from Mussolini to the President was delivered to the latter by the Italian Ambassador on the following day. The reply stressed that the nonbelligerency of Italy had effectively assured peace for two hundred million people; that Germany and Italy were opposed to the further extension of the conflict; that no peace was possible unless the fundamental problems of Italian liberty were solved; that as for repercussions which extension of the war would have on the three Americas, Italy had never concerned herself with the relations of the other American republics among themselves or with the United States and expected "reciprocity" so far as European affairs were concerned; and that when conditions permitted, and always based upon recognition of accomplished facts, Italy was ready to contribute toward a better world order.

In other words, Mussolini's reply was a polite but firm "No." He was not going to commit himself to any definite appeasement course, just on the eve of Germany's offensive against France.

Reports from Belgium and the Netherlands had already informed the Vatican that Germany was making preparations which indicated that those two countries might be invaded. The massing of large armies on the western borders of Germany left very little doubt as to Hitler's aims. In a private audience that he granted the Crown Prince Humbert on May 6, Pius spoke of the concern with which he viewed Italy's marked shift towards war. He expressed the hope that Italy would not intervene, since that move would spread the conflict to the shores of the Mediterranean and bring untold suffering to the people. According to Vatican prelates, the Pontiff pointed out that Italy had a great deal to gain by remaining neutral. France was willing to start negotiations to satisfy some of the Italian demands, while the United States, through her President, had manifested the same good will by offering Italy economic advantages. The Crown Prince was stated to have been so impressed by his conversation with the Pope that he saw Mussolini the same day and made a full report of it. He, as one of Italy's outstanding military leaders—the Italian dictator had placed him in command of one of the two groups of armies on national territory soon after the outbreak of hostilities—knew how pitifully unprepared the country was for a major war.

The Vatican was ready to act again as intermediary if its efforts were asked. The Pontiff had learned through Taylor of another message which Roosevelt had sent to Mussolini on May 14. In this message (I am quoting from the State Department publication) the President appealed to Mussolini to "stay wholly apart from any war." He said that the forces of slaughter, forces which denied God, forces which sought to dominate mankind by fear rather than by reason seemed to be extending their conquest against one hundred million human beings who had no desire but peace. He reminded Mussolini that the latter had it in his hands to stay the spread of the war to another group of two hundred million people. The President said that if this war should extend throughout the world, it would pass beyond the control of the heads of states and would encompass the "destruction of millions of lives and the best of what we call the liberty and culture of civilization."

Mussolini replied on May 18 that "Italy is and intends to remain allied with Germany," and that "Italy cannot remain absent at a moment when the fate of Europe is at stake."

Mussolini's answer to Pius' efforts was similar to the one given Roosevelt. The Italian dictator said that he regretted the time was not suitable for any appeasement moves, since in his opinion, he could see no basis for negotiations at that moment. He expressed agreement with the moral reasons that stood behind the President's initiative, and deplored as much as Roosevelt the horror and destruction brought about by war. Italy, he pointed out, had done everything in her power to prevent the spreading of the conflict but she had her own problems which no amount of mediation could solve. "Facts will speak," he told a crowd which had been commandeered, as usual, in Piazza Venezia on May 9, the fourth anniversary of the foundation of the Ethiopian Empire. As soon as the Nazi armies invaded Belgium, the Netherlands and Luxembourg, the official Italian attitude presented an alarming change. From the first stage of psychological preparation of the people, the campaign for intervention became aggressively anti-Ally. Now that France was engaged in a death struggle with Germany, Mussolini gradually abandoned all restraint. The old truculence which he had held temporarily in check reappeared. He knew that almost all of France's military resources had been marshaled for the battle with her hereditary enemy, and that she had no alternative other than to remain on the defense as far as Italy was concerned.

The rift between the Pope and Mussolini deepened and finally culminated in a serious crisis. As Fascist Italy gloated over the German blitzkrieg in the low countries, Pius took the most courageous decision of his Pontificate, on May 10, 1940 he officially pledged the moral support of the Holy See to Belgium, the Netherlands and Luxembourg in their struggle against Germany. The messages he sent to the sovereigns of those three countries were different in form but identical in substance.

"In a moment when, for the second time against its will and right the Belgian people sees its territory exposed to the cruelties of war," the Pontiff wrote to King Leopold of Belgium, "We, being profoundly moved, send Your Majesty and to the entire nation, so beloved by Us, assurance of our paternal affection and, while praying to the All-Powerful God that this stern trial may end with the restoration of full liberty and independence of Belgium, we send Your Majesty and your people Our apostolic blessing with all Our heart."

The key passage, which placed the Vatican on record before world public opinion as being opposed to German cold-blooded ruthlessness, was the one containing the remark that each of the three countries had been invaded "against its will and right." The Pope had been deeply shocked as news of the invasion reached him early in the morning of May 10, although the Secretariat of State made clear that it had regarded the development "not only possible but probable." Particular cause of sorrow, it was explained, was that Belgium's neutrality had been violated for the second time since 1914. That same afternoon, the views of the Vatican were even more clearly explained by Count dalla Torre, after the latter had a meeting with Cardinal Maglione.

"Belgium and Holland have kept their neutrality with scrupulous vigilance and strict loyalty," he wrote. "They have affirmed it repeatedly with the most authoritative statements; they have protected it with diplomatic notes which were very sound, despite accidental violations caused by either side; they have used aerial and anti-aircraft defenses without hesitation against all belligerent machines whenever it was necessary; when they were forced to mobilize and strengthen their armies they warned that they intended to oppose all attacks without discrimination from whatever side they might come. The German initiative has therefore no explanation. It confirms the sad experience of all similar precedents."

That evening 180,000 copies of L'Osservatore Romano, the highest number printed in its history, were sold within a few minutes after their delivery to the newsstands. Some of them, however, never reached their destination. A Vatican informant telephoned to The Times office to say that a cyclist, who carried a bundle of them, had been waylaid a few yards from the Sant' Anna entrance of the Vatican and lashed with barbed wire by four unidentified men. The copies had been burned on the spot. In Genoa, it was reported to the management of L'Osservatore Romano, a group of Fascists had mauled the driver of a truck carrying that day's issue. In Naples, all dealers who displayed the Vatican organ, were threatened with bodily harm unless they destroyed the copies that had been delivered to them and refused to accept future deliveries.

The papal messages were not, of course, printed in the Italian press, which had unanimously accepted Germany's pretext for the invasion. Ettore Muti, a friend of Ciano's who had succeeded Starace as Secretary of the Fascist party, sent confidential orders to the Fascists' clubs throughout Italy to start a terrorist campaign in order to discourage L'Osservatore Romano readers. Accordingly, groups of Fascists lingered unobtrusively near newsstands and, as soon as they saw someone asking for the newspaper, closed in on him and gave him a sound trouncing. In Piazza di Trevi, which is graced by the monumental baroque fountain built by Niccolo Salvi for Clement XII in 1735, two men were thrown in the water. At other stands, bundles of the newspaper were burned as soon as they arrived.

Finally, to avoid further incidents, the Pope gave orders to halt the distribution of L'Osservatore Romano in Rome. Anyone who wanted it could buy copies inside the Vatican, at the newspaper's offices. Shipments to other cities were made, but, to elude the vigilance of Fascists, the usual trucks were replaced by plain-looking automobiles bearing Italian license plates. The bundles were carefully wrapped to hide their contents. Yet, most of the issues were not delivered because the Government instructed the railroad authorities to seize the packages, despite the fact that the Lateran Treaty granted immunity to all Vatican mail and property. One railroad official, who agreed with the policy of the newspaper, allowed a few copies to go on one train. He was discovered, summoned to the local Fascist club and forced to drink castor oil.

The reprisals were taken after the Vatican's refusal to yield to three demands that Mussolini had presented to the Pope at the beginning of May. Il Duce wanted *L'Osservatore Romano* not to print foreign news that did not appear in the Italian newspapers, to abstain from using headlines apt to draw attention of the public, and to abandon its pacifist propaganda because, according to the Fascist doctrine, pacifism is synonymous with defeatism. Maglione rejected all three. The first, on the ground that it would violate the freedom of the Vatican press; the second, because it had no basis since *L'Osservatore Romano* had never used sensational headlines; and the third, because the specific mission of the Church is "to work in favor and in defense of peace, in accordance with the teaching of the Gospel." The negotiations having failed, Mussolini resorted to typical Fascist coercive methods. The Vatican protested but, as it was to be expected, Mussolini took the stand that the incidents had not been promoted by the Italian Government. The official reply was that they were due to the private initiative of individual citizens. There was no other recourse than to yield, unless the Vatican wanted to start an open fight. Since the issue with Fascism did not involve any religious tenets—the only ones upon which the Church accepts no compromise—Pius forbade publication of all political news. On May 16, the Vatican organ printed only the war communiques of the belligerent nations.

In an attempt to create an alibi for Mussolini, Farinacci came out the following day with an editorial that accused the Holy See of having made "common cause with the Netherlands and Belgium against the Germans. . . . In this way the Vatican gives another clear proof that it has taken a decided stand against one of the belligerents, and that it places itself against the Italian nation, which is bound to Germany by a pact."

The circulation of *L'Osservatore Romano* dropped from 150,000

copies to less than ten thousand in a few days. Italians who bought
it for its impartial reporting of news, were afraid to go near the
stands, and those who braved Fascist ire by asking for it at the
newspaper offices, soon dropped it because it no longer contained
the information they sought.

Of course, the Vatican could have chosen to defy Mussolini. Such a
gesture would, undoubtedly, have pleased the democratic powers and
the countries hostile to the Axis. But it must not be forgotten that
the Holy See, although a sovereign state whose territorial integrity
is guaranteed by a treaty, lies in the heart of Rome. It would have
been quite easy for Mussolini to adopt retaliations. He could have
justified them on political grounds, and I have not the slightest doubt
that Pius XII would have suffered the same fate as Pius VI and
Pius VII, who were kept prisoners by Napoleon because they refused
to yield to his demands. The Vatican would have been deprived
of all its means to influence the Catholic world. Mussolini felt he
did not need the support of the Church, because victory at a cheap
price appeared to be within sight. Since, in his opinion, war would
be over in a few months, the internal repercussions deriving from the
forcible muzzling of the Papacy would be offset soon by the booty
he expected from an Axis-dictated peace. He could have easily isolated
the Vatican from the rest of the world by cutting off the telephone
lines and by censoring its mail, as well as by controlling the movements of all prelates residing in it. He did not even need to apply
physical restrictions on the Pope. A few Blackshirts placed on guard
at the gates of Vatican City would have been enough. As to the
reaction of the Catholic world, a victorious Axis could snap its fingers
at it. Later, when he realized that the war was going to be a long
one, with victory uncertain, he took some measures, but did not dare
to go to extremes because he was afraid that a strong anti-Vatican
policy might have caused an internal crisis. By yielding on a minor
point the Holy See preserved the freedom of its diplomatic and
political action, with which it hoped to intervene whenever the
opportunity should arise in behalf of peace—its paramount goal.

The Vatican takes a long-range view of events. It knows that situations change and that even though the Church may suffer setbacks

and persecutions, millenary experience has shown that favorable conditions will eventually present themselves. Had the Pope been a prisoner of Mussolini's, the democracies would have lost a very valuable ally. Moreover, the Vatican had already made quite clear its anti-Axis attitude in Papal pronouncements, in editorials of its official newspaper, in broadcasts reaching the ears of all the peoples of Europe and of the Americas. Indeed, many impartial observers in Rome were impressed with the strong stand the Vatican took towards international events. Its criticism, although always inspired by moral and not temporal motives, was so open that it could hardly be conciliated with the policy becoming to a power that was not at war.

Twenty-four hours after the Nazi invasion of the low countries, the Ministry of Foreign Affairs released a statement on the control to which all Italian shipping was subjected. The Allied blockade had existed since the beginning of the war, and Mussolini's decision to make public a detailed account of how it affected Italy marked the beginning of the second phase of internal propaganda for direct intervention. The statement accused the Allies of arbitrary actions designed to foster commercial hegemony, and described the control as intolerable for a great power like Italy. It was written in such a manner as to arouse the anger of the people, but it failed in its purpose because thinking Italians understood the measure as a war necessity, which affected all nations equally, including the powerful and pro-British United States. The same day anti-Allied posters appeared for the first time in the streets of Rome and other large cities while the press intensified its drive to convince the nation that Germany was winning hands down, as, of course, she was then, and that the day of reckoning for the democracies was near.

The country, was rushed into an artificially created warlike atmosphere. The Fascist party organized anti-English demonstrations, which were explained as popular reaction against the Allied blockade. Youngsters were told to gather at their clubs, where they were assigned a leader, supplied with anti-Allied banners and sent parading through the streets or headed towards the British or French Embassy. I watched several of these groups—never more than a few hundred— and was struck by the lack of conviction of their manifestations. The young men, who for the most part were students, seemed to have a great deal of fun in the new Ally-baiting game devised by their political leaders. Hatred, which was what Mussolini wanted, was lacking. What would have been amusing, if the fate of 45,000,000 people had not been at stake solely because of the will of a dictator, was the effort the press made to present the demonstrations as spontaneous. Scorching anti-British editorials spoke of the "righteous indignation" caused by the British "tyranny" that "strangled" Italy in her own sea (Mare Nostrum). The familiar cries of Corsica, Jibuti, Tunis, Suez, Nice, which had not been heard since the tense summer of 1939 rang again throughout Italy as zealous political leaders vied each other in whipping up enthusiasm for the war.

The campaign gathered pace as Germany reaped success after success in France. The democracies were depicted as hopelessly beaten, decadent and powerless before the German Juggernaut. After the speeches made by Giunta, Grandi, Buffarini-Guidi and other leaders at the end of April, Ciano finally rendered a mediocre imita-tion of Mussolini for the benefit of the Italians in general and the Milanese in particular on May 19. I was not in Milan, but I saw a newsreel of the event a few days later. The mimetic powers of the young Foreign Minister were remarkable. He had learned many of Mussolini's antics—chin stuck out, chewing of the jaws, banging of the fist to emphasize a strong phrase, sarcastic inflections of the voice. He virtually announced that Italy was going to war. He felt quite safe in making that statement since the Germans, after break-ing through the French Ninth Army in the battle of the Meuse, between Namur and Sedan, had reached St. Quentin; Generalissimo Gamelin had been replaced by General Maxime Weygand; and the position of the Allies in France was just as black as in the days of the Battle of the Marne in 1914.

The Vatican took precautions to protect its property, and to shelter the representatives of the countries accredited to the Holy See who would be affected by Italy's declaration of war. Maglione sent out a circular in which he invited the diplomatic corps "to give immediate answer as to whether they intend to return home or take up residence in the Vatican." In the latter case, he explained, "The

Holy See will house only the head of the mission and a secretary."

Enrico Pietro Galeazzi, architect of the Apostolic Palaces, engaged workers to build anti-air raid shelters for ecclesiastics, laymen, and the Pope. The basement of a six-story building was fitted for the ecclesiastics. As a shelter for the lay population, Galeazzi used the Renaissance tower built by Pope Nicholas V, next to the Sant' Anna Gate, which has thirty-feet thick stone walls. The ground floor, of about eighty feet in diameter, can accommodate several hundred people. On the upper floors there is a steel-reinforced room where the Vatican funds are kept. The work of adaptation included food and water supplies, as well as some gas masks and air-conditioning devices.

The place chosen for the Pope's shelter was under the Courtyard of the Holy Office. Although Pius stated that he would not use it, he allowed it to be built because it would serve in case of an emergency for members of his household, Maglione, and other high prelates. The Pontiff's private elevator stops only a few yards from it, so that it can be reached in two or three minutes from the third floor where the Papal apartment is situated. A steel-armored room on the ground floor of a wing in the Belvedere Courtyard was also built, to protect the priceless manuscripts and rare books of the Vatican Library.

At the end of May and beginning of June, the Vatican, the United States, England and France attempted to stave off Italy's intervention.

On May 26, Roosevelt sent a third message to Mussolini through Ambassador Phillips who, however, was unable to see the Italian dictator personally. His requests for audiences were turned down on the pretext that the "Head of the Government is too busy," as Ciano explained to him.

The President, the State Department disclosed, referred to the Italian desire to obtain readjustments with regard to Italy's position and said that if Mussolini were willing to inform the President of Rome's specific wishes, he would communicate them to Great Britain and France. This would be done with the understanding that if an agreement were arrived at it would involve an assurance to the President by the French and British Governments that the agreement would be faithfully executed at the end of the war and that those Governments would welcome Italian participation at any eventual peace conference with a status equal to that of the belligerents; Mussolini would in a similar fashion assure the President that Italy's claims would be satisfied by the execution of this agreement and that the agreement so reached would avoid the possibility of Italy's entering the war.

The Ambassador discussed it with the Italian Foreign Minister who, with the approval of Mussolini, said that Italy could not accept the President's proposal; that Mussolini was resolved to fulfil his obligations under the alliance with Germany; that Mussolini desired to keep his freedom of action and was not disposed to engage in any negotiations which "would not be in accordance with the spirit of Fascism"; and that "any attempt to prevent Italy from fulfilling her engagements is not well regarded." The Foreign Minister informed Ambassador Phillips that Italy would enter the war "soon."

On May 30, President Roosevelt sent still another appeal to Mussolini. He warned the Italian dictator that if the war in Europe should be extended through the entrance of Italy, direct interests of the United States would be immediately and prejudicially affected. He reminded Mussolini of the historic and traditional interest of the United States in the Mediterranean. He said that his Government had never asserted any political interest in Europe, but had asserted its clearly defined economic interests; that through the extension of the war to the Mediterranean region the legitimate interests of the people of the United States would be gravely curtailed; and that such a possibility "cannot be viewed with equanimity." The President declared that the further extension of the war as the result of Italian participation would at once result in an increase in the rearmament program of the United States and in a redoubling of the efforts of our Government to facilitate in every practical way the securing within the United States by the Allied powers of all the supplies which they might require. In conclusion, he spoke of his desire to promote profitable commercial relations between Washington and Rome, as well as their respective policies and interests.

Mussolini replied to the President on June 1 through his Foreign

Minister. He confirmed Ciano's statement that the decision to enter
the war had already been taken, and stated it was "of no concern
to him" that Italy's entry would mean the redoubling of American
efforts to help the Allies. Finally, he said he preferred not to receive
any "further pressure" from the President; this would only "stiffen
his attitude."

During that period, Reynaud told François Poncet to ascertain
what Italy would regard as a satisfactory basis for discussion. He
needed an agreement very badly in view of France's critical military
situation. Churchill wrote a letter to Mussolini in which he stressed
that his government was willing to negotiate the solution of whatever problems might exist between England and Italy, and, to show
his conciliatory spirit, relaxed the control measures on Italian shipping at Gibraltar. Pius, who had been informed by Taylor of Roosevelt's efforts, joined the peace offensive of the democracies with a
last appeal in the form of an autographed message that Borgongini
Duca delivered to Ciano.

But Mussolini had made up his mind. France's defeat was a certainty and there was no need to tergiversate. Military preparations
were intensified. Troops were concentrated on the Italo-French
border, ships were forbidden to leave port, and those on the high
seas were instructed to take shelter in neutral harbors; blackout
regulations were published, and certain Italian regions declared military zones. Demonstrations occurred daily, and students were sent
to Piazza Venezia where they were told to clamor for Italy's intervention. Loud-speakers were placed in all the squares of Rome and
in those of other large cities, to relay the speech that was to announce
the Leader's final decision, and to spell Italy's ruin.

THIRTEENTH CHAPTER

Two weeks before Italy's entrance in the war, the majority of the Italians did not believe that France would be conquered. This view was held not only by the man in the street but by high Fascist officials as well. Mussolini was apparently the only one in the country who knew what the real situation was, because of the secret information that Hitler was giving him through the German Ambassador in Rome.

Many months later, Mario Ferraguti, who had been one of Il Duce's secretaries in 1926, when Fascism began the so-called "Battle of the Wheat" to make Italy self-sufficient in that field, told me of an audience he had had with Mussolini at the end of May, 1940. Ferraguti was a leading agricultural expert, and the Italian dictator wanted him to inspect Italy's wheat fields and to estimate that year's yield.

French Premier Reynaud had just made his disheartening speech announcing the surrender of the Belgian Army and describing France's situation as "very grave." Ferraguti was in the antechamber of Mussolini's office in Palazzo Venezia waiting to be received when two old friends of his, Italo Balbo, Air Marshal and Governor of Libya, and Buffarini-Guidi, Under Secretary of the Interior, arrived. They, too, had been summoned. Balbo, who had just flown in from Tripoli, had with him some strategic maps of Libya. He was worried. "I know why I have been called," he said. "The Chief wants to declare war, but we are in a very delicate situation. Look," he opened his maps, "we have absolutely no defenses except the desert. The French have a strongly fortified Mareth Line. The British have a railroad running from Cairo to Marsa Matruh, which they can use to supply their armies without too much difficulty. I have very few trucks, tanks, and men. If they [England and France] start a simultaneous offensive, I cannot hold out for more than two or three weeks."

At that moment, Balbo was told that Mussolini would receive him. There was a hasty good-bye, and the Air Marshal disappeared.

Ferraguti felt rather gloomy. Balbo's exposition was quite convincing. His turn came. He found Mussolini in the best of spirits—not a trace of worry. He was beaming all over. Ferraguti came out of the audience somewhat relieved, but still with doubts.

Two days later he met Balbo at the house of a friend. "Italo," he asked, "what happened during the audience?"

"He must know what he is doing," Balbo replied. "When I described the situation in Libya, he merely nodded and said, 'I know, I know, but don't worry. There will be events that will surprise you as well as everybody else.'"

I recount this episode to show that less than two weeks before Mussolini's decision, even Balbo had misgivings in regard to Italy's intervention. The people experienced the same feeling until the very last days. No amount of propaganda could have made them show enthusiasm for a war that did not already seem clearly won by Germany.

The Germans were at the gate of Paris, on June 10, 1940, and it was clear even to incurable optimists that France was rapidly collapsing under the mighty blows of the Nazi hordes. German Ambassador von Mackensen and General Eno von Rintelen, military attaché, had seen Mussolini the evening before and had given him the latest news of the military situation on the Western Front. France was no longer in a position to put up effective resistance, and Italy's intervention at that moment would undoubtedly hasten the moral and military debacle. The time was ripe to jump on the band wagon of victory. Again that morning, Mackensen had had an audience with Mussolini who told him that Italy would declare war on England and France in the afternoon.

The Italian dictator, as usual, announced his decision from the balcony of Palazzo Venezia. The square was by no means filled to capacity. There were only about thirty thousand people there when he appeared amidst the customary applause. I was standing not more than one hundred feet from the balcony, surrounded by students and Blackshirts. I had heard Mussolini speak dozens of times, and the ritual was always the same. The Secretary of the Fascist party would precede him by a few seconds, give the signal for the applause of welcome, then stand on the left side of the balcony, two paces behind the dictator, and shout, "*Saluto, al Duce!*" The salute was timed with Mussolini's appearance.

While the Secretary of the party motioned for silence, Mussolini would begin to speak in an even tone. Whenever he wanted an applause he would raise his voice in rapid crescendo. Words would pour forth, machine-gun-like, to convey the impression of uncontrolled emotion. The crowd would go wild.

This day the speech fell flat. It was sober and unconvincing, and as cold and impersonal as the report of a chairman at a board of directors' meeting. It was the poorest I had heard him make both from the point of delivery and substance. Although he struck his usual pose, short, bowed legs slightly apart, hands sometimes resting on hips, face grim, I felt that Il Duce was not sure of himself. The way he uttered his words indicated that his decision was the result of a rational calculation opposed by his political intuition. I may be wrong, but he sounded and looked like a man who was afraid of the gravity of his own action; who, in the back of his brain, had doubts as to the ultimate outcome of the war. This time he could not bluff his way through. He had to deliver, and he knew that if the war lasted more than six months, he would be powerless. Hitler had told him that France was beaten and that England would not go on fighting alone. It sounded logical. It was the chance he had been waiting for in order to get a lot with a minimum of risk. Yet, there lingered subconsciously the uneasy feeling that perhaps what looked so convincing might be adversely altered by factors which he sensed but could not single out. To me, his speech betrayed a conflict between instinct and brain.

But that was not all. His declaration of war at a time when France was prostrate and helpless was a cowardly act, just like kicking a man when he is down. It was, as Roosevelt said with a phrase that struck the proud Italian dictator to the core, "A stab in the back!" It seemed, then, a shrewd, clever move, but it was as contemptible as playing a poker game with marked cards in cahoots with an equally crooked partner. As far as Italy was concerned, the situation was no different in regard to France from the one in 1915, when Mussolini as a young man had written fiery editorials advocating intervention in favor of the nations which he was now fighting. He was reneging that phase of his political life. Still, it was not this that bothered him, for he had no moral principles; it was the criticism of world public opinion. Years of undeniable successes in the field of international politics had led him to believe he was a great man. He had attained power and had become accustomed to it. Now, his ultimate goal was to attain an outstanding place in history, and that depended on the results of the decision he had just announced. He was afraid.

The Italian people heard the declaration of war with mixed feelings. They thought it was going to be a brief conflict, and that with France out, they would be safe. The Fascist propaganda barrage in the weeks preceding intervention to explain Italy's war aims had had little effect. What had convinced them was Germany's smashing victories in Poland, Norway, Belgium, Holland, and, now, France. Though they had little confidence in their own strength, they felt that with such a powerful ally, Italy could not lose. A joke that reflected this attitude was heard currently in Rome.

An Englishman was boasting to an Italian about his country's military strength, "We have thousands of airplanes, scores of thousands of machine guns, tanks, and . . . ."

"That's nothing," interrupted the Italian.

"What do you mean 'nothing'? What have you got?"

"We have an ally that has got all that and more!"

A few thousand Italians, marshaled into line by their leaders, dutifully marched to the Quirinal Palace, official residence of the Italian sovereigns, at the end of Mussolini's speech. They hailed King Victor, who, having been notified in advance that a demonstration was to take place, had left Villa Savoia, in the outskirts of the capital, where he normally lived, and was waiting at the Quirinal. In response to the shouts of the crowd, he appeared on the balcony of his palace, surrounded by Crown Prince Humbert and other members of the House of Savoy. He saluted the people with both hands, but did not smile. His Majesty was also worried.

It was after sunset when I arrived at the Vatican. The Courtyard of Saint Damasus was deserted except for a few papal gendarmes on duty. An atmosphere of gloom and sorrow seemed to pervade the magnificent halls and loggias. At the Secretariat of State, on the top floor, I was told that "the attitude and responsibility of the Vatican are entirely separate from those of the Italian clergy and Catholics. While the Holy See is responsible toward the Catholics of all nations, and, therefore, its attitude must be inspired by this responsibility, the Italian clergy and Catholics have specific duties to their country and will, as always, fulfill them generously."

This statement was in keeping with the traditional attitude of the papacy in regard to war. Since the Church recognizes the authority of the State, it advocates the allegiance of the citizen to the legally constituted government, whether he be a cleric or a layman. On the other hand, the Vatican, as the administrative and guiding body of the Church, is international in character because it represents the interests of all Catholics regardless of their nationality, and must, therefore, maintain complete neutrality.

Italy's declaration of war placed the Vatican in a delicate position. Bernardo Attòlico, who had succeeded Dino Alfieri as Ambassador to the Holy See, handed to Maglione a series of requests formulated by Mussolini himself. The Italian dictator knew how strongly the Vatican had opposed Italy's entrance in the war and took measures designed to neutralize papal influence on the people. He asked that the Holy See apply a blackout, suppress all official war communiques which *L'Osservatore Romano* had been publishing up to that time, and limit the daily broadcasts of the Vatican City station to those in the Italian language.

The Pope submitted to these demands. Had he acted differently, he would have laid himself open to the charges already too frequently made, that the Holy See was siding with the Allies. In view of the fact that the papal state was physically within Italian territory, there was nothing else he could do. Had Pius refused to conform with blackout regulations, the Vatican would have been a useful beacon for English and French planes raiding the capital. The Italian people themselves would have resented it.

All the Vatican apartments were fitted with heavy curtains. As a result, the light issuing from the second window on the third floor of the Apostolic Palace, which belonged to the Pope's study, was no longer seen at night from St. Peter's Square. Similarly, the large window panes of the loggias on the Courtyard of Saint Damasus showed only very dim blue light.

L'Osservatore Romano hinted at Fascist pressure by announcing that "in the present circumstances we find it impossible to continue as we have up to now the publication of all official communiques by belligerent countries." At the same time, preparations were made to house the heads of missions accredited to the Holy See of the countries with which Italy was at war.

The Secretariat of State requested the Italian Government to maintain all the customary prerogatives and immunities to the diplomatists of belligerent countries accredited to the Vatican, and to allow them to retain their seats on Italian territory. The request was based on Article XII of the Lateran Accord which guaranteed such treatment. Mussolini's refusal confirmed the fact that he could disregard treaties as easily as his German partner when they did not suit him.

Count Vladimir d'Ormesson and Francis d'Arcy Osborne, the French and British ambassadors, placed themselves under Vatican protection two days after Italy's intervention. Casimir Papee and Adrian Nieuwenhuys, the Polish and Belgian ambassadors joined them a few days later. The diplomatists were given apartments in the Hospice of St. Marta, not far from the entrance known as the Arch of the Bells, on the left side of St. Peter's Square. When they arrived at the Vatican, the Secretariat of State informed them that they could not receive visitors without special permission, leave Vatican City, and have direct contact with their governments.

The Pope was determined to give Mussolini no excuse for complaints. He issued strict orders to avoid any breach of political neutrality. Residents were forbidden to carry on political discussions of the international situation in any public premise inside the Vatican. The papal gendarmes were charged with the task of enforcing that order, and they kept a close watch on residents and visitors in a drive against "fifth columnists." Foreign students were barred from the Vatican Library, to foil possible attempts at espionage on the part of foreign powers. Censorship was established. Two of the three post offices were closed. Mail was examined by members of the congregation of Don Orion, which also controlled the telephone exchange. To avoid possible profiteering, the price of all commodities was increased by 40 per cent. Before the war, Vatican prices were nearly 50 per cent lower than those in Italy; the new measure brought them almost to the same level. In addition, the sale of spaghetti and tobacco was restricted. Nuns, who replaced the lay employees, exercised constant supervision to prevent infractions.

At night, the Vatican firemen were permanently mobilized to inspect all buildings inside the grounds to make sure that no lights were showing. The first person found guilty of transgressing papal orders was Monsignor Arborio-Mella di Sant' Elia, Papal Master of the Chamber, a very stern disciplinarian himself, who scrupulously enforced rules over those who were under his authority. Monsignor Mella forgot to black out his windows one night and was fined fifteen dollars. Many people who had felt the severity of that prelate were quite pleased.

Foreigners who wished to visit residents were obliged to file an application, which remained at the Vatican police bureau, and state the reason for their visit. If the reason were found unsatisfactory, they were not admitted. At the same time, posters in all public places such as the Vatican bar warned customers to remain inside the premises only for "the time strictly necessary for the purchases." Those who disregarded this order were fined. Plain-clothes men mixed among the people and listened to what was being said. They reported to the Vatican police any information that might indicate the presence of informants in the pay of foreign powers.

All bishops were notified that they owed allegiance to their country and should co-operate loyally as long as this co-operation did not conflict with religious principles. There were some of them who were Fascist sympathizers, such as Monsignor Evasio Colli, Bishop of Parma and head of the Central Bureau of Catholic Action, who appealed to all members of that organization to do their duty. This he summed up in three words, "Pray and Work." Monsignor Carlo Margotti, Archbishop of Gorizia, issued a pastoral letter in which, according to the press, he urged the Italian people and clergy to obey and trust Mussolini in the war Italy was waging for the "welfare of the country." I never saw the letter, but I have no reason to doubt its existence, since it was never denied by Margotti or by L'Osservatore Romano, as far as I know.

A passage of the letter said that all Italians should "lift our reverent thoughts to the ever-victorious King and Emperor and to the undefeated Duce, to whom we have entrusted the fate of our armies and nation. . . . The Italians can no longer be kept within the unjust frontiers of the peninsula and are seeking on their sea the outlet assigned to them by Providence."

Contrary to its habit, L'Osservatore Romano ignored the letter, as well as a speech that Cardinal Ildefonso Schuster, Archbishop of Milan, made on July 25, when he prayed that, "God be with our dear soldiers and aid them in the faithful accomplishment of their duty."

I quote these passages because they indicate the loyalty with which the Italian clergy co-operated with the Fascist Government at the beginning of the conflict. This attitude in no way differed from the ones adopted by the national clergics of other countries toward their governments. The reason is that today's priest does not consider himself an individual apart from the life of the nation. He is a citizen, and, as all citizens, supports his government in times of crisis. This attitude is part of his mission as the "shepherd of souls." He has the duty of bringing comfort to and of alleviating the suffering of his flock.

One of the Pope's first diplomatic moves, soon after Italy's intervention, was to request the French and English Governments not to bomb or shell Rome. The Vatican pointed out that there were more than four hundred churches in the capital as well as many seminaries, monasteries, convents, and other religious buildings that could hardly escape damage in the event of air raids. Both governments gave satisfactory replies although they refused to commit themselves definitely. Osborne was received in a private audience by Pius and informed him that Premier Winston Churchill realized the sacred character of the Italian capital. He said Churchill would "do everything in his power not to bomb the city, and under all circumstances, rigorously to respect its religious monuments and buildings." Quite rightly, the British Premier wanted to be free to bomb Rome's outskirts, if strategic reasons made it necessary.

Fascist officials with whom I spoke were none too happy when they learned that England would abstain from bombing Rome. An enemy air raid would have been a powerful propaganda weapon for them. Mussolini could have exploited the solidarity which Catholics all over the world felt for the Papacy, just as he attempted to when the Allied air force raided the Italian capital for the first time in July, 1943. Further, it cannot be excluded that, had an English raid taken place, Mussolini would have followed it with one of his own, and blamed his enemies for it to arouse the indignation of Catholics.

In view of the somewhat evasive British reply to his request, the Pope decided to stay in Rome for the duration of the war, and, despite the hot weather, gave up his annual vacation in Castel Gandolfo which he had planned to take early in May. The various Fascist measures made it increasingly clear that Mussolini was preparing for intervention, and the Pontiff hoped that he could restrain the Italian dictator from taking the fatal plunge.

During the same period, the Pontiff appealed, both publicly and privately, to Hitler and Mussolini to show generosity in regard to defeated France. He warned in one of his speeches that clemency alone could prevent the breeding of hatred that inevitably follows the imposition of harsh terms on the vanquished.

"In the present hour," the Pope said on July 10, "there is the danger that the noble and legitimate feeling of love for one's own country may degenerate in the soul of many men to revengeful passion— an unceasing pride in some, and an incurable rancor in others. While defending faithfully and courageously his country, a Christian must, however, abstain from hating those whom he is obliged to combat. . . . Bloodshed through force too often breeds rancor. The rancor of the riven soul is as deep as an abyss that gives on to another abyss, just as wave is followed by wave, and calamity by calamity. . . . Therefore, one must first of all forgive, but above everything else, remove the desire for revenge."

The Vatican regarded the Franco-Italian and Franco-German armistice terms as very stiff. High prelates pointed out to me that they were very much concerned over the fact that both documents lacked a clause limiting the special regime to which the victors had subjected France. The Axis powers, in other words, had refused to give any pledges as to the extent of their interference with the new government headed by the octogenarian French marshal, Henri Philippe Pétain. With the approval of the Pope, Maglione sent a letter to the president of the "Social Week" of Portugal, a Catholic congress that was held in Lisbon at the end of June, in which he stressed that "the social teachings of the Church are more urgent and important than ever in this age when, under the impulse of a new political paganism, no less loathsome than the ancient, people are involved and abandoned to the chaos of passions and war. Catholics must dedicate all their energies to the return of peace with honor, justice, and charity." It was a broadside fired at Germany. The Vatican saw clearly through Hitler's plan to weaken France irremediably by refusing, among other things, to release one million five hundred thousand French prisoners. By keeping these men separate from their families, he lowered the already critical French birth rate, and hoped to make Germany's historic rival a nation of old and weak people who would be unable to bring about their own resurrection after the war. In the first few months following the armistice, the Pope repeatedly praised the old marshal who had pledged support to all institutions likely to stem the corruption of morals; but his entreaties, in this case also, were fruitless.

Despite her strong anti-clericalism, France is a Catholic nation, and it is easily understood why the papacy was doing whatever it could, both in the political and spiritual fields, to support it. Moreover, as I have said, Franco-Vatican relations had been very cordial in the immediate pre-war years. Not even the Socialist Blum Government had deviated from what had become an accepted policy of collaboration with the Church. In a letter to the French episcopate at the end of July, Pius invoked the "reawakening" of the country which he felt could not fail to occur in view of its resources "so numerous and powerful."

At the same time, the Vatican began negotiations for a concordat with Vichy, in the hope of obtaining the repeal of the French anti-clerical laws. It asked for full freedom of the religious orders and congregations, the re-establishment of religious teaching in schools, the recognition of Catholic Action, and finally, the return of Church property confiscated by the State when the anti-clerical wave swept the country in 1904, and brought about the severance of French-Vatican relations a year later. Cardinal Pierre Gerlier, Archbishop of Lyon and head of the clergy in non-occupied France, and Monsignor Rene de Fontenelle, a very able prelate who enjoyed Maglione's confidence were the intermediaries between the Vatican and the Vichy Government. No announcement as to the outcome of these negotiations was ever made, but this is not surprising since I was told in the beginning that the Pope intended to wait and see what the attitude of post-war France would be towards the religious question. The conversations were regarded as preliminary work.

The Vatican was attacked during that period by Farinacci because of its "Italophobe policy" as shown by its favorable attitude toward Vichy. The Fascist extremist interpreted L'Osservatore Romano's articles praising Pétain's work of reconstruction as betraying the Vatican's desire for the victory of Great Britain over the Axis.

Elated over the collapse of France, the Italians felt quite confident during the first months of the war that England would surrender. Their press told them that it was a matter of weeks, and editorials appealed to the traditional common sense of the English people to end a war they could never hope to win. Mussolini himself waited. The Italian Air Force and Navy which, according to Fascist spokesmen in the prewar days, were going to blast the British off the Mediterranean, were surprisingly inactive: a few bombing raids and no naval operations. The only story of any importance that came out of Rome in the first month of war was Balbo's death when his plane was shot down over Tobruk, Libya. The Italian official communique claiming that the Air Marshal had been killed during an enemy bombing raid was false. But equally false was the British contention that Mussolini had planned the assassination of his collaborator in order to get rid of a feared rival. Some of Balbo's intimate friends made a thorough investigation and gave me a detailed account of the Fascist leader's death.

It happened like this. Balbo had entertained some friends in his Tripoli castle. It was about four in the afternoon of June 29, when he decided to make a sudden inspection trip to Tobruk. He invited his guests to come along. Nello Quilici, his nephew, and several others accepted. Quilici was the editor of *Il Corriere Padano*, the newspaper owned by Balbo. He was strongly anti-German. His and Balbo's lives were as closely interwoven as the roots of the tree with the earth.

They drove to the Tripoli airport in Balbo's big, black Fiat limousine. The bomber was ready. It was an obsolete Savoia Marchetti 79. It could carry about twelve people as well as a small load of bombs. The cockpit bristled with machine guns. It was not a fast plane as planes go today; its top speed was less than two hundred miles per hour. Before climbing on board, the Marshal summoned one of his adjutants.

"Tell Tobruk I'll be there in three hours."

He left for his death trip with the usual jovial smile and hearty manner which had given him countless friends in Italy and had made him so popular that the jealous Duce had decided to relegate him to a colony. During my trip to Libya in the fall of 1938, Mussolini's name was seldom mentioned. When an Italian spoke of "*lui*" (him), it was Balbo. In Italy, "*lui*" was always Mussolini. Even the Arabs liked the Marshal—as much as Arabs are capable of liking anyone who has robbed them of their land.

The adjutant attempted to telephone to Tobruk, but the line was dead. The British had just carried out a raid, and bombs had put the overland lines out of order. The adjutant tried to telegraph. That, too, was impossible. "Pretty bad raid," they thought in Tripoli.

Balbo piloted the plane himself. He loved to dive into clouds and see the shadow of his bomber and show off his ability as a pilot. I flew with him once, and he turned the trip into a roller coaster ride.

It was sunset when the plane sighted Tobruk. It was the kind of sunset that makes those who have lived in Africa long enough to see

some of them want to stay forever. Balbo often watched them from
the terrace of his Tripoli castle built on a strip of land that jutted
far out in the sea. However, he did not want to stay in Libya. He was
a man of action and not a dreamer. Italy was the arena of his ambition. He missed the political strife, the restful evenings with his intellectual friends, and the atmosphere of conviviality created by the generous wine, the beautiful women, and the good rich food. He often
flew unexpectedly, in five or six hours, from Tripoli to Ostia—more
often than Mussolini liked. Just a telephone call from Tripoli to his
special office of "Marshal of the Air" in the ministry of aeronautics
in Rome, announcing his arrival, and the three-room suite he always
kept on the first floor of the Hotel Excelsior would be packed with
friends to welcome him.

The crews of the San Giorgio, the old destroyer the British had
sunk in the harbor of Tobruk, were nervous. The Italians had dragged
her into shallow water, filled her with concrete, equipped her with
anti-aircraft guns, and turned her into a fortress. The British had
rained bombs over her day after day, but the concrete had formed
a solid block with the steel structure. That day, too, the British had
tried to blast her. The last raid ended twenty or thirty minutes before
another plane was sighted. A British bomber? The gunners started
firing.

I can almost hear Balbo, who was a master at profanity, cursing
the San Giorgio crews. I can "see" him getting madder and madder
at their stupidity. And, of course, there was no thought in his mind
of turning tail. Shells were whizzing past him, dangerously close. The
plane was flying high—about nine thousand feet. Balbo liked to fly
high.

He dove, straight for the San Giorgio. The fools would see in a few
moments that it was an Italian plane and cease firing. But they never
gave him a chance. They were blind with fear, their nerves shaken,
their hearts beating faster and faster as the plane approached with
increasing speed. They did not want to be strafed. They must shoot
that plane. It's a question of "him" or "us." And they fired, fired,
fired. The shells hit the gasoline tank. The crews were happy and
proud. The plane was catching fire. It lurched, in that clear, cobalt

sky, and added the color of its flames to that of the dying sun. It made a brighter patch of red right there in the crystal clear air. It banked and fell on the golden sand edging Tobruk from inland, and burned only a few yards away from the boxlike, one-story, white-frescoed houses on the outskirts of the town. Thus died Balbo, recklessly, as he had lived, killed by a blunder which threw hundreds of thousands of Italians into mourning. He was one of the very few Fascist leaders who admired Americans and wanted Italy and the United States to be friends.

Balbo was very popular in Italy despite the fact that for years his name hardly ever appeared in the newspapers. He had laid the foundations for Italy's air force way back in the early twenties, and had thousands of faithful officers in that branch of the armed forces who would have unhesitantly followed him in any enterprise. Of course, he, like many other Italians who had supported Mussolini at the inception of the Fascist movement had taken a leading part in the so-called punitive expeditions the Blackshirts carried out against their political adversaries. Balbo's name had been linked with the murder of several people, during the campaigns of terror which he had organized in his native province of Ferrara. He had been accused of stealing millions of lire during his political career. Morally, he was as devoid of principles and as greedy as a *"condottiere"* of the fifteenth century.

But, a great deal of water had flowed under the bridge. The revolutionary days were gone, and Balbo who had attained wealth and power, developed into a potential opposition leader. He knew the extent of his influence but never used it. He was biding his time, and had he lived, I wonder whether Mussolini could have remained in power until the summer of 1943, when Libya and Tunisia were already irreparably lost; Sicily invaded, Sardinia, and the Italian mainland subjected to the devastating bombing of the Anglo-American air force.

At this point, I should like to relate the views expressed by Italian and German officers on Libya's strategic situation in the summer of 1940. According to them, France's decision not to continue the war from North Africa and the rest of her empire was one of her greatest military blunders. Italy, as Balbo himself stated, had nothing with which to oppose the French and English armies in her colony, and an offensive on two fronts would have wiped out the badly equipped Fascist troops in a few weeks. Italian generals admitted to me that they were jittery over that possibility during the first month of war when they did not know whether the French empire would carry on the war independently of the motherland. They were deeply concerned over the large French army in Tunisia, fully equipped with planes and tanks, which, even if the Germans had taken the whole of continental France, could have beaten Mussolini before his ally was in a position to give effective support.

Since Hitler was not able to invade England in the summer of 1940, there is no reason to suppose that he could have invaded French North Africa in that same period. Indeed, his chances of success were even slimmer because, in the latter case, he would have had to face a trained army across a much vaster expanse of water than the English Channel, as well as the French fleet. The Italians presented no threat, for how could Mussolini, who was not able to take Malta, hope to beat the French in Tunisia and fight the English in Egypt?

I do not need to explain what the advantages would have been with Libya in Allied hands. Anyone could visualize them in the summer of 1943, when that vitally strategic territory was conquered by the Anglo-American armies. France could have saved herself in Africa, but it would have taken moral courage and foresight. These qualities she once had were destroyed by the social and political disintegration that caused her downfall. These, as I said, are not my views, but those of Axis officers.

Instead, the immobilization of the French Army in Tunisia enabled Marshal Rodolfo Graziani, who had become the commander in Libya after Balbo's death, to launch an offensive against Egypt in the middle of September—fully three months after the declaration of war— and advance as far as Sidi Barrani, a few miles from the Italo-Egyptian border. Italy's weakness was clearly shown when General Archibald Wavell routed the Fascist Army ten weeks later, took Cyrenaica, and finally, early in 1941, halted at El Agheila, on the fringe of the Sirte desert a few hundred miles from Tripoli!

Graziani himself unmasked Italy's appalling lack of preparedness in his report on the war in Africa published on December 23, 1940. He attributed Wavell's successful counter-offensive launched on December 9, to the "crushing superiority of the enemy's armored units." The Italian infantry divisions, lightly supported with tanks and artillery, and lacking trucks, were encircled and cut off one by one by the faster and stronger armored British Army. This proved that Italy had no mechanized forces to speak of at the beginning of the war, and that, as Balbo had feared, Libya would have been hardly more than a military walk if the French had also attacked from Tunisia.

FOURTEENTH CHAPTER

Since the feared French intervention failed to materialize, Mussolini and the Italian people themselves thought in that summer of 1940, that they were sitting on top of the world. The Axis was triumphing both in Europe and in Africa. Italy had conquered British Somaliland early in August; Germany was launching mass air raids on Britain, which was reported rocking under the incessant bombings. It was, the Italians felt, a matter of weeks before the war was over.

In view of Italy's success in British Somaliland, and the terror that German might had spread among Europe's smaller nations, Mussolini decided that the time was ripe to start the conquest of the Mediterranean.

The first indication of the Italian dictator's schemes came to me from the Vatican. Parish priests in Istria, a region bordering on Yugoslavia, and in cities along the Adriatic litoral, had reported to Rome that police agents had been quietly canvassing families asking what accommodations they had for "refugees." These were Italians residing in Dalmatia who would have to leave Yugoslavia before the outbreak of hostilities. Then there occurred two anti-Yugoslav demonstrations in Florence and in Rome, which were quickly halted, however. At the same time, word came from Meran and Fiume that large contingents of infantry, cavalry, and mechanized troops were being massed in those towns. Eventually, Italian officers who were sent to the Italo-Yugoslav border told me that all preparations had been made for the attack, when suddenly they were ordered to withdraw. No explanation was given. Their impression was that Hitler had stayed Mussolini's hands. The German general staff was stated to have been much more interested in an Italian offensive against Egypt, at a time when England was heavily engaged in fighting the Nazi air force at home.

As a preliminary to his African campaign, Mussolini attempted to coerce Greece into joining the Axis camp. The means he used was so puerile that not one Italian I spoke to was taken in. The Albanian official newspaper *Tomori* of Tirana, which had replaced the *Drita* of the Zog regime, accused Athens on August 11 of having murdered an Albanian "Irredentist" called Daut Hoxha. Every newspaper in the country screamed insults at Greece for the "barbarous crime," in a stupendous outburst of rage that would have seemed genuine to anyone who was not familiar with the orchestralike manner in which Mussolini directed his press. Visitors from Tirana told Edda that Hoxha, a shepherd, had been killed in a fight over some sheep. He was a notorious bandit sought by the Greek police for murders he had committed many years before. The pretext was, therefore, a very flimsy one, but it was made to serve Mussolini's purpose. The reason behind the very violent attacks of the Fascist press was to force Greece to renounce formally the British guarantees of her independence and territorial integrity. This was meant to be only the beginning of a series of requests which would eventually include the control of all Greek harbors and bases.

The firm attitude of John Metaxas, Greek premier, who manifested his willingness to fight rather than to yield, and Germany's intervention as a pacifier were said in Rome to have been responsible for it. Since Greece could not be blackmailed, Hitler's opinion still was that Italy should concentrate on Africa. In this case also, the anti-Greek campaign was allowed to peter out for a few weeks.

Graziani's successful offensive in September made the seizure of Greek naval and air bases a coveted objective for their control would improve Italy's strategic position and enable her to strike at the British fleet, which was a serious threat for Libya where Mussolini was planning to start a new offensive.

A close relative of one of the high officials who attended a session of the Grand Council of Fascism at the end of September gave me the story of how Italy's invasion of Greece was planned. My experience in covering foreign news is that the usefulness of one's sources is gradually developed over a number of years during which mutual liking and confidence are tested. I had half a dozen good Italian friends in important posts who eventually would tell me what had happened on certain occasions. It was hardly ever possible to obtain confidential information as decisions were being taken, because they had a sense of responsibility, but when events were so long past that they had become history, they would willingly give explanations. This, I may add, is the reason why I cannot quote people, for if I did, my friends would be placed in a dangerous position.

All the Italian cabinet ministers, Marshal Pietro Badoglio, who was chief of the general staff, Sebastiano Visconti-Prasca, commander of the Italian forces in Albania, and many other officials attended the meeting. Mussolini opened the session by stating that Greece must be made to yield Salonika, her bases in the mainland and in Crete. This would give the Italian Air Force and Navy the possibility of attacking with greater effectiveness the British convoys to Egypt, prevent the supplying of Wavell's forces, keep the enemy fleet in Alexandria harbor and relieve Graziani's army of the shelling by British naval units which had impeded the logistical work necessary for the next offensive against Matruh.

Greece, he said, should be to Italy what Denmark was to Germany, an unwilling but very useful collaborator whose geographical position was as strategically important in the Mediterranean as that of the Nordic country in the Atlantic. If she refused, however, Italy would wage war. Since this was a distinct possibility, he had instructed Ciano to undermine the potential enemy from within. Albanians who resided in Greece and knew many of the generals and politicians had been engaged as agents. They had guaranteed the co-operation of some of the Greek military leaders who would surrender as soon as the Italian Army in Albania crossed the border. A report sent by the brother of Gemil Dino was particularly optimistic. Gemil Dino himself was an Italophile Albanian and the son-in-law of Sheftek Verlaci, then Albanian premier. He was one of the conspirators who had prepared Albania for the Fascist invasion in April, 1939. Mussolini had given him the rank of ambassador, as a reward for his treachery —the only Albanian in the Italian diplomatic service who enjoyed that title.

Mussolini predicted that Greece would be conquered in two weeks. Wavell was still in the process of organizing his forces in Egypt since the original British plans in that theater of war had been upset by the collapse of France which had eliminated the army in Tunisia. In view of this situation, Italy would have time to prepare the Greek bases without too much interference from the enemy. He asked Badoglio to endorse the plan of campaign submitted by Visconti Prasca. On Badoglio, as chief of the general staff, rested the final decision.

The Marshal refused. He pointed out that Italy had only seven divisions in Albania totaling sixty thousand men, very little artillery, tanks, machine guns, and auxiliary units. One division would have to be stationed on the Albanian-Yugoslav border as a precautionary measure; two would have to be kept in reserve to garrison the country. That would leave four divisions to start the war with. The Greeks, according to Italian military intelligence, had fifteen divisions. The terrain was strategically favorable to them.

Mussolini replied that numerical and military inferiority on Italy's part would be offset by the political results expected of fifth columnist work already done in Greece.

"It may be, but I don't base military campaigns on political considerations. I base them on guns and men. I refuse to sign the order, and I wish to resign," Badoglio was quoted as saying. He got up to leave. Mussolini left his chair, went over to him, and spoke along the following lines:

"The responsibility for the campaign will be mine. I don't want you to resign because the whole world will then think that Italy is traversing a military crisis. This is inopportune especially at this moment when our armies have had successes in Libya, Kenya, and British Somaliland."

Badoglio, and this was his mistake, yielded. He was a patriot and realized that what Mussolini said was correct. His resignation would have been interpreted as a sign of dissension between the Fascist regime and the Army.

The invasion of Greece was Mussolini's second greatest politic-military blunder. The first was intervention. The general opinion seems to be that it was Ciano who suggested it. This is not true. The man responsible for it was Mussolini himself. Ciano was made the scapegoat in order to save whatever shreds of prestige were left to

the Duce after the Italian Army, betrayed by the Fascist Party and
the Government, was sent to fight a well-equipped enemy in a condition of appalling inferiority. The Italians were pushed steadily back
after the first week of the war, and hung on throughout the winter
to a few key positions in the western part of Albania, until the Germans came to their rescue from the north in the spring of 1941.
Just to give an idea of how bad conditions were, Italian Army
ordnance officers were sent out to buy all the woolen socks, under-
pants, gloves, sweaters, and like apparel in department stores. These
supplies were then flown to the soldiers in Albania who were being
decimated by the freezing temperatures in the mountains. When I
toured the Albanian battlefields, in the spring of 1941, an Italian
medical officer confided privately that in one military hospital at
Berat nearly thirty thousand soldiers had been treated for congealed
feet. Italian casualties in Albania were estimated at more than ninety
thousand and 60 per cent of that number was due to frozen limbs and
to sickness caused by what was regarded as famine because of inadequate supply services. In one sector called Monastery Hill because of
an ancient convent that had existed in the vicinity, an Italian division
lived on top of a hill throughout the winter, in trenches only four feet
deep that were exposed to constant cross fire from three surrounding
mountains. It was a vital link in the Italian defensive line and, had it
been taken by the Greeks, Valona and Tirana could not have been
defended. That division was reformed three times. At the end of the
war, fifteen thousand Italians had been killed or wounded on that
single spot.

As a sop to popular indignation, the press announced that the
Italian Foreign Minister had taken a leave of absence to fight at the
front. This "front" was a comfortable hotel in Bari, in the Italian
province of Apulia where Ciano made his headquarters with some of
his cronies, such as Alessandro Pavolini, Minister of Press, and Ettore
Muti, Secretary of the Party, their wives and several female friends.
Weather permitting, Ciano would pilot a bomber over Greek positions as wing leader of a squadron called "La Disperata," which was
named after a squad of Florentine Blackshirts who beat up and administered castor oil to socialists before the March on Rome. After

dropping his daily ratio of bombs, he would return to the hotel and spend the afternoon and evening playing bridge, smoking American cigarettes, drinking Scotch whiskey, or reading American magazines of which he was fond. That was his idea of fighting. His name disappeared from the newspapers for months, in hopes that, in time, people would forget about him. When reverses followed reverses, Badoglio resigned. Farinacci accused him of being responsible for the debacle in Albania. The Fascist Party started a whispering campaign to save its own skin and shift on to the elderly Italian Marshal, the popular anger and criticism that was rampant in Italy at the time. Badoglio wrote a letter to Farinacci, of which I have a copy, placing the responsibility squarely on the Government. He walked into Mussolini's office on December 9, and told the dictator that unless he stopped the whispering campaign, he would see that the real version of the Italian debacle would reach the Italian people. Badoglio was regarded as a hero by the Italians because of the masterly way in which he had directed the war in Ethiopia. Mussolini did not dare to antagonize him and bring out in the open the proofs of his own guilt. The campaign stopped. Not only that, an official communique was issued the same day which emphasized that "Il Duce received Marshal Badoglio in a formal call and entertained him in a cordial colloquy." The word, "cordial" was inserted to show the people that the military leader was not responsible for the reverses. It was also meant as a direct reply to Farinacci's slanderous editorial.

The Vatican kept an attitude of complete aloofness in the months following Italy's intervention. Pius was too experienced a statesman not to realize that nothing could arrest the spreading of the war. However, he made the views of the Holy See clear in regard to several problems. He exhorted all belligerent nations to humanize war by abstaining from indiscriminate bombing of the civilian populations, from the use of gases, and from persecution of the people in the occupied areas. Further, when Mussolini seemed bent on creating an "incident" because of the murder of Daut Hoxha, he had L'Osservatore Romano deplore the deliberate lies of the Fascist press whose attitude the Vatican newspaper termed "grave and severe." It was not more than a hint, but it indicated the sympathy of the Holy See for

Greece which was loyally striving to remain neutral. As a matter of fact, the Papal Secretariat of State knew in advance of Mussolini's plans to blackmail Athens. On August 7, three days before Stefani, the Italian official agency, reported the Tomori editorial that unleashed the press campaign against Greece, the Pontiff appealed indirectly to Mussolini in a speech delivered during a public audience granted to about one thousand people. He urged the abandonment of propaganda that fostered hatred among nations.

"Besides the writings that spread impiety and bad morals," he said, "we cannot omit to mention others that propagate falsehoods and cause hatred. Would God that history recorded no war provoked by an ably spread lie."

Another proof of Papal concern over Axis domination of Europe was had when Hitler announced his intention to create a "new order," which envisaged a federation of the European states under the aegis of Germany and Italy. A Vatican broadcast on September 16, scored "those who alleged they would be able to establish a new order in the world. Those who state this are preparing the destruction of the peoples whom they allegedly want to make happy. It is a world order which is as dry as the desert, an order which is the same order as the order of the desert. It is being achieved by the exploitation of human life. What these falsehoods call life is no life. It is dissolution—it is death."

In other pronouncements, the Vatican disclosed that Germany had refused to permit the Nuncio in Belgium, Monsignor Clemente Micara, to perform his "religious mission" and help prisoners and other unfortunates. L'Osservatore Romano pointed out that during the First World War when Belgium was also invaded by Germany, the same Monsignor Micara, who was secretary of the nunciature in Brussels, had been free to pursue welfare activities with satisfaction to the Belgian authorities and the Germans in occupation.

But the strongest stand against Nazism came in a broadcast of November 20. The Vatican speaker refuted a statement published by the Spanish newspaper, Alcazar, that National Socialism was not contradictory to Christian ideals. A survey of Hitler's anti-Christian policy since 1933, proved beyond all doubt, he said, that the assertion was false.

Nazi literature had attacked Christianity and the Catholic Church as a whole, as well as its personnel and institutions. It had even attacked the most essential dogmas of the Church. Religious education had been wiped out in a campaign carried out with the "greatest possible efficiency." Monasteries in Austria had been closed down; all the goods of the religious bodies had been confiscated; from German-occupied Poland alone four hundred priests had in those very days been brought into Germany.

"How can anyone assert that both within and without the Reich National Socialism has shown its respect for religion?" asked the Vatican.

In a homily he delivered on November 24 in St. Peter's, the Pope prayed for the establishment of "an order of things more just and more harmonious." The next day, Italian newspapers distorted the meaning of that passage. They called it a "fair and realistic remark," and printed an extensive summary of the sermon tending to give the impression that the papacy was supporting the Axis, which had contended all along that it was fighting for "living space" in a world whose wealth was controlled by the selfish democracies. L'Osservatore Romano tartly explained that the Pontiff had already made clear in previous pronouncements his views of the war, and stressed another passage of the homily which admonished nations "not to do to others what they would not want to have done to themselves," thus implying a condemnation of Axis invasion of European countries.

Still, in the latter half of 1940, relations between Italy and the Vatican, although strained by the war, had not yet degenerated to open hostility. At the beginning of the conflict, Mussolini felt he was winning, and, therefore, cared little as to what the Vatican said or did. Moreover, the Pope had been extremely correct as far as his political neutrality was concerned. He had always based his criticisms and reproaches on moral grounds in order to defend church principles and interests while leaving the Italian clergy free to collaborate with the armed forces. Even when the Axis had attempted—and failed—to draw Catholic Spain within its orbit, the Vatican had remained silent. Serrano Suner, Spanish foreign minister, had had meetings with Hitler and Mussolini at the end of August, but he had abstained from seeing the Pope. *L'Osservatore Romano* had merely noted the snub and let it go at that. Again, when the Axis was courting Soviet Russia in an attempt to make her adhere to the tripartite pact signed with Japan on September 27, 1940, the Vatican did not stir. The reason for this attitude was that the Pope did not wish to make worse the lot of Catholics in an Axis-dominated Europe by openly opposing Nazi and Fascist policy. He was powerless politically. England was fighting with her back to the wall; the United States was still outside the conflict and in the early stages of military preparedness. Thus there seemed to be no hope of halting the triumphant Italo-German coalition.

The Italian rapprochement with the Soviet early in November deserves to be stressed because it shows Mussolini's lack of all moral principles. The Fascist press, which less than a year before had inveighed againt Russia for her invasion of "little Finland," threw the usual political somersault, and warmly praised a speech made by Mikhail Ivanovitch Kalinin, chairman of the Russian Presidium, at the beginning of November.

It termed it "sober and energetic," and one newspaper emphasized that Kalinin could not have outlined in fewer words or in a more concise and eloquent manner such a realist policy which in one year of war "has succeeded in ensuring his country the greatest number of successes." Another editorial spoke of the continental bloc formed by Japan, Germany, and Italy, "together with their friend, the Soviet Union!"

An explanation for this cordial attitude was given by the German Embassy in Rome. Russia, I was assured, would sign an agreement with the tripartite powers before the end of the year.

Then came the reverses in Egypt which, coupled with Mussolini's bungling of the war against Greece, caused profound discouragement among the Italians. Popular anger against the Italian dictator was stronger than at any other period of his career, with the exception of the crucial fall and winter in 1924, after the assassination of the Socialist deputy, Giacomo Matteotti, by Il Duce's henchmen. In markets, streets, cafés, restaurants, everywhere I went, Fascism and its leader were openly criticized. Newsreels showing German victories and British defeats had to be withdrawn because audiences applauded at the wrong places, that is, when British troops appeared on the screen. The OVRA (Secret Political Police) listened and reported, but Mussolini was wise enough not to make matters worse by ordering wholesale arrests. Hitler had promised to help him in the spring, and so long as there was no organized opposition, he preferred to let the people have their emotional outlet until such time when the Greeks would be defeated.

Relations between the Fascist Government and the Vatican became worse at the beginning of 1941, as the Italians realized that what the officially inspired propaganda had maintained was being proven hollow by events. They began to regard the papacy, which had championed the cause of peace as the only power that could, perhaps, save them from complete ruin. They had been promised a short war, and its end, instead, was nowhere in sight. Nice, Savoy, Corsica, Jibuti, Suez, Tunisia, looked like mirages in a desert. Food shortage was becoming serious. Germans were pouring into Italy to help the battered Graziani army in Libya. Nazi soldiers and automobiles were seen everywhere in Rome, a visible proof of Italy's humiliating military inefficiency. Two German motorized divisions were shipped to North Africa, and the sending of this large force required a complex logistical organization that had its headquarters in many hotels of the capital and branches in the harbors of the South.

Germany had conquered Poland, Norway, Belgium, Holland, France. Italy had been beaten in Greece and in Libya, and was gradually losing her Ethiopian Empire. The Italian people wanted to know why they had been plunged into a war that had resulted only in shameful defeats and fruitless sacrifices. Such was their psychological reaction in that bleak 1940–41 winter. What was the use of fighting when one did not have the weapons and had to rely upon those of an ally? Not until they were faced with the naked truth about their unpreparedness did the Italians see the magnitude of Mussolini's blunder.

The strength and solidity of nations are tested in times of war when resources are strained to the utmost in the greatest effort made by all the social forces forming the collectivity. Italy collapsed morally that winter because nineteen years of Fascism had failed to bring about national unity. Italian intellectuals hated the regime so deeply that they saw in Italy's defeat, the only way to rid themselves of a system that had, in their opinion, caused only harm because it had been built to serve the ambition of one man—Mussolini. Today's Italian is by nature a pacifist. His philosophy of life in a nutshell is that man must work to live and not live to work. In other words, he regards his occupation as a means that enables him to pursue his inclinations. The peasant, for instance, works hard all week in order to spend Sunday afternoon with his fellow workers at the town's *osteria*, playing *boccie* and drinking wine. This peasant, who represents at least 70 per cent of Italy's population, has for centuries led a simple life and has to a certain extent kept himself aloof from the industrial revolution. Of course, there are two other classes: the aristocracy and the bourgeoisie. The aristocracy was anti-Fascist because many of its members were devoted to the Papacy and viewed with alarm the alliance with anti-Christian Nazism, which was contrary to their religious, sentimental, and cultural traditions.

The bourgeoisie, both middle and upper was overburdened with taxation as a result of the cost of the campaigns in Ethiopia, Spain, and, of course, the Second World War. To the middle-class Italian, whose life was perforce restricted because of his modest salary and low standard of living, Mussolini's ambitious schemes meant only more hardships and tightening of the belt. The Italians, naturally, would have liked to acquire territory and wealth, just as all other human beings, but their common sense and innate intelligence made them realize that Italy, because of her geographical position and lack of natural resources, could not hope to play the role of a world power in competition with empires of such magnitude as the British, the American, and even the German.

The Italian bourgeois, who was reared in the hatred of the Teuton whom he has fought for centuries and as late as the First World War, never fully accepted the alliance with Germany and the presence of soldiers in his country with swastika bands on their arms. However, in the earlier phases of the war, the dislike for the Nazi was tempered by admiration mingled with fear. Hitler's astounding military victories impressed even the least politically minded Italian.

Mussolini himself was a changed man that winter. I heard him deliver two speeches—one on November 18, and the other on February 23—which revealed the psychological crisis he was traversing. The pride, truculence, and assurance, as well as the smarting sarcasm and contempt for the democracies which characterized his prewar pronouncements, were absent. His popularity was gone and so was his faith in his political vision, his belief in his ability to keep Italy independent and, above all, his dreams of Mediterranean conquest. Anyone who had known and followed him realized that the swashbuckling supremely confident Duce had been replaced by a pavid, irresolute, bewildered man. He was apologizing for Italy's military defeats.

In nearly two decades of absolute control of the peninsula, Mussolini had failed to imbue his countrymen with the imperialist spirit so predominant among the Germans. The Ethiopian campaign in 1935 was decidedly unpopular at the beginning, and it was supported by the people only when the British Government decided to apply sanctions against Italy. Even after it was conquered Ethiopia meant very little to the average Italian. She was a strange and remote land. It took all the means at the disposal of Fascist propaganda machine to induce Italian farmers to settle there and, despite the expenditure of more than twenty billion lire (one billion dollars at the official prewar rate of exchange) Ethiopia was never a profitable enterprise for Italy.

The same lack of enthusiasm showed itself when the Italian dictator decided to intervene in the Spanish Civil War. Of course, there were youngsters who volunteered for service in Spain, but the majority of the people rued Italian intervention in the civil war because of the international tension that followed it. Their nerves were on edge after the serious crisis in European relations caused by the invasion of Ethiopia. When popular support failed, many Blackshirts were induced to leave Italy because they were told that they were going to Ethiopia. Mussolini had to resort to stratagems to send troops to

Franco's Spain. So, in the middle of the voyage, the ship just veered toward Spain. There, the soldiers who fought on Franco's side were paid an average of $1.50 and the officers $5 a day.

The last time I had a fleeting glimpse of Mussolini was in May of 1942 when he reviewed some troops in Rome's Via dell' Impero. Always plump, Il Duce was then definitely fat, so fat, indeed, that in the winter of 1941 he had stopped playing tennis and had also cut down his horseback riding. His 1935 double chin had become a triple chin; his clean-shaven head showed that his scant hair, if it were allowed to grow, would be white. His face which once was virile and forceful, was now flaccid.

The powerful dictator who in the summer of 1934 stopped Hitler's attempt to annex Austria by sending Italian divisions to the Brenner Pass had been forced since the beginning of the war to receive orders from von Mackensen, the German ambassador to Rome. Mussolini still ruled Italy, of course, because in twenty years of his regime he had been able to secure control of all the forces of the State. But his power was based only on the support of a comparatively small group of men who knew that his fall would spell their own doom. This minority had fought a losing battle not only on the international but the domestic front, because the Italian people had shown apathy toward the war, lack of confidence in their leaders, dislike for the Nazi ally and, above all, an unbreakable resistance to the Fascist doctrine of force and Mussolini's policy of aggression.

In his November 1940 speech Mussolini acknowledged the country's desire for peace and warned that "certain universalistic pacifism of unbalanced minds is being watched and fought; it is out of order in this effort of steel and cannon." In his February speech, he urged the people to nurse a feeling of "cold, conscious, implacable hatred against the enemy in every heart and every home, for it is an indispensable element to victory." That speech was the start for a campaign against the clergy, who refused to accept the dictatorial command to foment hatred. In January, 1941, two Catholic weeklies published in Padua and Udine were suppressed on the ground that they were writing pacifist propaganda. The distribution of the text of a prayer for peace, which was contained in a speech that the Pope delivered to the

Roman patriciate and nobility on January 5, was forbidden because it spoke of a "just and durable peace." Monsignor Giovanni Cazzani, Bishop of Cremona, who issued a pastoral letter in March stating that "war is the punishment of God to nations that abandon the Christian faith and deny the existence of the Lord to embrace idolatry," was warned not to deliver similar sermons in the future. Fascists seized all copies of the letter which was printed by a local press.

In contrast with Mussolini's campaign of hatred, the Pope, however, continued to advocate peace in every public utterance. Orders went out from the Vatican to the Catholic press to fight what prelates termed "anti-Christian feelings." The official newspaper of the Italian Catholic Action of the University Students was seized and suspended for one month in March 1941 because it condemned hatred as a "base feeling" and urged its readers "to silence those who speak words of hatred because they bring dishonor to the country." L'Osservatore Romano itself joined the battle with editorials that appeared from time to time throughout that year. In one article it stressed that "there is no need to foment hatred which poisons the spirit and deadens the generosity of heroism."

These were the first ominous rumblings of a tension that was to lead to an unofficially declared war between the Vatican and Fascism.

FIFTEENTH CHAPTER

Shefket Verlaci, Albanian premier, Selim Mborja, Secretary of the Albanian Fascist Party, Mileq Bushatti, minister of the interior, and several members of the so-called Albanian Parliament, were received by Mussolini on January 13. They had asked to see the Italian dictator because the internal situation in Albania was very grave. Koritza and Argirocastro had fallen into Greek hands, thousands of Albanian refugees had poured into Tirana, aggravating the already acute food shortage and housing problem. Malcontent was widespread. The hatred which the people had nursed for the Italians was increased tenfold by the war reverses on their soil. As a consequence the puppet Albanian Government was very unpopular.

Two hours after the audience, a member of the Albanian delegation met Edda and gave her a full account of it.

Verlaci, as premier, was the spokesman for the group. He told Mussolini that he wanted to resign. The position of his government was indefensible, he explained, because the people were blaming it for the debacle.

Mussolini pulled a detailed map of Albania from a drawer, spread it over his desk, asked the delegation to gather around him, and proceeded to show that the Italian Army held key defensive positions, which the Greeks could not hope to capture. This is the gist of what he said.

"We are securely entrenched here. You must not fear any further Greek advances. Tirana will not be conquered. In the spring, the Germans will come to our aid and start an offensive against Greece from the North."

"I don't see how it can be done," Verlaci replied. "I know the Yugoslavs and am sure that they will not allow either you or the Germans to go through their territory."

"You'll see that I am right," Mussolini retorted. "Do not fear. We shall beat Greece. Therefore, I don't want you to resign."

Mussolini was right, except in one thing. It was not Italy that beat Greece, but Germany. The maximum Italian penetration on Greek soil when the armistice was signed in April 1941, was four miles in only one sector! Verlaci could not know, of course, that Germany would force Bulgaria to allow the passage of the Nazi Army in the spring, and that she would invade Yugoslavia. As a matter of fact, Mussolini himself knew only of the German plans in regard to Bulgaria.

The Belgrade coup d'etat on March 27, which ousted the Cincar Markovitch government was as much of a surprise to him as it was to Hitler.

"Accounts from all over Yugoslavia say that the country has accepted the announcement of the Yugoslav participation in the system of reconstruction with general tranquillity and calm," wrote Turin's *Gazzetta del Popolo* the very same day the revolution broke out in Belgrade. Everyone of the Fascist morning newspapers followed a similar line. The editorials had been written the day before, when Markovitch had signed in Berlin the protocol pledging Yugoslavia's adhesion to the Tripartite Pact.

As Hitler smashed Yugoslavia in less than two weeks, overran Greece in three, routed the British Expeditionary Army dispatched to Athens' aid, and conquered Crete, the Holy See watched with anxious eyes the trend of American politics. Whenever I went to the Vatican, prelates would ask me for the latest news from the United States. The prevailing opinion then was that England could not win the war alone. The only hope for the salvation of Christian civilization, I was told, was American intervention. An influential prelate handed me a fifteen-thousand-word report, which reached the Vatican at the end of July, describing the anti-religious persecution that Hitler had lauched in Slovenia, one of Yugoslavia's regions. For its brutality and ferocity, it was equal to, if not worse than, the one in Poland.

The Slovenes belong to the Slav race, along with the Croats, Serbians, Bulgarians, Czechs, Slovaks, Poles, Ruthenians (Ukrainians) Russians. They are among the most civilized European peoples. At the end of the First World War, Slovenia was divided among three countries: Yugoslavia, 6,096 square miles with 1,165,000 inhabitants; Italy, 2,306 square miles with 420,000; Austria, 1,374 square miles with 98,000. In addition, there are 11,000 Slovenes in Hungary, while 440,000 have emigrated to other continents, especially the United States, so that the whole race totals about 2,100,000 people. The Slovenes in Yugoslavia were 94 per cent Catholic. Before the German invasion, the diocese of Maribor consisted of 654,000 souls, with 254 parishes, 474 members of the secular clergy, and 109 of the regular clergy. The diocese of Lubliana totaled 565,000 inhabitants, with 275 parishes held by 546 secular and 175 regular clergymen. The Italians occupied some of that territory, with 350,000 inhabitants, and the Germans the rest with 215,000 people.

In less than three months, the Gestapo had arrested, killed or expelled six-sevenths of the clergy from the diocese of Maribor. Of the 254 parishes, 91 were held by a single priest, the others had been closed or taken over by the authorities. In the district of Ptuj, for example, which had thirty parishes with fifty-seven priests and eighty thousand Catholics, there remained only three clergymen, two of whom had already retired from active duty because of old age, so that only one, fifty-seven years old, was carrying on the apostolate.

In the diocese of Lubliana, the territory occupied by the Germans had 128 parishes with 215,000 faithful. At the end of June 1941, 137 priests had been thrown in jail, 74 expelled, and 37 others had fled. That left only nine priests for a population of 215,000!

Franz Steindl, who was appointed head of the Nazi political organization after the end of the war with Yugoslavia, announced on May 10, Hitler's order to him: "Germanize these territories."

Consequently, Steindl not only began to stamp out religion, but he arrested and expelled all Slovene intellectuals, closed their universities and schools, and confiscated property which was subsequently assigned to Germans brought from the Reich. Before the war, Slovenia boasted of a university, academy of science and arts, conservatory of music, eighteen preparatory schools (gymnasiums and lyceums) with thirteen thousand students; six schools for teachers; forty-six schools for craftsmanship; and eight hundred sixty-eight elementary schools, in addition to professional, technical, commercial, agrarian schools, two theological seminaries, and the like. These various institutes were frequented by two hundred thousand students. There was no illiteracy in Slovenia.

Teaching in elementary schools was resumed at the end of May but in the German language. It was made compulsory for all boys from ten to fourteen years of age. German teachers replaced Slovenes, and proceeded to Nazify the youth. The daily four-hour course began with the ceremony of the salute to the Nazi flag, followed by the song of the Hitler Youth which was sung by the whole class. The second part of the program included gymnastic exercise and the teaching of German warlike songs. The third hour was dedicated to the teaching of the German language by means of a specially devised pictorial system since the Slovene youth does not understand German. At the end, the boys witnessed the ceremony of the lowering of the Nazi flag and sang again the Hitler Youth song.

To give an idea of the system adopted by the Nazi authorities to smash the Catholic organizations in a few weeks, I shall relate two of the many episodes listed in the report.

At 11 P.M. a group of Gestapo agents, between twenty and twenty-four years of age, arrived at the Convent of the Ursuline Sisters in Mekinje, near Kamnik. They demanded dinner, molested some of the younger nuns, drank copiously, and at about two o'clock of the following morning announced that the convent was sequestrated. They gave the terrorized sisters two hours in which to pack up their belongings. At 4:30 A.M., a bus took the nuns to another convent in Sticna, a few miles away, while the Nazi authorities decided what should be done with them.

In Maribor eight Gestapo agents and a woman entered the refectory of the Franciscan fathers while the latter were having dinner. The leader of the group ordered everybody to fall into line while the woman recorded their names. The fathers were told to take one blanket, a spoon, and a glass each, and were confined to the Melje barracks. As this was going on, German workers arrived at the convent and began to adapt it for the use of the German authorities. According to the report, everyone of the convents and monasteries and religious houses were sequestrated.

As to the Slovene youth, the Germans while educating the children to the Nazi creed, in some cases went to the extreme of sterilizing youngsters by artificial radiations. The report mentions Jesenice and Jezersko as two of the towns where this type of Nazi brutality was recorded. Moreover, pretty girls were told they would be sent to work in German factories. Fearing that this might conceal base motives, they hastened to marry Slovene boys. The number of weddings increased to such an extent that the Germans in some of the occupied towns forbade further marriages.

The Nazi policy of de-Christianization was carried out in other countries, such as the Netherlands, which Hitler obviously intended to incorporate in the Reich. A pastoral letter dated August 15, 1941, which was read in all the Churches of Holland on August 24, disclosed that the Germans had abolished religious teaching in schools, reduced the salary of clergymen by 40 per cent, and disbanded organizations such as the Catholic Boy Scouts, the Young Guard, the Crusade, as well as the Catholic Workers' League. The letter, which was signed by J. de Jong, Archbishop of Utrecht; P. A. U. Hopmans, Bishop of Breda; A. F. Diepens, Bishop of Bois-le-Duc; J. H. J. Lemmens, Bishop of Ruremonde; J. P. Huijbers, Bishop of Haarlem, forbade the clergy to give communion to all Netherland Catholics who belonged to the Nazi party or to Nazi-controlled organizations. A similar situation existed in the Reich proper where on July 6, the German bishops published a collective pastoral letter in which they stated that "the existence or the suppression of Christianity in the German Church is at stake."

No wonder, therefore, that the news of Germany's attack on Russia, June 23, was described by the Vatican as the most encouraging anti-Nazi development since the beginning of the war. By shifting his war machine to the east, Hitler, according to the Holy See, had implicitly admitted that he could not beat England. The Vatican hoped that the German-Soviet war would give the British Empire and the United States time to strengthen their military preparations.

Italy, as it was to be expected, joined Germany against Russia. Mussolini deluded himself into thinking that the Vatican would support his decision, and told Bernardo Attòlico, Italian ambassador to the Holy See, to urge upon Pius a public endorsement of what the Axis press described as "a crusade against Communism."

Attòlico saw Maglione to whom he suggested that the Pope send a letter to all Catholic bishops in the world with instructions to encourage the formation of volunteer forces to fight the Soviet. I have not been able to ascertain what Maglione's reply was, but subsequent events left no doubt as to the Pope's attitude. Still, Mussolini had hopes that Pius would agree to some gesture of solidarity because when *L'Osservatore Romano* published the news that the Pontiff would speak on June 29, which was the feast of the Saints Peter and Paul, the Fascist press gave prominence to the announcement. This was very unusual. As far as I can recall, a papal speech had never been publicized in advance. Moreover, the government-controlled radio station made arrangements to broadcast the speech simultaneously with the Vatican station. It was clear, therefore, that the Fascist Government intended to draw the attention of the people to the Vatican.

Pius' address, although it dealt a great deal with the war, contained not even an indirect reference to the Axis-Soviet conflict. Mussolini was furious. He realized that the Pope's refusal was in itself a proof of the concern with which the Vatican viewed a Nazi victory. This was all the more apparent since Communism was admittedly the arch foe of the Church. A high prelate who cannot be further identified for obvious reasons, explained what, in his opinion, were the reasons that had induced the Holy See to remain aloof from the German-Soviet war.

"Atheist Bolshevism," he said, "is less preoccupying for the reason that, although it has forcibly eliminated God, man cannot live without believing in a superior being. On the other hand, Nazism has replaced God with a pagan theory which, though it does not meet his spiritual needs, yet gives him something to look up to.

"When the time of reconstruction comes, it will be more difficult for the Church to eradicate the false neo-pagan theory of the Nazis from the consciousness of the masses than to instill in the soul of the atheist the belief in God, for this belief will answer a natural craving of man's soul, while the neo-pagan masses may not feel it equally strongly."

Of course, the Vatican did not underestimate the danger represented by the spreading of Communism through Russia's victory in Europe. Yet, being a conservative force, the help of which is invaluable during a period of postwar reconstruction, it felt that both the United States and England would find it to their advantage to collaborate with the Church. Theoretically Communism and Nazism are anathema to the Holy See. But between the two evils, the papacy up to the time I was in Italy, felt that Hitler was a far more deadly enemy than Stalin. For one thing, he had control of the whole of Europe and was winning in Russia. The Vatican thought that, even if the Nazis should, in the long run, be beaten, devastation brought by the war on Russian soil and the losses in wealth and men would monopolize for many years the attention of the Soviet political leaders who would thus have no time or opportunity to foster the spreading of Communism in the international field. Had Hitler won, however, he would have been in a position to consolidate the work of de-Christianization that Nazism had been vigorously pursuing since the beginning of the conflict in all the subjugated countries. This, I was told, was the practical and realistic outlook, which was, of course, in contrast with the theoretical principles. But in analyzing Vatican policy, or any other policy for that matter, one must always distinguish between theory and practice. Of all the world powers, the Church is the one which, though maintaining absolute rigidity as far as its religious tenets are concerned, has shown the greatest elasticity in the field of practical politics. Being a universal organization, it adapts its policy to the particular circumstances, and its methods vary in accordance with the given environment.

A case in point is that of Spain. The papacy had been accused of supporting Fascism because the Spanish clergy sided with Franco and the Vatican gave the Insurgents its moral support, during the Spanish Civil War. The Vatican never concealed its sympathies for the Spanish dictator, but it always denied that it was in favor of one ideology as against another. In an earlier chapter, I tried to explain how Pius XI backed Franco in Spain and fought Hitler tooth and nail in Germany. But this policy was not due to a desire to foster the Fascist ideology. To the Holy See, Franco represented the man who was defending the Church in Spain, and the only objective of Vatican policy, as I have already stated, is that of spreading Catholicism and obtaining for its religious bodies favorable working conditions. True, this aim sometimes coincides with those of governments that are totalitarian in character, and therefore, in contrast with the fundamental concepts of democracy. But what does this prove? Can anyone deny that many Latin-American "republics" are undiluted dictatorships? Still the Church was persecuted in Mexico under dictator Plutarco Elias Calles' regime and prospered in every other country in the Western Hemisphere. Pius XII himself collaborated very closely with President Roosevelt, the head of a democratic nation overwhelmingly Protestant, which was fighting Italy and Germany!

What is often forgotten is that the Church is willing to collaborate with any government that will ensure it the possibility of carrying out its apostolic mission, and that it combats ideologies when their practical application harms religious interests. It fought Hitler, but it collaborated with Mussolini when the latter's policy did not affect the Catholic faith. It did not hesitate to fight Mussolini when his policy hampered the work of the Church.

Having realized that the Vatican, far from supporting him, had clearly shown that it considered Fascism one of its enemies, Mussolini took reprisals. He placed the Vatican under strict surveillance. Policemen were posted outside its gates, and reported on all visitors to the Holy See. Secret informants, found among the lay Vatican employees, watched the movements of prelates. Since the telephone exchange of the Holy See is connected with the Italian system, OVRA agents listened in on telephone conversations. Vatican mail was opened, and its contents photographed.

Under these conditions, the coverage of Vatican news became a difficult assignment. Correspondents were forced to adopt the methods of secret agents themselves so as not to jeopardize the personal safety of their informants. Matthews and I communicated with our

Vatican sources by means of letters signed with an alias and delivered by hand. Since the anti-American feeling in official quarters was becoming daily more acute because of Roosevelt's open pro-British policy, I stopped going to the Vatican altogether. Americans were regarded as unofficial enemies by the Fascists and any Italian seen with me was courting trouble. I would set an appointment with our informants for late at night, when Rome's strict blackout made detection almost impossible. We would walk in the dark, through solitary streets, in the vicinity of the Vatican, and before leaving we would agree on the time and place for the next meeting.

Another system used was to meet in the house of an anti-Fascist friend early in the afternoon, when the janitor of the building was having his siesta. This could not be done very often because it was rather dangerous both to our informant and our friend, most janitors having instructions from the OVRA to keep a close watch on the tenants and to report on all visitors. Despite these conditions, our sources would willingly co-operate because they were anxious to make the attitude of the Vatican towards the conflict clear to the democracies.

Italy was not the only power that wished to have the support of the Holy See in the war. The United States was keenly interested in knowing what the attitude of the Pope was in regard to the Axis-Soviet conflict. Harold Tittman, who was attached to the office of Myron C. Taylor, saw the Pope and Cardinal Maglione the first week in July. Those two audiences were never officially announced. Tittman, from what was said at the time, conveyed a State Department suggestion that the Holy See abstain from gestures which might be construed as favorable to the Axis in its war against the Soviet. Both Pius and Maglione were stated to have given satisfactory assurances, since the attitude of the Vatican on this particular question coincided with that of the powers hostile to Germany.

The similarity of views held by both the Pope and Roosevelt in regard to the European war made even closer the already very cordial relations existing between the two leaders. Taylor, who had returned to the United States the previous fall to recuperate from a serious illness, suddenly came back to his post in September. He was the bearer of a Presidential message to the Pope, the contents of which were not divulged. Yet, one of *The Times'* informants who had excellent contacts with the Secretariat of State gave us a version which I was told was substantially accurate. I could never get official confirmation of it because both the Vatican and the State Department had not at the end of 1943, made public diplomatic documents that could throw light on the status of their relations.

Roosevelt, according to this version, asked the Pontiff to issue a statement that would encourage Catholics throughout the world to support Great Britain and Russia in the war they were waging against Nazism. The President was said to have pointed out that the American Catholics were disoriented at the moment, since they regarded the German-Russian struggle as that of two powers, both of which were hostile to the Church. As a consequence, their interest in a British victory was waning because it would also mean a Russian victory, which they feared as much as a German victory. An indication from the Vatican, showing that it regarded Nazism at that particular moment a much graver threat than Communism would, in the President's opinion, help considerably to solidify the pro-democratic feeling in the United States.

The Pontiff meditated his answer for five days. His reply was given to our office as negative on September 16. The gist of it, it was explained, was that the Vatican, being a body that represented interests of Catholics of all nations, could not take sides in a war that involved Catholics in both camps. The following days, Vatican sources gave me a more detailed explanation of the Pope's stand, which was in keeping with the tradition of the Church.

It is a well-known fact that the Roman Catholic faith condemns violence as an end in itself but does not exclude the defense of legitimate interests. St. Augustine, whose views are still basically those of the Church today, asserts that war is a "divine deed" and abstains from judging whether it is "good or bad." It is a secret of God. In his opinion, God uses war to punish those who are guilty, to test man, and to purify all. It is an instrument of the Divine Providence because it awakens dormant energies and gives new impetus to man's idealistic aspirations. Soldiers are not murderers because they do not avenge private injuries. They are the defenders of the law, and, therefore, of the welfare of the community.

War, however, must be condemned when it is fought for "greed" and it originates from "lust for conquest," when, in other words, it is fought not for the defense of the interests of the nation but for domination of other countries.

"The spirit of the Gospel," said a Vatican broadcast on September 23, "is not to be confounded with an unconditional pacifism. Places will occur where not only it is permitted, but where it is a duty to resist with force the invasion of an unjust aggressor.

"More than that, it may be a duty to wage war for the vindication of a vital right that has been wantonly violated by an enemy nation. Any contrary principle would guarantee impunity to tyrants, robbers, or those for whom the might of arms makes right, and who condemn the law-abiding to an intolerable labor.

"Far removed from that criminal weakness is the genuine spirit of Christianity, that to defend and to bring to triumph the order of justice and morality has been always foremost, and whose glory it has been to offer the blood of her beloved to defend that order.

"Nor must we today be too quick to dismiss the idea that a modern state would wage war for the precise purpose of destroying those principles of law and morality that Christian culture has given to mankind. When that is the case, we all have the duty to go out and meet all the agonies of war. They will, after all, be far less than the collapse of Christian civilization."

In this conception of the war one may find the key to the attitude of the Vatican in the present conflict. Although the Pope has abstained from taking sides, he has on several occasions—as I have attempted to show—condemned the Axis on doctrinal grounds. He has not, of course, specifically singled out the powers which, in the opinion of the Church, are guilty of having unleashed the conflict. The reason must be found in the fact that there are Catholics in every one of the belligerent nations. A papal condemnation of one side would without doubt have serious repercussions among the Catholics of the power or powers condemned. It would not only assume an extremely important political significance, but it would be used by the nations exonerated from the accusation as a powerful means of propaganda to undermine the morale of their enemies. The clergy of the accused party would be placed before the grave dilemma of either declaring the Pope wrong or of reneging their country. The Pope, then, would have discriminated between "innocent" Catholics and "guilty" Catholics. Although it is impossible to foresee what the aftermath of that situation would be, it is easy to imagine that the moral solidarity of the accused Catholics with the Vatican would be shaken. In any case, the consequences would be very grave, since it cannot be excluded that the individual today often feels that he is first a citizen and then a Catholic, and places the interests of his country at war before those of his Church.

When a nation goes to war, it wants to win. The heat of battle unleashes passions that develop nationalist spirit to its most acute form. But, in moments of despair, when everything seems lost, man looks for supra-human help. It is then that he draws nearer to his Church to find solace for his unhappiness. The Italian people certainly did not want to go to war. Tired of many years of war in Ethiopia and in Spain as well as of international tension, they wanted to be left alone. They followed with unreserved support the Vatican diplomatic activity in behalf of peace. Moreover, the ingrained dislike they harbored for the Teuton ally made it even more difficult for the Fascist regime to stir up enthusiasm. But when they were in the fighting, and they were winning, moral considerations were superseded by the mirage of physical gains which they hoped to attain by victory.

In a speech delivered on October 6, 1940—when Italy was winning —to the girl members of the Italian Catholic Association, Pius remarked that even in Italy "indifference to God and divine things was noticeable."

"Believing themselves, through having conquered the greatest goods here below, that they are less immediately dependent on a sovereign Lord," he said, "ungrateful men forget that all is a gift from God—even the forces of nature that they have conquered, as well as their intellect and strength which are the means of their success and their victories."

In the case of the Italians, success was short-lived, however. An intelligent, laborious, humane, very civilized people, they had none of the martial-like spirit of the Germans and no ambition to dominate the world. Unlike the First World War, which was truly felt and supported by the whole nation, the one they found themselves in, in 1940, they regarded as a war of their Fascist ruling class—the war of a minority which had imposed its will over the majority and failed to convince it.

When the reverses came, they looked at the priest, who had been advocating peace, as their friend. They manifested their solidarity with, and interest in, the activity of the Holy See in many ways. Papal speeches and pronouncements were read and commented upon in the large city as well as in the village. When L'Osservatore Romano was found inadequate as a means for the dissemination of the Pontiff's constant appeals for peace, a group of parish priests started a sheet called La Parola del Papa (Word of the Pope). This small-sized newspaper carried no editorial comment. It merely published papal speeches, whenever they were made. It started with a circulation of five thousand copies, in the summer of 1941, and by the time I left Italy, in May 1942, it had topped the two hundred thousand mark. One of its editors whom I was able to meet during my five months of internment in Siena, told me that the Parola del Papa was sent to parish priests throughout Italy, who distributed it among the faithful. In this way, the masses were kept fully informed of the activity of the Pope, and the favorable reaction to his entreaties for peace gave the Church an accurate picture of the national feeling toward the conflict.

Petty Fascist hierarchs in small provincial towns and villages attempted to stop the distribution of that newspaper. They arrested priests as "defeatists" and sent them to the "confino." But the pacifist feeling was gaining ground steadily, and La Parola del Papa was expected to reach a circulation of five hundred thousand copies by the end of 1942.

SIXTEENTH CHAPTER

The week before Pearl Harbor, the Japanese diplomatists in Rome launched a strong let's-be-friends drive which had as its objective the American newspapermen and the members of the United States Embassy. They probably did not know themselves that their ships had already left Japan to attack the United States' base in the Pacific when they were showering us with invitations to "six o'clock" teas. My impression is that the Germans and the Italians in Rome did not know. They professed to be as surprised as we Americans were to hear of Pearl Harbor. That treacherous attack smashed overnight all their carefully planned diplomacy to keep the United States out of the war until Russia was beaten and Europe built into what they hoped would be an impregnable fortress.

I remember the German correspondents, already gloomy over the failure of their armies to smash decisively Russian military strength after a full-scale summer campaign, huddling into a corner of the Foreign Press Club to discuss the situation with their Japanese allies. One of them came over to me as I was debating with some American colleagues whether the United States would extend the declaration of war to include Germany and Italy, or prefer to fight Japan alone.

"I want to say good-bye to you," this German whispered as he drew me aside—he was anti-Nazi and had given me some pretty good information from time to time, but, after all, as he had many times explained, one has to live. "We shall declare war on the United States within the week. We can't do anything else. We hope to win before you become too strong. We think that your naval power in the Pacific has been smashed and that the Japanese will be able to keep you busy until we can liquidate Russia."

I remember the affable, smiling, and living example of Japanese hypocrisy and treachery, Yoshiniori Maeda, correspondent of the *Asahi*, a rabid nationalist who even despised his German colleagues as members of an "inferior race," walking into the office of *The New*

York *Times* the day after Pearl Harbor "to sell" us the story that Italy was not going to declare war on the United States.

"I have just conversed with the Japanese Ambassador," he told Herbert Matthews and me, "who has had the honor of being received by His Excellency, the Foreign Minister Count Ciano, this afternoon, and His Excellency told him that Italy will make no hostilities against the United States."

He was the same man who, exactly seven days before, had approached us with a broad, friendly grin. "I am sorry to displease you while you are working," he had said. "My chancellor wishes you to make him the honor of partaking the tea at six o'clock, Wednesday, December 3, within his home."

Matthews and I had looked at each other. Then Matthews had replied: "You may tell you chancellor that we shall come if possible."

Next morning we told our Embassy people about the invitation. Colonel Norman Fiske, the shrewd military attaché who was worrying the Italians because of the military information he was able to gather in Italy, had remarked, "I received an invitation myself from the Japanese military attaché. It's for Saturday."

Captain Laurence McNair, the naval attaché who seemed to know the position of every Italian warship at any given moment, had blithely added, "Me too, Friday, from the naval attaché."

The following Monday, we further learned, several of the United States Embassy secretaries were to go to the Japanese Ambassador's home.

The general feeling among the Americans in Rome was that the Japanese were afraid. Their invitations were taken as an indication that the worried Tokyo Government was attempting to propitiate Americans in a desperate effort to avert war. After all, negotiations between Cordell Hull and Saburo Kurusu were continuing in Washington, and, according to the daily radio bulletins received at the United States Embassy, Washington was taking a strong stand. We went around feeling rather cocky and superior to our yellow-skinned colleagues, who, on the other hand, must have been laughing at us. It was a mistake in psychology of the kind the democratic powers had been making for many years before the outbreak of the war because they had underestimated their enemies.

The party in honor of the American correspondents was lavish. The chancellor was very charming, although he did not quite succeed in hiding the fact that the "six o'clock tea" was an excuse to get us drunk. On several tables of the dimly lit, over-furnished apartment there was enough liquor to keep us in an unconscious state for a month. Prominently displayed I saw bottles of a very expensive brand of whiskey. In Italy whiskey cost thirty dollars a bottle those days, and it was getting scarcer by the minute. On another table there were bottles of champagne, rum, gin, rye, and an assortment of Italian liqueurs including Strega and Benedictine. No trace of tea.

One of the Japanese offered me a drink. It was the strongest cocktail I ever tasted in my life. It must have been 99 per cent gin and one per cent vermouth. I put the glass down.

"What, no drink?" asked the alert chancellor.

"If you don't mind, I'd rather wait awhile," I said.

"Of course."

The Japanese wanted to know a great many things from us. Did we think that the United States would go to war? Were the isolationist forces strong? What did we think of Roosevelt? How was production going? The Axis would never win the war? Yes?

Whatever Matthews, Massock, Eleanor and Reynolds Packard, and I said was welcomed with polite smiles and a guttural coughlike laugh which was to signify appreciation and interest. The slant-eyed chancellor was speaking of the United States with such a feeling of friendliness and admiration that one would have thought he was a fifth-columnist working for the democracies to undermine the Italian morale. As time went on our Japanese colleagues, who had wasted no time in swallowing several cocktails and were now gradually liquidating the whiskey, became more and more friendly. I was slapped repeatedly on the back amidst peals of laughter for something which the Japanese thought was very funny. It was a friendly atmosphere, indeed.

Then as we were getting a little fed up, one of us asked a Japanese correspondent, "if it came to a showdown, do you think the American fleet could beat the Japanese fleet?"

In one instant, the mask of friendliness vanished. Eyes flashed and mouths, which had been laughing at the slightest provocation, closed in two rigid lines.

"I think that not even the American and British fleets together can beat our navy," was the haughty reply.

Packard, who had been phoning, saved the situation by saying that he had to go down to the office to write a story. We all started leaving.

"I am sure that we shall be able to patch up our little differences," the chancellor said as he was escorting us to the door. "The Japanese people don't want any quarrel with the United States."

We said good-bye.

"No, not good-bye," the chancellor said, bowing. "We shall see each other soon again."

It was four days before Pearl Harbor.

The day after the United States declared war on Japan, I found that Vatican officials, while chagrined over the fact that the conflict had become world-wide, realized that American intervention was the only hope for the restoration of freedom to the enslaved European continent.

"Today, the Axis has lost the war," was the way a prelate summed up the general impression.

Because of its information service represented by the periodical reports of bishops and diplomatic representatives throughout the world, the Vatican was fully acquainted with American potential and actual strength. It did not doubt for a moment, therefore, that the United States would prove to be as decisive a factor in World War II as it was in World War I.

The Secretariat of State, where the reports are read and filed, is composed of no more than thirty officials and clerks who, despite the fact that they dedicate a great deal of their time to prayer and spiritual matters, are distinguished for their highly trained minds and realistic outlook on temporal problems. Its quarters were originally mere attics on top of the Apostolic Palace. They were adapted as "temporary" offices in 1870, when the Secretariat, which was housed in the Consulta Palace, next to the Quirinal in Rome, was transferred to the Vatican as a consequence of Italy's seizure of Rome.

Less than forty-eight hours after Pearl Harbor, the Vatican had already been informed by the nunciature in Berlin that Hitler would honor the tripartite pact signed the previous September and join his eastern ally in the war against the United States. Monsignor Borgongini Duca, nuncio to Italy, had also made inquiries in Italian official circles and his information indicated that Mussolini would follow his partner's lead.

* * *

From the way the German correspondents at the bar stared at me, I knew I was entering Rome's Foreign Press Club for the last time. There could be no mistake. The day about which I had been forewarned had come. Hitler and Mussolini were to declare war simultaneously against the United States. The Japanese correspondents were all smiles. They were fraternizing with the Germans and probably gloating over Pearl Harbor. One who always had professed he favored Japanese-American understanding greeted me as I climbed the stairs to the first floor. I could think of nothing to say.

On the first floor were the members' mailboxes, working rooms, and telephone booths for long distance calls. It was noon and only a few newsmen were busy writing. Four ushers sat around, idle. I had known them for years, and they had done me a thousand favors; they had paid my taxes, the electric light and telephone bills; they had bought me cigarettes, drinks, and newspapers. All I did was to supply the money and they took care of the rest. They were so obliging that they had become almost indispensable. I liked them and they had shown a discreet preference for me over the other American correspondents, probably because I spoke their Roman dialect. Before me, they had served my father when he was United Press manager in Rome.

I opened my mailbox and took out a lot of useless papers—old clippings, photos, communiques, newspapers—which had piled up over a period of many years. I glanced at the ushers, and I sensed that they, too, knew. The Germans must have told them. They just stared at me and kept silent. They were afraid of being reported, although war had not yet been declared.

What I was doing was a familiar sight to them. They had seen the French, British, Dutch, Belgian, Russian, and Polish correspondents clean out their mailboxes, too, when Hitler had invaded one country after another and Mussolini had been forced to obey the dictates of his master and declare war in turn.

I sorted my papers, then I went over and placed a hundred lire bill on the ushers' desk. "Have a drink on me, tonight, just for old times' sake," I said.

Via della Mercede was as usual. It did not seem possible that on a day when my whole life was going to be changed by the decision of one man, things and people around me should have the same familiar aspect. Across the narrow street, the wizened old woman was still selling newspapers piled on a small wooden bench against a wall. She smiled at me, but, of course, she did not know. The café around the corner at Piazza San Silvestro was as crowded as usual. I ordered an Americano—a drink made of vermouth and bitters with a dash from a syphon. Only in Italy is it known by that name, and I had never been able to find out how it got that title. The bartender asked me whether the Lazio was going to beat the Roma next Sunday in what promised to be the season's best soccer match. The war to him was only a side show.

On the Corso, Rome's main street, I felt that things were going to happen. Romans were converging on Piazza Venezia from all sections of the town. Small groups followed their Fascist leaders like so many sheep. It was a familiar sight which repeated itself every time a so-called "spontaneous" demonstration was scheduled for Mussolini. It was almost one o'clock when I walked on to Piazza Venezia.

The beautiful square was about half full. Most of the crowd was milling beneath the balcony of Palazzo Venezia where Mussolini would appear. It was a typical Roman December day, almost warm, with a clear sky. I made my way through soldiers, Blackshirts, civilians, women, students, and policemen. It was an unusually quiet crowd save for a few hundred students who were having the time of their lives. For them, it was literally a Roman holiday. They held banners aloft showing caricatures of Roosevelt and Churchill. One pictured Roosevelt on a throne and wearing an emperor's crown. A Fascist was clubbing him on the head. The caption underneath said: "Down with Del—ano." The splitting of the President's name has a vulgar meaning in Italian and had been adopted with great relish by the Fascist press. Another cartoon depicted Churchill, with the big red nose of a typical drunkard, reclining on a couch with a cigar in his mouth and a bottle of whiskey in his hand while on a corner British soldiers silhouetted against a desert landscape were being killed by stalwart Fascists in hand-to-hand fighting. The caption said: "Churchill at work."

I took a place almost directly under the balcony. I wanted to have a good look at Mussolini. Two army officers were on my right, one of them with crutches, probably wounded during the war with Greece. On my left stood two dark-haired girls of the working class. They were enjoying the antics of the students. It was a real show for them, better than the movies.

It was almost one thirty, and the people were becoming impatient. Someone started clapping and the throng joined in as in a theater when the performance is delayed. The students chanted "Du—Chay, Du—Chay." It was not applause. It was a signal for Mussolini to hurry up because in the square below there were twenty thousand people who had had to forfeit their lunch in order to form a crowd that would give him an excuse for speaking. A band of the Fascist militia grouped on the left corner of the palazzo sought to keep the crowd quiet by playing Mascagni's beautiful *Hymn to Rome*.

Well after two, Mussolini came out. The people shouted and applauded. When the band played *Giovinezza* everyone stood at attention. Then the roar again swelled the square. Mussolini leaned with his hands on the edge of the balcony and looked at the crowd. He did not smile as I had seen him do on other occasions. He motioned for silence. Slowly, the people quieted. He started speaking. It was war all right. The crowd listened in silence. There was no applause at the end of each sentence as in former speeches. There was nothing to be enthusiastic about. It was war with another power, and Mussolini himself had said not long before that war with the United States meant a long, hard conflict with world-wide repercussions!

"He lisps," I overheard the officer with the crutches whisper to his friend. "Listen, he pronounces the 'S' as though it were 'SH.' He is nervous. I wonder why."

"What do you mean, 'who?'" the other replied. "You would be nervous, too, if you had to declare war on the biggest nation in the world."

At the end of the speech, the crowd applauded but it did not linger in the plaza. People were hungry and hurried away to their homes. Mussolini took three bows—that is, he appeared three times on the balcony after pretending to withdraw. It was, however, a pretty cold show—a far cry from the forty-two bows he took at his master performance on May 9, 1936, when he proclaimed the Ethiopian Empire.

Although it was late, I started to walk along the Corso to the San Carlo Restaurant. I wanted to take in every detail of that charming street which I might never see again. I was now an enemy alien. It seemed as though people looked at me knowingly. I had the uneasy feeling of being among enemies. I went past the *Giornale d'Italia,* and it reminded me that Virginio Gayda, the editor, would have a pretty dull time after we, the Americans, left Rome. Of late, he had been writing editorials virtually for the American correspondents. He obviously enjoyed our rage over his slanders concerning Roosevelt and the American people. If we were no longer here to publicize his editorials by quoting him every day, how would he feed his ego?

Newsboys under the Galleria Colonna, which faces Palazzo Chigi, the Italian Foreign Ministry, already were out with the extras. "War with the United States," the headlines said. People were not paying much attention to them.

As I was crossing Largo Goldoni an Italian returning from the demonstration was hailed by a friend who inquired what had happened.

"Nothing," he said. "We have just now declared war on the United States."

This reply was not intended for sarcasm. It was the attitude of resignation in regard to the war so common to most Italians. The people were simply tired. They had been on tenterhooks for almost seven years and now were callous. First Ethiopia, then Spain, Munich, Italy's intervention, war against Russia, and now, this one against the United States. One enemy more or less did not make a great deal of difference.

The San Carlo Church, which was across the street from the restaurant, was open. I stood for a moment gazing at its impressive baroque architecture. The bells tolled three o'clock. The restaurant was almost deserted. When I saw the familiar oak-paneled walls, the massive cupboard, and the smiling face of Raffaello, my waiter, the feeling of uneasiness left me. I was in a friendly atmosphere.

"Is there any food left for an enemy?" I asked in English.

Raffaello spoke a little English and loved to show it off. He had seldom addressed me in Italian during the many years I had gone to San Carlo. But this time he was excited and spoke his native tongue.

"Signor Cianfarra, e' terribile! Dove andiamo a finire. Where are we going to end?" he himself translated. "What's going to happen to you?"

"Mussolini will decide that, I suppose. I am his country's guest, you know. How about some lunch? I am very hungry."

"Si, si, of course. I have something for you. Maccheroni alla matriciana. They are good. You know, meat gravy and goat cheese on top. I ate them myself."

"In that case I'll take them. And after?"

"I should advise stuffed roast duck. It melts in your mouth, Signore."

Raffaello continued. "This war, it is terrible, Signore. It is ruining business. We don't want it, but what can we do? I hope the United States finishes the war soon. You are big and strong. How long will it last?"

"Many years, Raffaello. How about a piece of cake?"

"No good. Too dry. Better take fruit, Signore. An apple, they are not too bad. We would have better ones, if we did not send our best to the Germans."

I had fruit, and ordered the barley concoction which the Italians had adopted as a substitute for coffee which had disappeared from circulation many months before. It was pretty hard to get it even on the black market. Only occasionally I would be able to blow myself to an *espresso* at half a dollar a cup.

It was a long time before Raffaello came back. I took a sip and stared at him. "Raffaello, this is real coffee!"

"Si, *Signore*. Just my gift to you. So you'll remember Raffaello when you are back in the States, maybe. You are probably the last American customer I shall serve for a long time, *Signore*."

The luncheon was good, despite the fact that the macaroni was virtually all bran, with only a suspicion of flour. It cost me the equivalent of two dollars and ten cents.

We shook hands. It seemed very silly, but I hated to go. Our good-bye had about it an air of finality. The San Carlo church bells tolled. It was four o'clock.

The police came for me an hour later as I was cleaning the drawers of my desk in *The New York Times'* office. They were very polite. It appeared that Cavaliere Rocco Aguesci, the Head of the Foreign Squad, wanted to have a brief, friendly chat with me.

At police headquarters, Aguesci was embarrassed as he told me that I was to be detained there until—taken to jail! "Orders from the Foreign Ministry," he said. "It will be only for a few days, I am sure."

I was put temporarily in an adjacent room where I found Richard Massock of the Associated Press. We waited a long time. Finally two plain-clothes men escorted us to a cab. One sat between us, the other in front.

The jail was a huge building not far from the Tiber in an over-crowded quarter of the poor. On top of its massive doors was inscribed, *Regina Coeli*—Queen of Heaven! Inside they stripped us and took all our possessions save cigarettes and matches. Then they gave us back our clothes and led us through several gates. We halted somewhere on the ground floor and were handed sheets, blankets, one straw-filled pillow, one aluminum pitcher for water and a soup bowl. We climbed two flights of iron stairs and marched along a passageway covered with a wire net. There were cells on either side. The warden opened one of them and pushed us in.

"You'll get dinner later," he said.

It was nearly ten when Herbert Matthews of *The Times* was brought in. There were three cots in the cell, nine feet long and six feet wide. One blue lamp shed only a faint light upon the dank stone floor and the stained walls which many years before had been whitewashed.

I inspected the verminous straw mattress. There was a depression in the middle of it where only the rough linen casing lay between the body and the iron bed. The mattress had been used so much that the straw had formed tufts as hard as stones. I lay down reluctantly, fully dressed and with my coat on. I was very cold. I stared at the grime-covered, barred windows. It was depressing. We hardly spoke. A pang of memory turned my thoughts to my father. I had followed in his journalistic footsteps to the Queen of Heaven where seventeen years before he had been imprisoned for anti-Fascist sentiments.

After two days in jail, the American correspondents in Rome were taken to a cheap boardinghouse called Pensione Suquet in Corso Umberto, and then sent to a first-class hotel in Siena. During the five months I spent in internment I managed to keep in touch with some of my Vatican friends, through acquaintances I had made in Siena. The Italians left us free within the city limit, and we could, therefore, go to cafés, restaurants, movies—anywhere we liked. A Vatican prelate, who happened to spend a few days in Siena, sent word to me that I could see him in the rear of a shop, of which I was a steady customer. I was very glad to talk to him because there was a question that was weighing on my mind, and he could give me the answer. The Italian press had announced on March 27, that Japan and the Holy See had established normal diplomatic relations. It had published a statement made by the Japanese Foreign Minister which said that "in order to render closer the friendly relations existing between Japan and the Holy See, the Japanese Government has decided to appoint Minister Harada as its official representative to the

Vatican. In view of the present situation and the presence of many Roman Catholics in the Japanese empire, the establishment of friendly relations and of direct contacts between Japan and the Vatican, assumes a particular significance."

The Italian press had interpreted the event as a "Japanese diplomatic victory over the United States and a clear reply to the false enemy propaganda which pretends to affirm that Japan is the destroyer of any religious faith." It stated that there were two hundred thousand Catholics in Japan and Korea, sixteen dioceses, three hundred twenty-four churches, one hundred thirty monasteries and convents, one thousand priests, one thousand two hundred twenty nuns, and one theological seminary with one hundred students.

According to Florence's *La Nazione*, at the beginning of the negotiations that led to the Vatican-Japanese agreement, Washington had lodged a "strong protest with the Secretariat of State through its representative, Myron Taylor, while attempting to influence the Holy See by means of an intense anti-Japanese propaganda on the radio."

"What is the reason behind the Vatican decision?" I asked the prelate.

"Since the United States entered the war," he replied, "many things have happened. English and American possessions in the Pacific have fallen in Japanese hands. You have lost the Philippines. Thousands of Anglo-American soldiers have been made prisoners. His Holiness has been deeply concerned over their welfare. As you know, one of the most important activities of the Vatican today is to alleviate the suffering of prisoners. Before the establishment of normal diplomatic relations, Monsignor Paolo Marella, the apostolic delegate in Tokio, found it very difficult to carry out the welfare activities required by the turn of the war in the Far East. Japan's appointment of a minister to the Vatican, has greatly facilitated the work. The Vatican Information Service now may communicate directly with Tokio, and has a regular diplomatic channel through which it can materially aid the plight of the Christian soldiers. Since a great deal of the financial means necessary for this work comes from the United States, you may see for yourself that the Vatican has now become the link between Washington and Tokio."

Humanitarian reasons, he said, were the only ones that had prompted the Pope to accept a Tokio representative. The Holy See, of course, had foreseen that the Axis press would use the development in Japanese-Vatican relations for propaganda purposes, but an exhaustive explanation had been given to Harold H. Tittman, who had taken up residence in the Vatican when the Axis declared war on the United States. Washington had been kept informed throughout the negotiations with Tokio, and Tittman had delivered to Maglione a note which gave assurances that the State Department fully understood the papal move.

The work of relief of the Vatican Information Bureau, which Pius XII organized one month after the outbreak of the war, had reached considerable proportions in the spring of 1942, owing to the spreading of the war to the Pacific. The bureau stemmed from a similar organization formed by Benedict XV at the end of 1914, during World War I. Pius XII delved into the experience he acquired when as nuncio to Munich he directed Vatican assistance to prisoners in Germany, to make the 1939 edition of the service an efficient welfare agency with ramifications in all the important war centers.

In the fall of 1939 the office was composed of a few prelates and had its seat in the Secretariat of State. Its task then was to meet inquiries as to the fate of scores of thousands of Polish refugees and soldiers, who were missing as a result of Germany's invasion of Poland. The search concerned not only the Nazi-occupied territory but also neighborhood countries, such as Hungary, Lithuania, Rumania and Latvia, where thousands of homeless and destitute Poles had sought shelter.

When Germany subjugated Norway, Belgium, Holland, Luxembourg and France the requests for information increased from a few hundreds to over two thousand daily. Italy's intervention in the summer of 1940 brought the war to Greece, North and East Africa; and the requests skyrocketed to several thousands. They were mostly from worried relatives of Italian soldiers and civilians in Albania and

Africa, or on Italian ships that had been sunk in the Mediterranean.

The growing volume of work forced the transfer of the bureau from the Secretariat of State to a building in Piazza Santa Marta, within Vatican City. The initial handful of clerks swelled into nearly a hundred and fifty clergymen and nuns, under the direction of Bishop Alexander Evreinoff, of the Bizantine rite, who was assisted by many high prelates. Evreinoff was the logical person for the post because of his command of more than a dozen languages.

Vatican officials told me in November 1941 that from June 1940 to September 1941 they had received 367,306 requests for information, 148,105 of which they had answered either by letter or telegram. In view of the difficulties of communication, the remoteness of some of the battlefields, and the many obstacles of a juridical and military nature, the Holy See made extensive use of its powerful radio station to convey the requests to countries it could not hope to reach quickly or easily. During the same period, Vatican broadcasts asking the whereabouts of 58,205 missing civilians and soldiers, totalled 36,105 minutes. The transmissions were beamed on Cairo, the information center for the Near East and Sudan; Mombasa, for Kenya and Tanganika; Bangkok, for Indo-China, Dutch East Indies and Thailand; Leopoldville, for Belgian Congo, French Equatorial Africa and South Africa; London, for England; Ottawa, for Canada; and Addis Ababa, for Ethiopia.

After Pearl Harbor, Washington and Tokio became two of the most important centers of information. Papal representatives abroad supervised personally the work of relief. In the United States, Monsignor Amleto Cicognani, Apostolic Delegate, who is regarded as one of the ablest members of the Vatican diplomatic service, visited during 1943 prisoner-of-war camps in Missouri, Tennessee, Georgia, North Carolina, Indiana, Maryland and other states.

When a new camp is opened, the papal representative contacts the local bishop to provide immediate spiritual care for the internees. Usually an army chaplain is appointed to this task, or else the services of near-by priests are enlisted. These clergymen distribute rosaries, crucifixes, medals, holy cards and prayer books. At the same time, arrangements are made to facilitate the correspondence of the prisoners with their families abroad, because the sending and reception of such communications is a very important factor in sustaining prisoner morale. Forms of the Vatican Information Service are freely supplied and prisoners may write as often as they wish. The messages, however, must not exceed twenty-five words, and are restricted only to personal information. In September 1943 alone, the Apostolic Delegation in Washington forwarded to Vatican City for eventual delivery to the addressees 32,000 messages from Italian and German war prisoners. Since it was expected that their number would increase with the steady advance of the Anglo-American forces in Europe, Monsignor Cicognani's office, at the end of 1943, placed an order with the printer for one million correspondence forms.

Another of the tasks of the Vatican bureau is that of alleviating as far as possible the mental suffering of prisoners who in civil life pursued professional or artistic activities. The Apostolic Delegation in Washington fulfilled countless requests for books and periodicals on specialized subjects, and provided materials for painting, as well as musical instruments including pianos, violins, cellos, guitars and mandolins. English grammars were also in great demand, for a great many of the prisoners wished to turn their forced stay in the United States into an opportunity to learn a new language. When Monsignor Cicognani visits a camp, he invariably leaves with the commanding officer a lump sum for the prisoners and orders the purchase of at least one radio, often two or three according to the number of prisoners, as personal gifts from the Pope. The system of the Washington branch of the Vatican service is typical of the one adopted by all other nunciatures and delegations in belligerent countries.

After nearly five months of internment, all the American correspondents in Siena were taken to Rome on May 3, for their departure on the diplomatic train to Lisbon. We were given rooms at the Grand Hotel, where the American diplomatists had been confined since December 11, while awaiting the conclusion of the negotiations between the State Department and the Italian Foreign Ministry for the evacuation of their respective nationals.

We stayed two weeks in the capital, during which I quietly put in several hours of solid work a day to obtain information as to the

attitude of the Vatican in regard to the war. The American newspapermen, unlike the diplomatists, were treated with a certain
amount of consideration by the Italian authorities. We were the
boys who were going to write stories about Italy and Fascism, after
our departure, and the shrewd officials went out of their way to
make things easy for us. Instead, the diplomatists confined in Rome
had an 11 P.M. curfew, were constantly watched by a policeman
twenty-four hours a day, forbidden to go to movies and theaters, or
have contacts with any Italians, we, in Siena, after the first few days,
had not even been watched. A policeman would from time to time
come to the hotel and check on us, but he never interfered with our
movements.

In Rome, we also had a policeman, but he would wait in the lobby
of the hotel, whereas, the ones assigned to the diplomatists would be
stationed in front of the rooms so that no one could visit the
Americans without being seen. This slight difference in treatment
proved very useful to me.

Edda, who was left free to do whatever she wanted, probably because the Italian male, au fond, believes that women have no political sense and are interested only in household questions and in the
breeding of children, contacted our friends in the Vatican. She gave
them the number of my room, the floor on which it was, and the
safest time at which to see me. This was usually late in the morning
when most of the policemen on duty had left the hotel to escort
the internees. The visitors would walk through the lobby, take the
elevator to the second floor and calmly enter my room without
knocking, after making sure that no one was in sight.

Despite the reverses suffered by the United States and England in
the Pacific, the attitude of the Vatican had remained one of implacable hostility towards Germany, I was assured. The Holy See,
while officially maintaining political neutrality, feared that an Axis
victory might be followed by a campaign of de-Christianization
throughout Europe. No compromise was possible between the
Vatican and Nazism. The reason was given me in the form of a
Vatican memorandum which consisted of eleven points summing up
Hitler's anti-religious policy as follows:

1) State monopoly of the education of youth, and exclusion of religious teaching; 2) Racial laws which, especially in their sanction of sterilization, are in complete contrast with Catholic principles; 3) Methodical confiscation of ecclesiastical property under the pretext of patriotic and national needs; 4) Absolute suppression of freedom of Catholic Action activities; 5) Abolition of the freedom of the press and suppression of most of the Catholic newspapers and periodicals; 6) Constant anticlerical campaign of the Nazi press; 7) Trials against the clergy and religious orders for alleged immoral practices and for the exportation of funds needed for missionary work; 8) Systematic atheist and neo-pagan propaganda by exponents of Nazi policy (Goebbels, Rosenberg); 9) Persecution of the episcopate and clergy, such as attacks against Cardinal Faulhaber, and confinement of priests to concentration camps; 10) Application of racial laws, and pitiless anticlerical persecutions in Poland, Austria, Bohemia, and Yugoslavia; 11) Political pressure on Italy to obtain adoption of antiracial and anticlerical policy.

The attitude of the Vatican in regard to Italy was different, however. Ideologically the conflict with Fascism was not so sharp as with Nazism. Mussolini had not gone to Hitler's extremes and attempted to stamp out religion. Italy's Catholic tradition had restrained him. Whereas Nazism excluded the collaboration of the Church with the State, Fascism accepted it, although with limitations. The autonomy of action which the Church theoretically asks of the lay government as an essential condition for the free exercise of its mission, was denied. Fascism arrogated to itself the right of controlling the actions of the citizen in the social sphere which included educational, welfare, and recreational activities. However, it allowed the Church and its organizations to participate in the national life on condition that it abstained from pursuing aims in contrast with those set by the totalitarian state. It recognized in the Church a social force which was part of the nation.

But as Germany's influence on Italy began to be felt, Mussolini altered his policy whenever it suited his convenience. He was not anti-Catholic, like his partner, but anticlerical. He did not attempt to make the Italians a nation of atheists or pagans, but to weaken the authority and power of the Vatican, which is the defender of religious rights and interests in the international field. This is one of the reasons why the Holy See, I was told, welcomed the destruction of the Fascist regime and wished a victory of the Anglo-Saxon powers.

Both in England and in the United States, my friends pointed out, the Church enjoyed the freedom of action which it lacked in the Axis countries. The lay government in those countries permits the citizens to organize themselves in accordance with their own convictions and interests. The Church enjoys no favoritism, but at the same time, it is not discriminated against. It has recognized rights equal to those of other religious organizations, and its status before the lay power is that of a private corporation. Although the State does not grant diplomatic recognition to the Vatican because such gesture would imply a distinction in favor of the Catholic Church, and therefore, a discrimination against other religious societies, on the other hand, it leaves the Vatican free to appoint its own representative to the local episcopate. While in the Axis countries, the Church was either persecuted or restricted, in the Anglo-Saxon world, it was free to establish schools, recreation centers, hospitals, and engage in many other forms of social and religious activities.

Moreover, the Vatican did not overlook the fact that four-fifths of its missions are in British territories and possessions, where they are prospering unhampered by the civil authorities. Missionary work is a very important activity of the Catholic Church, for it is the vanguard of the religious offensive of Catholicism in the world.

In the light of these explanations, could anyone doubt, Vatican prelates asked, that the papacy was in favor of an Anglo-Saxon victory?

SEVENTEENTH CHAPTER

After the Axis declaration of war against the United States, the collaboration between the Vatican and Washington continued to be as close as circumstances permitted. This happy state of affairs was strengthened by the all-out support the Roman Catholic clergy gave to the nation's war effort. The American archbishops and bishops met in Washington in November 1942 for their annual general meeting, at which 102 members of the hierarchy participated, and issued a "Statement on Victory and Peace" that advocated the prosecution of the war until the defeat of the Axis powers.

"Our country," it said "has been forced into the most devastating war of all time. This war, which is the absorbing interest of all the world, involves unquestionably the most important moral issue of today. Some nations are united in waging war to bring about a slave world—a world that would deprive man of his divinely conferred dignity, reject human freedom and permit no religious liberty. We are associated with other powers in a deadly conflict against these nations to maintain a free world. This conflict of principles makes compromise impossible. . . . From the moment that our country declared war we have called upon our people to make the sacrifices which, Catholic doctrine, the virtue of patriotism, justice and charity impose. In every section of this nation the voices of our bishops have been heard. Their instructions, their pastorals, their counsels, their appeals for prayers are an encouragement and an inspiration to their flocks. Our priests as chaplains on the war fronts have inspired confidence in the men whom they so zealously serve."

A few weeks earlier, Myron C. Taylor, Roosevelt's personal representative to the Vatican, had flown to Italy for a series of conversations with Pius. Both the Holy See and Washington gave not the slightest indication as to what his mission was, and the world will have to wait a very long time before elucidating documents will be

published. If and when they will appear, they will have only historical value.

One of Taylor's tasks was to obtain information regarding the
extent of anti-Nazi opposition and sabotage in the countries dominated by Germany, as well as of the morale of the civilian populations, and of the armed forces in Germany, Italy and the other
powers that had adhered to the tripartite pact, Rumania, Hungary,
Bulgaria. From the beginning of the war, as seen in earlier chapters,
the Vatican had been receiving a remarkably accurate picture of the
internal situation obtaining in all European countries, except Russia.
Priests in the cities, as well as in the villages, sent their reports to
the bishop of their diocese and, somehow, despite the very strict
watch exercised by their conquerors, the reports would reach Rome.
Except for a few high officials, no one knows how they were smuggled through Nazi-ridden countries where thousands of police kept
clergymen under constant surveillance. The details of this amazing
job of reporting will in all likelihood never be disclosed for the Holy
See can guard secrets better than any other power in the world. It is
a safe guess that a wealth of extremely valuable information was
made available to Taylor, who conveyed it to President Roosevelt.
It was a great contribution to the Allied war effort, because it enabled
Washington to gauge accurately conditions in Europe. Our propaganda overseas was undoubtedly influenced by confidential knowledge
of the internal situation in the various countries. This knowledge
permitted us to use policies we knew would be more apt to create
psychological reactions tending to undermine the enemy's war effort.

It is not to be wondered, therefore, that one of the first steps the
Germans took on occupying Rome, after Italy's unconditional surrender, was to isolate the Vatican. Nazi troops were placed all round the
papal city with instructions to forbid access to it to all persons not
provided with a special permit. The decision was prompted by politico-
military, and not anti-religious considerations. Hitler wanted to muz-
zle Pius. Thus, he forbade all Vatican broadcasts as well as news in
L'Osservatore Romano not dealing with religious subjects, and at the
same time sought to discover what the papal sources of information
were, by keeping a close watch on visitors. It can hardly be doubted

that he was especially concerned with preventing reports on the subjugated countries and Germany proper from reaching the Holy See, and from there, the outside world.

I offer this explanation on the basis of remarks I heard the Germans make during the war years I spent in Italy. Nazi officials were furious at the Vatican, and said so openly, but they abstained from following their words with actions because they foresaw the ominous repercussions that reprisals against the papacy would cause among forty-five million Catholic Italians, who, moreover, were only passive allies.

How highly Washington valued the contacts with the Vatican was proved again when Archbishop Francis J. Spellman, Archbishop of New York, went to Rome in February 1943. Monsignor Spellman's reputation in the Vatican, where he had spent many years as an official of the Secretariat of State, was very flattering. He had enjoyed the confidence of Pius XI who, at the time of the struggle between the Vatican and Fascism over the education of youth, entrusted him with the text of the encyclical *Non Abbiamo Bisogno*, which Spellman smuggled out of Italy and released in Paris at the end of June 1931. The Pope feared Mussolini would prevent the publication of the document in Italy, since it criticized many aspects, etc. of the Fascist doctrine and denounced some violations of the Lateran accord.

On February 20, 1943, Spellman arrived at the Vatican, where for three days he had conferences with Pius. His presence in Rome originated rumors that inevitably crop up when an important personage is sent on a secret mission. There was talk of a separate peace move by the smaller European nations, based on the fact that during the same period the Pope also received the secretaries of the Hungarian and Argentine legations. But one of the most remarkable stories, which had wide publicity in the United States press was that the American Archbishop intended to discuss arrangements for the Pope's departure from Italy. Brazil was suggested as the new haven for the Head of the Catholic Church.

While such a possibility cannot be entirely excluded, anyone familiar with Vatican affairs would know that at no time since the beginning of his pontificate did Pius entertain plans to leave Vatican

City. When Spellman visited him, Italy's situation, though difficult, was not yet desperate. It was less critical, for instance, than that of Britain after Dunkirk. Moreover, both Mussolini and Hitler were anxious to avoid steps that might cause a strong reaction among Italian and German Catholics. Had the Pope been forced to abandon Rome, the United Nations would have been provided with an invaluable propaganda weapon against the Axis, inasmuch as the whole world would have regarded that move as a proof that the Pontiff had decided to support openly the democracies. Moreover, the Vatican could no longer have hoped to become an intermediary between the belligerents.

Apart from the traditional, moral and political considerations that made the departure inconceivable in the circumstances existing at the time, there were some concrete economic factors which, though of lesser importance, had to be taken into account. To carry on its spiritual mission the church must have money. As already explained, the 1929 Lateran Treaty gave the papacy a billion lire in state bonds and 750,000,000 lire in cash as compensation for the loss of the Papal States in 1870. It is, of course, true that if the fate of the Church had been at stake, the Vatican would not have hesitated to forego this sum. On the other hand, the lira may have been worth nothing in neutral and democratic countries, but in 1943 it still circulated in Italy and Nazi-dominated nations.

Then there were the incalculable treasures in the Vatican palaces and museums. The Pope would have had to leave behind these treasures. Not only this, but he would have lost his temporal kingdom, for one may be sure that Mussolini would not have hesitated to annex Vatican City.

It may seem paradoxical, but the position of the Pontiff vis-à-vis the Axis powers improved as it became increasingly clear in the spring and summer of 1943 that the tide of the war had turned in favor of the United States. A member of the Italian diplomatic service, who was very intimate with several high Fascists, told me before I left Italy that Mussolini regarded the Pope as the only man who, when all hopes for an Axis victory were gone, might soften Italy's defeat. Pius, he said, was a political asset because of his potentialities as a mediator. The Italian dictator never did have a chance to avail himself of Vatican influence and prestige because events, which he was unable to control, swept him suddenly from power.

On July 10 the Allied forces invaded Sicily, where they met only scant resistance. That region was one of the least advanced of the Italian Kingdom. The majority of the people still lived under a feudal system which Mussolini had sought to change, with little success, in 1939 when he split the latifundia, or large estates, among the poverty-stricken peasants. He launched a ten-year plan that called for the building of 20,000 rural houses spread over 1,500,000 acres. The plan was never carried out because of its prohibitive cost and the resistance of the politically influential landowners.

Sicilians had always been lukewarm Fascists. Early in the war, reports reached me in Rome that British intelligence had very useful collaborators among the people living in Sicilian coastal towns. English agents would leave Malta aboard swift launches and dock under cover of darkness at some deserted spot where Italian informants were waiting for them with news concerning the movements of ships and troops. Thus, the English, for instance, knew several weeks in advance that a German Air Corps was to arrive in Sicily during the 1940–41 winter, and were able to take effective precautions to ensure the safety of ships transporting supplies to Malta, the besieged island which was less than twenty minutes by plane from Sicilian bases. Other reports described how the bodies of murdered Nazi soldiers were found in fields or country roads, so much so that curfews had to be imposed in some towns.

Allied troops had hardly landed on Sicilian soil than Pius received a message from President Roosevelt assuring him that "churches and religious institutions will, to the extent that it is within our power, be spared the devastations of war during the struggle ahead. Throughout the period of operations the neutral status of Vatican City, as well as of the papal domains throughout Italy will be respected."

Nevertheless, nine days later Rome was bombed and the Basilica of St. Laurence Outside-the-Walls was seriously damaged. The news shocked the Catholic world and untold numbers of lovers of art and culture, regardless of their faith. Many members of the American episcopate minced no words in condemning that unprecedented step. Cardinal William O'Connell, Archbishop of Boston and dean of the Catholic hierarchy in America, referred to it as a "sad event" and left it "to the conscience of those responsible for it" as to whether or not it was a military necessity. Bishop Joseph P. Hurley of St. Augustine, Florida, declared that "every decent Christian thought and sentiment within me cries out that we have made a tragically mistaken decision." Archbishop Edward Mooney of Detroit expressed "surprise and regret," as did many other prelates.

The Pope refused to go to his private shelter in the basement of the Apostolic Palace and witnessed the two-and-a-half hour raid from a window of his study. More than five hundred American bombers participated in the attack and dropped twelve hundred tons of explosives. As soon as the all-clear signal sounded, Pius left the Vatican in a closed automobile to inspect the damage done to the Basilica and to the surrounding tenement houses of what was one of Rome's most crowded districts inhabited chiefly by laborers.

St. Laurence Outside-the-Walls was first built in the sixth century by Pope Pelagius II, but it underwent so many enlargements and modifications by subsequent popes, notably by Honorius III in 1216, that nothing of the original structure remains except the choir of today's larger structure.

Pius voiced his protest in a letter addressed the next day to Cardinal Francesco Marchetti-Selvaggiani, Vicar General of the District of Rome. He complained that the Basilica had been "in very great part destroyed" and recalled his repeated appeals to both groups of belligerents "to respect the inviolability of peaceful citizens and monuments of faith and civilization."

"We thought ourselves justified in hoping," the Pope said, "that in the face of such evident reasons, the authority with which, however unworthily, we are endowed, the universal recognition of our completely impartial stand above the conflict and of the right and constant charity of activity which we have exercised on behalf of all, without distinction of nationality or religious belief, that all those considerations would have secured us the consolation among such bitterness of finding a reception by the contending parties. But, alas, this so reasonable hope of ours has been disappointed."

Rome and Berlin, as it was to be expected, attempted to use the raid as a means to stir Catholic sentiment against the United Nations. Axis broadcasts announced that the Pope was preparing a note of protest, and that Giovanni Battista Montini, Head of the Congregation of Ordinary Affairs, had already discussed the bombing with Harold H. Tittman, United States representative to the Holy See.

The maneuver was soon spiked. The Vatican radio, in a broadcast to Germany on July 22, branded these Axis reports as having "no foundation in fact whatsoever." The statement said that Pius had limited himself to visiting the bombed district, and to writing a letter to the Vicar General of Rome. It stressed that the letter was "not addressed to one of the belligerents, but to both sides," and recalled previous papal appeals for the humanization of warfare, as well as condemnation of the destruction caused by air raids in other countries.

The papal stand on the bombing of Rome aroused considerable criticism in non-Catholic quarters, which accused the Pontiff of having failed to show an equal interest in the fate of churches in Allied countries. News from London on July 30, however, disclosed that as early as January 1943 the Pope had appropriated $50,000 of Holy See funds for the restoration of Roman Catholic Churches in England damaged or destroyed by the Nazi Air Force.

Until May 1942, the time of my departure from Italy, Rome proper could not by any stretch of the imagination be called an industrial city. It was, of course, the seat of the Government and, therefore, a justifiable target for air raids, but its contribution to the nation's war effort was negligible. In its immediate outskirts there were, instead, some undeniably important military objectives, such as a Breda plant, which produced weapons, and three airfields: Ala Littoria, Ciampino and Centocelle. The last two were about six miles from the city, and the first less than two miles from any populated quarter.

The San Lorenzo marshaling yards, the destruction of which the Allied High Command gave as the main reason for the raid, though an objective, were not so strategically important as one would think. Troop trains hardly ever formed there, since the capital had no facilities for quartering large bodies of soldiers. Much more important as a railroad junction was Aversa, not far from Naples, where the two main lines from the northern regions running along the Mediterranean and the Adriatic litorals, converged on their way south. With the Aversa yards destroyed, no trains coming from the north could reach the boot of the peninsula or Sicily by using the line along the Mediterranean.

I cannot enter into a discussion as to whether or not Rome's military objectives justified the raid, and whether the results obtained offset the adverse moral and political repercussions in the civilized world, because when the bombing occurred I had been away from Italy for more than a year. It may well be that since the middle of 1942, Rome had become an important military center. I certainly would not put it past Mussolini to exploit for military purposes the unique position of Rome, as the seat of the papacy and the cradle of Christianity. However, should this not be so, I have no doubt that the raid was dictated more by political than military considerations. The Allied general staff probably sought to provoke an internal collapse in Italy by carrying aerial warfare to her capital, a city that all Italians venerate.

Soon after the first raid, Pius and President Roosevelt made it clear that they had repeatedly tried to protect Rome from aerial attack. Roosevelt stated at a White House conference that he had been "very anxious to have Rome declared an open city, but the Fascists would not do it; and on the contrary, Rome had become, and probably was then, a very important military center." It seems clear, therefore, that the ultimate responsibility for the bombing rested on Mussolini, who provoked it through his refusal to heed papal and American suggestions.

As scores of panic-stricken Romans were fleeing from their city, and the victorious Allied Armies were steadily occupying Sicily, King Victor Emmanuel announced on July 25 Mussolini's "resignations" and the appointment of seventy-two year old Marshal Pietro Badoglio as Prime Minister.

The Italian dictator had just returned from northern Italy, where he had had a three-day meeting with Hitler. He fell because his partner was unable to give him the military support necessary to cope with the Allied forces in Sicily, and to stave off the internal political unrests that had followed the military reverses. Germany could no longer spare matériel and men which she needed in order not to weaken her over-extended army from the Baltic to the Mediterranean, from the Atlantic to the Black Sea, and to resist the ever-increasing Russian pressure in the East. Mussolini wanted enough troops to push the Allied forces in Sicily back into the sea. Instead, all that Hitler could offer was to fight a gigantic delaying action throughout the length and breadth of Italy. It was his implied admission that he was beaten and that he was forced to sacrifice Italy and risk the tremendous moral repercussions which the end of Fascism would cause in Germany and in all the other nations which had adhered to the Tripartite Pact, such as Rumania, Hungary, Bulgaria. Thus, the military implications of Mussolini's fall far transcended the political implications.

That he had no choice is shown by the fact that Hitler had already saved Mussolini twice during the war. The first time was in the 1940–41 winter when the Fascist Armies in Libya were pushed as far as El Agheila on the fringe of the Sirte Desert by the triumphant British troops led by Sir Archibald Wavell. Mussolini had virtually no equipment with which to fight a mechanized war. Hitler dispatched two motorized divisions to North Africa and pushed Wavell back to the Libyan-Egyptian border. The second time was in early spring of 1941, when Hitler's troops invaded Greece to save the beleaguered Italians in Albania, who had been barely able to escape a debacle by managing to keep a few key positions.

Therefore, Hitler had no illusions as to his ally's strength. Italy could not wage a modern war alone, unless she were allied with the powers that controlled the Mediterranean. For example, she needed a minimum of one million tons of coal a month to keep her industry running. Before the outbreak of the European conflict, despite Mussolini's celebrated policy to make Italy self-sufficient, she still imported 70 per cent of her raw materials from countries outside continental Europe and the Mediterranean. With Germany no longer able to support her, she collapsed.

Contrary to what is generally believed, Germany had a very small number of troops in Italy as late as May 1942. What started the legend that the country was held in check by hundreds of thousands of Nazis placed at strategic points was the colossal logistical machinery built by the Nazi high command to feed and supply its divisions fighting in Libya. German soldiers were seen in Rome, as well as in other cities and especially in the southern harbors, but they were either going to or returning from Libya. After a few months of fighting in a hot climate to which they were not accustomed, these troops were pulled back to Italy where they were granted a period of rest. Many of them had to be cured of tropical illnesses, such as amoebic dysentery. At the same time, a steady stream of troops poured in from the Brenner Pass, to replace the German casualties in Libya.

Hitler did not have to occupy Italy because Mussolini was politically, economically and militarily bound to him. What the German dictator had was a firm grip on the Italian industry through the presence of German experts in every plant connected with the war effort. They controlled and decided the use of the raw materials Germany was supplying to her poorer partner.

Had Italy been de facto occupied by German military forces, how would it have been possible to oust Mussolini? Surely the effective political pressure which Berlin could have exerted by virtue of the physical domination of the country would have been sufficient to foil any attempt on the part of anti-Fascist elements to change a regime whose maintenance was of paramount importance to Hitler. The appointment of Badoglio, who had steadfastly opposed German interference in Italian affairs, and the subsequent purging of Italian political leaders who had supported Mussolini's pro-Axis policy, were a very serious blow for Germany. Hitler himself admitted in a speech delivered at the beginning of September that Berlin had been caught napping and, branded the Italian King and his new premier as traitors.

The German dictator attempted to obtain political control of Italy and to overthrow the House of Savoy and the Government in September 1943 when German troops suddenly occupied Rome, but he found that the royal family and Badoglio had fled. He also announced the formation of a new "Republican Fascist Party" headed by Mussolini who, according to Berlin, had been "rescued" from prison by his Nazi friends. Even this desperate move failed to bring results, however, owing to the landing of American troops in Salerno, which brought the Allied forces dangerously near Rome.

Mussolini's fall, then, proved conclusively that Italy was a willing *collaborator* and not a *victim* of Nazism, as the misguided Anglo-Saxon propaganda, based on wishful thinking, had led the world to believe for years. When I speak of Italy, I am, of course, referring to her ruling class and not to the people as a whole. Mussolini remained in power as long as he was supported by his immediate collaborators, who formed the controlling minority of which he was the exponent. These men were loyal to him because it was only through their leader that they could hope to retain the power they had acquired. Mussolini could not have promoted pro-German policy without the acquiescence of his collaborators who controlled the social forces that composed the state—money, land, industry and commerce; the judiciary and the military. The only force that had resisted Fascist control was the Church. But, as far as the national clergy was concerned, Mussolini had been able to secure the collaboration of the majority of its members. The Vatican, although it sought to prevent Italy's intervention, carefully abstained from fomenting opposition to Italy's war effort.

In its domestic implications, Mussolini's end was the result of the lack of confidence which his incompetent leadership of the war had originated in the Fascist ruling class. He had nothing to show on the profit side, and, when he was no longer able to secure German military help, he was doomed.

His overthrow occurred with a minimum of political disturbances. There were pacifist demonstrations in the large cities as well as scuffles between Fascist extremists who refused to accept the end of a political regime by which they had benefited. This was another proof of the deep gap existing between the ruling class and its leader. Although Badoglio disbanded virtually all Fascist institutions and established a military regime, many of Mussolini's former collaborators willingly rallied to his side, and helped him to prevent a revolution by maintaining discipline among the millions of people that formed the national structure.

To cite but one example: Mussolini had created a well-organized and well-equipped Fascist militia, which numbered hundreds of thousands of men. Had this force received orders to oppose Badoglio, the inevitable result would have been civil war. Instead, not only did it not fight for its leader, but it meekly accepted disbandment.

By eliminating Mussolini, King Victor Emmanuel, who had been forced to play a purely nominal role in Italian affairs for twenty-one years, emerged from the comparative obscurity to which the strong personality of the former Italian dictator had relegated him. His sanction of the change from a tottering political regime to a military dictatorship composed of men faithful to the crown, was the fourth major decision in the forty-three years of his reign. A typical constitutional monarch, he always abstained from taking a hand in the politics of his country and intervened only when the internal situation was such that the responsibility for the decisive step was placed on him.

His first decision was in 1915, a few days before Italy's entrance in the first World War. Antonio Salandra, the prime minister who was openly pro-Ally, provoked a cabinet crisis to eliminate his strongest political opponent, Giovanni Giolitti, ex-premier who had a great parliamentary majority and was championing neutrality. If the King accepted Salandra's resignation, it meant that Italy would continue to remain neutral; if he refused, it meant intervention. Salandra was confirmed in office, and Italy joined the Allies against the Central Powers.

While the Italian Army was in full retreat after the severe defeat suffered at Caporetto in 1917, a war council was held at Peschiera. Italian and Allied Generals had reached a unanimous decision that Italy's line of defense should be on the southern bank of the River Adige, which involved the abandonment of Venice to the enemy. The King again intervened. He opposed the decision and argued that a stand could be made on the River Piave, north of Venice. He won his point and, eventually, the war.

In October 1922 the King took a decision that changed the course of Italy's history. Mussolini had mobilized his Blackshirts for the March on Rome. The spineless Facta Government drafted a bill proclaiming martial law and announced it to the nation through a communique released by Stefani, the Italian official agency. At the same time, General Pietro Badoglio told his sovereign that he could disperse Mussolini's Blackshirts in a few hours. There seems to be no doubt among historians that Badoglio was right. However, the King feared that repressive measures against the Fascists might lead to civil war. In making his deal with Fascism, the King saved his crown. The Duke of Aosta, his cousin, who had openly supported the Fascist movement, was stated to be in Perugia as the Blackshirts marched on Rome, awaiting the moment to seize the throne. Moreover, Victor Emmanuel remembered what had happened in the winter of 1921 at the inauguration of the new Parliament. As he began reading the crown speech, all the socialist deputies walked out of the chamber while the Republicans shouted that they would be glad "to escort Your Majesty with a brass band to any border" if he abdicated. It was a stormy session which showed that there were powerful political factors in Italy bent on ridding the country of the House of Savoy. In accepting the premiership, Mussolini pledged his support to the monarchy.

I don't include among the King's decisions, Italy's declaration of war in June 10, 1940, because his role in this case was merely that of signing the decree submitted to him by Mussolini. It was not a decision; it was the logical outcome of a policy which the Italian sovereign had supported for nearly twenty-one years.

In the years immediately after the establishment of the Fascist dictatorship, the rumor spread that Humbert, Prince of Piedmont, was one of Mussolini's bitterest enemies. The King was not linked with the rumor because he, after all, had been responsible for putting the dictator in power, and was, from all appearances, collaborating with him. One of the facts given as evidence of Humbert's anti-Fascist feelings was that the newly created Grand Council of Fascism in its December 1925 session had granted Il Duce extraordinary powers including that of ratifying the successor to the throne. The Italian constitution states that, in accordance with the Salic law, the first-born of the male sex has the right of succession to the crown. This right, however, must be ratified by Parliament. What Mussolini did was to extend the power of ratification to the Grand Council of Fascism, as Italy's supreme advisory body. When that decision was announced, it was believed all over Italy that the Italian dictator wanted to eliminate the Crown Prince as a successor to the throne.

Members of the Roman aristocracy with whom I discussed the question, explained that the rumors of Humbert's hostility to Fascism were being assiduously fed by court circles. Noblemen would whisper in people's ears the latest anti-Fascist joke which they said the Crown Prince, who was gifted with natural wit, had just recounted. The purpose of the campaign was purely a matter of policy. The royal family, like everybody else, did not know whether Fascism were going to last. Mussolini might be overthrown or assassinated. In that case, anti-Fascist forces would, undoubtedly, come into power. The King, because of his policy of collaboration with the dictator, might be forced to abdicate. Obviously, an heir who was supposedly anti-Fascist would have greater chances of succeeding to the throne, thus insuring the continuation of the monarchy.

Victor Emmanuel was thirty-one years old when he became king in tragic circumstances. He was born in Naples on November 11, 1869, and was an only child. At a ceremony held in Monza, northern Italy, on July 29, 1900, an anarchist called Gaetano Berschi assassinated his father, Humbert I. The then Crown Prince was cruising off the coast of Calabria with his wife on his private yacht, when the semaphore on Capte Spartivento signaled the message: "King seriously ill." As he was putting to port, a torpedo boat appeared on the horizon under full steam. Its flag flying at half-mast conveyed the news. Four years earlier, in October 1896, he had married Princess Helena Petrovitch Niegoch, beautiful daughter of the King of Montenegro, whom he had met at the court of the Czar during one of his visits to Russia. Russia was in those days the fulcrum of pan-Slavism and claimed a sort of spiritual protectorate over all the Balkans. Young princes and princesses visited the court of the Czar where they received their final education. Helen bore him five children: Princess Yolanda Margherita Milena Romana Maria, 1901;

Princess Mafalda Maria Anna Romana Elisabetta, 1902; Prince Umberto Nicola Tommaso Giovanni Maria, 1904; Princess Giovanna Elisabetta Antonia Romana Maria, 1907; Princess Maria Francesca Anna Romana, 1914.

Physically very small, he is only five feet three inches tall, Victor Emmanuel has none of the belligerency that is sometimes associated with little men, although the shortness of his stature is a source of embarrassment to him and he does not like to see reference to it, as in cartoons.

Modest, retiring, unassuming, he and the Queen wish to live their own lives far from crowds. "The fact that I am King," he said when he ascended the throne, "does not deprive me of the right, which I share with all other citizens of living quietly in my own home, free from the indiscretions of others." To him, Queen Helen is not "Her Majesty," but "my wife"; the royal princesses, not "Their Highnesses," but "my daughters."

Helen is as simple as her husband. She has strong clannish feelings for her old-time friends, many of whom she supported because they had no means of livelihood. When the Second World War broke out and Poland was divided between Germany and Russia, the Queen learned that Princess Radziwill, an intimate friend whom she had first known as a young girl at the court of the Czar, had been evicted from her castle in Russian-occupied Poland and taken to a Moscow jail. Helen wrote a personal letter to Hitler to ask whether he could intercede with Stalin and have the noblewoman come to Rome. Hitler wrote personally to the Russian dictator, and the completely destitute princess, as well as her two sons, was freed. The Queen housed her in an apartment in Via Panama, located in one of Rome's most elegant residential sections.

Because of their dislike for pomp, the Italian sovereigns prefer to live in Villa Savoia, a large estate in the suburbs of Rome, rather than in the Quirinal which is the official royal palace where they give receptions only on exceptional occasions, such as the wedding of a relative, or the christening of a grandchild. Parsimonious by nature, the King, who is one of the wealthiest men in Europe, runs his household with great simplicity. An engineer who had the job of supervising the electrical system at the Villa Savoia, told me that every summer, before leaving for his country estate at San Rossore, near Pisa, Tuscany, the King decided to economize on electricity, and all the lights in the palace were removed and replaced with one single bulb—just enough for the servants not to bump on furniture as they passed through the halls.

When wealthy, attractive, Crown Princess Maria Jose, sister of King Leopold of Belgium, went to Naples with Humbert and started entertaining on a lavish scale, a Neapolitan nobleman asked the King for a private audience. "Your Majesty," he said, "the members of the Neapolitan aristocracy realize that Her Highness is young and very sociable. But to keep up with her, our women have been spending far too much money in new dresses. We cannot afford it." The King promptly wrote a letter to his daughter-in-law and told her that she was, of course, free to do whatever she liked in private life, but that at official ceremonies, Italian princesses wore "only one new dress a month." And that was the end of it.

A studious sovereign, whose hobby is numismatics, Victor owns the greatest private collection of ancient coins in the world, more than one hundred thousand. Just before the war, he published a monumental work on the history of Italian coins called, Corpus Nummorum Italicorum, which he began writing in 1897. His grandfather, Victor Emmanuel II, who created Italy's unity through a series of wars for independence in the nineteenth century, was christened "Father of the Country." His father, Humbert I, a rather colorless sovereign, was christened "The Good." King Victor, himself, because of the fact that Italy, up to the time of her intervention in 1940, had won every war—against Turkey, 1911; Austria, 1915; Ethiopia, 1935—was commonly referred to as "The Victorious."

Tall, dark and handsome, Humbert was a dashing prince and the exact physical opposite of his father. As a young man he was quite appreciative of feminine beauty, and his good looks gave him the reputation of a lady-killer. Stories of his escapades were heard for years all over Italy, especially in Turin where he was first stationed as a garrison officer. An excellent and passionate dancer, he mastered new steps in record time and did not fail to exhibit them when his father who frowned on such levities was not around. His love for fun fostered the legend that he was unintelligent. This is far from true. He has a good brain and is now a student of military strategy. When he began getting hold of himself and buckling down to the serious business of preparing for the responsibilities of a future sovereign, he changed his habits greatly. Military life became his main interest; skiing and swimming, rather than dancing, his recreation.

As Mussolini wiped out all opposition, securely establishing his regime, and it became clear that Fascism was in Italy to stay for an unpredictable length of time, the House of Savoy not only stopped the anti-Fascist whispering campaign, but officially manifested its support to the regime. They, as all members of royal houses, were conservative and favored, therefore, the maintenance of a political system which had proved itself to be no danger to the monarchy.

The most impressive manifestation of royal collaboration with Mussolini came at the time of the conquest of Ethiopia. Queen Helen led the officially promoted campaign for the voluntary dona-tion of gold to the country in January, 1936, by handing over her marriage ring to the Fascist authorities in a solemn ceremony held on the steps of the monument to Victor Emmanuel II in Piazza Venezia. The campaign was Mussolini's idea to rally popular support behind the Ethiopian adventure and to acquire much-needed gold to defray part of the cost of the war. It was a clever psychological, as well as practical move, since the League of Nations' decision to apply economic sanctions on the Fascist aggressor had deprived Italy of all her foreign trade and alarmingly depleted her already very meager gold reserve.

Crown Princess Maria Jose, although she was expecting a child, served as a nurse aboard a hospital ship. Humbert reviewed troops and Blackshirts sailing from Naples on their way to East Africa, and, for the first time, greeted them with the Fascist salute. However, he was not satisfied with playing a passive role. He wanted to fight and begged his father to give him command of a unit. He was so insistent that, according to what members of the aristocracy close to the Ital-ian court told me, a joint council of the royal family and of the Fascist Cabinet, including Mussolini, was held.

At the end of the meeting, it was decided that Humbert could not risk his life because he was at that time the sole direct heir to the throne. His marriage with Maria Jose in 1930, had produced only a girl, Maria Pia, in 1934. As to the other members of the secondary Savoy lines, Aosta and Genoa, the Duke of Spoleto, and Count of Turin, of the Aosta branch, and the Duke of Genoa, Duke of Bergamo, and Duke of Pistoia, of the Genoa branch, were bachelors. The only ones who were married were the Duke of Aosta and the Duke of Pistoia, the latter of the Genoa branch. Moreover, they were all older than Humbert, himself, who was thus more likely to have an heir than his distant relatives. As it happened, Maria Jose gave birth to Victor Emmanuel, Prince of Naples, in February 1936.

Nevertheless, the House of Savoy was represented in the war against Ethiopia by the Duke of Bergamo and his younger brother, Duke of Ancona, as officers in command of two regiments. After the African conquest, the Duke of Aosta, cousin of the King, succeeded Marshal Rodolfo Graziani, as Viceroy of Ethiopia, and when Mussolini plunged the country into the Second World War, fought the British Army in Africa to the finish. He surrendered in 1941, when he had no longer any means to offer resistance, and died as a prisoner of the British in the spring of 1942.

His brother, the Duke of Spoleto, accepted the crown of Croatia on May 18, 1941, after the Axis had invaded and dismembered Yugoslavia. The crown was offered him by Ante Pavelitch, poglavnick or leader of the newly formed Croatian State and already well-known as the man who plotted the assassination of King Alexander of Yugoslavia in 1934. As it turned out, it was only a symbolic gesture. Spoleto, who had taken the name of Tomislav II and thus revived a dynasty founded by Tomislav I, Croatia's first King in the Middle Ages, never went to Zagreb, the capital of his kingdom. In all fairness to him, I must say that intimate friends of his told me of his reluctance to accept the crown. Devoid of political ambition, he much preferred to court women, play polo or loll lazily on the golden sands of the magic-like island of Brioni in the northern Adriatic, which was regarded more or less as his private kingdom. On July 31, 1943, less than a week after Mussolini's fall, he announced his "abdication."

Mussolini, who thought that he would be in power forever, went out of his way to enlist Humbert's collaboration to the Fascist regime and give him every opportunity to indulge in his militarist passion. The Crown Prince would some day become King, and the Italian dictator expected to collaborate with him as closely as with his father. At the 1938 summer army maneuvers held near Avellino, southern Italy, and at those of the following year in Piedmont, northern Italy, Humbert was in command of the "blue" army and, of course, successfully solved all tactical problems by defeating the "red" army. In September, 1939, Mussolini appointed him commander of one of the two groups of armies into which Italy's land forces had been divided. The commander of the other group was Graziani. It was the highest active military post after those of Chief of the General Staff, which was held by Badoglio, and of Minister of War, held by Mussolini, himself. Then, at the time of Italy's intervention, Humbert was in charge of the Northern Army that attacked France. Again, early in 1943, the news was published that he had been assigned to the command of the Italian Army on the Russian front. Of course, there have been times when the King and Mussolini did not see eye to eye on certain questions. I know of two instances, and in both cases a compromise was achieved.

Mussolini wanted to remove the coat of arms of the House of Savoy from the Italian flag and replace it with the Fascist lictor. The King refused. Mussolini then suggested that both the lictor and the Savoy crown appear on the tricolor. The suggestion was accepted.

The second disagreement was caused by a bill passed by the Italian Parliament which gave Blackshirt officers a rank equal to army officers. The King vetoed it, and the measure was never put into effect. As a compromise, *Blackshirt* officers were granted equal rank "nominally." *De facto* they were one rank below the army officers. To give an example, a captain in the Fascist militia was only a lieutenant in the regular Italian Army.

There were no hard feelings, however. The King made one of his most significant pro-Fascist gestures in the summer of 1938 when he, who has among his titles those of King of Italy, Emperor of Ethiopia, King of Albania, King of Sardinia, King of Cyprus and King of Jerusalem and Armenia, laid two wreaths over the tomb of blacksmith Alessandro Mussolini and rural teacher, Rosa Maltoni, the dictator's parents, in the cemetery of Predappio, the little village where the man who was to rule Italy for twenty-one years was born on July 29, 1883.

To a friend who delicately hinted that the Italian people thought he was identifying himself too closely with the dictatorship, the King summed up his policy toward Fascism in these words: "When the ministers are strong, the Crown can be weak; but when the ministers are weak, the Crown must be strong." His July 25, 1943, proclamation to the Italian people showed that he had thought the moment had come for the Crown to be strong.

Badoglio was the logical choice as Mussolini's successor, at a time when the country was losing the war. He was regarded as the ablest Italian general and enjoyed the respect of all army leaders. Moreover, because of his conquest of Ethiopia and of his well-known anti-German feelings, he was popular among the people.

After his resignation as Chief of the General Staff in December 1941, he wrote a letter to Farinacci, who had accused him of being responsible for the Italian routs in Albania and bluntly stated that he had always opposed German domination in Italy. "All my directives were inspired by the concept of independent action," he said. "Collaboration? Yes. Submission? Never."

Badoglio's retirement in 1941 was a serious blow for Italy, not only because the services of an experienced general were lost, but also because high officers, who had risen with the old Marshal from the Army ranks and were loyal to him, resented the appointment of General Ugo Cavallero as the new Chief of General Staff. Cavallero was chosen by Mussolini because he had identified himself with the Fascist movement since its inception. In the early twenties he had been Under Secretary of War, a post he was forced to relinquish because his name was involved in a scandal over profiteering of army supplies.

On the other hand, Badoglio was famed for his integrity. Born of peasant stock in Grazzano Monferrato, Piedmont, on September 28, 1871, he had risen the hard way—on his merits. For years his wife's parents, who belonged to the upper-bourgeois Giobbe family, closely connected with the Vatican, refused to consider the young lieutenant of humble origin as a suitor. They thought he had no future. He was incorruptible, but wanted wealth and security. This ambition was fulfilled soon after the end of the war with Ethiopia. A grateful Mussolini gave him the title of Viceroy of the newly conquered land, ten million lire, which in 1935 was the equivalent of about seven hundred thousand dollars and a villa in Piedmont. The King created him Duke of Addis Ababa.

Reared in the monarchist tradition, Badoglio was always one of the staunchest supporters of the House of Savoy against the political encroachments of Fascism. If a scandal did not break out over Mussolini's bungling of the war with Greece in 1940–41, it was due to King Victor Emmanuel's intervention. The Italian sovereign begged the Marshal not to publish documented proof of the Italian dictator's irresponsible leadership, and to abstain from polemics.

Despite rumors that the Pope was attempting to negotiate an armistice between Italy and the United Nations, the Vatican, continued to maintain its attitude of complete political neutrality, even after Mussolini's fall, and carefully avoided interfering with Italian affairs. President Roosevelt and Prime Minister Churchill had reiterated their demand for unconditional surrender, and declared that Mussolini's disappearance from Italy's political stage had not altered the situation. After these statements, there was nothing that the Pope could do. His experience enabled him to gauge the tremendous responsibility befalling anyone who would attempt to induce a virtually beaten nation to surrender. Whatever the terms the Vatican might have been able to secure for Italy, they would have hardly pleased the Italians. And eventually the Pope, as the mediator, would have been blamed for them.

Therefore, Pius limited himself to denouncing the totalitarian form of government and to voicing his support of democratic ideals.

"The Pope," said a Vatican broadcast on July 28 "indicts attempts to subordinate juridical and legislative activities to the requirements of particular groups, classes or movements, as these must be subordinate only to the establishment of justice and to the service of society as a whole. . . . The life and activities of all must be protected against arbitrary human action. This means that no man has any right on the life and freedom of other men. Authority is sublime in its essence, inasmuch as it is the embodiment of a virtue granted by God, but it cannot be at the service of any arbitrary power. Herein lies the essential differences between tyranny and true usefulness. . . . The Pope condemns those who dare to place the fortunes of whole nations in the hands of one man alone, a man who as such, is the prey of passions, errors and dreams. . . . It is, therefore, essential that a pre-established set of laws be placed above the governor and the governed, all outside the reach of arbitrary action."

Italy's surrender was announced in a communique issued simultaneously by General Eisenhower and Badoglio on September 8, 1943. It was the inexorable epilogue of Fascist policy. Mussolini, the first of the twentieth-century dictators, left Italy weaker and more impoverished than at the time in 1922 when he seized power. His fall marked the end of an era which proved the fallacy of one-man rule over a highly civilized people. To quote Shakespeare, his dictatorship was as "hollow as a ghost."

EIGHTEENTH CHAPTER

Poland had just been conquered by Germany when Pope Pius XII, in keeping with the tradition of the Roman Pontiffs, presented to the world a five-point peace program which was contained in his 1939 Christmas message. In subsequent speeches, notably the one delivered to The Sacred College of Cardinals on December 24, 1941, and in his encyclical *Summi Pontificatus*, the Pope amplified his conceptions of a "just and honorable peace" in accordance with Christian principles.

He advocated the right of all nations to life and economic independence—big and small, strong and weak. Minorities, he said, must be protected and not oppressed; access to natural world wealth must be given to all nations on the basis of a just distribution; treaties must be respected; general disarmament achieved; peaceful methods for the settlement of international problems adopted.

In his conception, a peace which is based on force, that is, the armed superiority of a victor nation over the vanquished is ephemeral and bound to fail. It would inevitably plunge the world in a third catastrophe. The rebuilding of the post-war world cannot be conceived without moral principles, and the solution of international problems must be approached on a plane which excludes pride, hatred, ambition, in order to consider only the real human values. In other words, the Pontiff maintained that either peace will be Christian—that is, in accordance with the eternal principles of Christian morals, or there will be no peace.

In the following lines I shall attempt to give what I believe to be the Vatican interpretation of the five papal points, in the light of conversations held with authoritative Vatican prelates while I was in Rome, and of officially inspired articles by Professor Guido Gonella, one of the most intelligent interpreters of Vatican policy, which appeared from time to time in *L'Osservatore Romano*.

THE RIGHT TO LIFE OF ALL NATIONS

This first point of the papal program, which was outlined in the 1939 Christian message, was further expanded in December 1941. In order that the life and independence of nations be respected, no attempt must be made to curtail "freedom and territorial integrity," the Pope said.

Freedom is held by the Vatican to be a natural right. It is necessary because without freedom there is no responsibility. State freedom implies autonomy and independence. Autonomy is intended as internal sovereignty which is exercised within the territorial limits and in the relations between State and citizens. Independence is intended as external sovereignty, that is, as a sphere of action within which the State affirms its will in its relations with the other members of the international community. Independence is, therefore, the freedom of a state in its relation with other states, and excludes all foreign interference. Without freedom there is no independence, and independence without security is only fictitious independence.

However, that foreign policy which considers the particular advantage of a people as the exclusive aim of state action runs counter to the reciprocity of rights and duties between nations. It denies healthy international co-operation which tends to achieve the common good in the family of nations. Freedom and territorial integrity must be secure in order to be fruitful. This feeling of security may be found only in a clear conception of international justice and in the avowed respect of other nations' rights, which create the indispensable atmosphere for constructive action. Lack of security is the curse of international relations.

Doctrines which uphold the right of force are to be condemned because they take into account only physical capacity and not ethical values, which predominate in the conscience of the individual, regardless of his material strength. Right—in the world of moral relations—has a value of its own which is not related to the greater or lesser capacity of asserting it, because those who are wrong may also have strength. Consequently, force should not be used as an instrument of foreign policy except, of course, in the case of legitimate defense. For this reason the Pope affirmed that "the will to live of a nation must not represent the death sentence for another."

Territorial extension and capacity for defense vary from nation to nation but the right to life is identical for everyone. Therefore, even the small nations have a right to the respect of their political freedom and to the efficient safeguarding of their neutrality in the conflicts between nations, so that they may freely co-operate with other nations without being subordinated to force.

PROTECTION OF MINORITIES

After outlining this point in his 1939 Christmas message, the Pope, probably bearing in mind the persecutions and the ruthless policy of oppression and extermination which the Germans were pursuing against the Poles, the Czechs and the Yugoslavs under their domination, expanded it considerably in December 1941.

"In a new order founded on moral principles," he said, "there can be no place for (1) open or subtle oppression of the cultural and language characteristics of national minorities, (2) contraction of their economic capacities, (3) limitation or abolition of their natural fecundity. The more conscientiously the state respects the rights of its minorities, the more safely and effectively it can demand from its members loyal observance of their civil rights, which are equal to those of other citizens."

In other words, the Pope advocated the preservation of the four national rights of the minorities: culture, language, economic capacity and natural fecundity, and at the same time affirmed the necessity of reciprocal loyal relations between state and ethnic groups.

His appeal was directed to the conscience of the states and to the loyalty of the minorities. The states should grant equality of rights and freedom to their citizens and make no distinction between majorities and minorities. The latter, on the other hand, must loyally perform their duty towards the states. Once the mutual respect of rights and duties is achieved, minorities would no longer agitate for secession and attempt to create a state within the state. The states, in turn, would abandon the policy of coerced assimilation, having realized that the spontaneous fusion of ethnic elements does not weaken the race, and that harmony is vitally necessary for order and peace.

The states should grant to the minorities the right to learn the mother language, and the minorities should loyally learn the language of the state to which they belong, instead of using their own language and education to combat the state of which they are an organic part. Moreover, the financial burdens of the minorities should be equal to those of the majorities, as well as the economic benefits granted by the state. No policy tending to limit or deny the right to life, in contrast with the Christian preaching, *crescite et multipli-animi*, should be adopted.

NATURAL RESOURCES AND ECONOMIC CO-OPERA-TION

The Pope condemned in his 1941 Christmas message the "narrow, selfish considerations which tend to monopolize economic wealth and raw materials in general use, to the exclusion of nations less favored by nature." His fundamental idea, which was inspired by the writings of Saint Thomas (*Summa Theologica*) is that although ownership of resources may be private, their use must be open to all. Private property is not an end in itself. It is not meant for the sterile enriching of the few but, instead, for the fulfillment of the needs of the many. Property is a right but, at the same time, a duty. It embodies an obligation towards the community. The individualist doctrine sacrifices the common good to the private good, while the papal contention is that private good must be subordinated to the common good as a necessity of social justice.

These ethical principles cannot be ignored in international relations which are, in substance, relations between men or groups of men. Every individual is a member of the human family; every state is a member of the collectivity of states. But the states, after all, represent only groups of individuals whose economic welfare must be promoted. According to this conception, frontiers are barriers which divide, not bridges which unite. Therefore, state organization must not lead to the segregation of a group of men from the rest of the world but must, on the contrary, be a step forward in the organic process of co-operation between national groups. In other words, the particular interest of a state, as a member of a group of states, cannot but be subordinated to the general interest of the collectivity of states.

The main reason for the world-wide economic crisis, which reached a climax in the present war, must be ascribed to the selfish considerations which have denied the social importance of resources and have given preference to the particular interest of the individual nation at the expense of the international interest as a whole. The consequences of this policy have been economic defense on the part of the individual states, as expressed in measures forbidding exportation of goods, lifting of customs barriers, creation of monopolies, artificial barriers to the international movement of capital, dumping, closing of colonial markets and the like.

Finally, the aim of a selfish economic policy is the attainment of the greatest possible massing of wealth. This is a narrow policy which ignores far more important and noble aims of the human life.

DISARMAMENT

The solution of economic problems, the Pope warned, is strictly linked with the abolition of war and the progressive limitation of armaments. Armament programs have had a direct and powerful influence on state economy and have been responsible for serious crises. Expenditures for military preparedness have considerably increased budget deficits. To offset these deficits, the states have lowered the standard of living, raised customs barriers, adopted control of currency and other measures which have contracted international exchanges. On the international plane, wealthier states not only have abstained from aiding those less wealthy for fear that aid would materially increase the military strength of a potential foe, but have attempted to corner the supply of all those materials which might be transformed into war weapons.

Thus a progressive limitation of armaments is necessary. But, to attain this objective, treaties must be respected and international institutions created with the specific task of guaranteeing the respect of treaties.

Disarmament must be not only material, but spiritual. The mere elimination of weapons is not enough. People must forego the habit of arming, the wish to arm, the passion for arms. To attain this moral maturity, the collective conscience must be freed from the psychosis of war. Obligations between peoples and international guarantees must be regarded as a substitution of strength, not an addition to it.

If moral disarmament is not achieved, the real and efficient limitation of armaments will be only a chimera, for it is not so much the weapon which makes the warrior, as the warrior who makes the weapon. This is an essential premise of spiritual nature for gradual and loyal disarmament. However, nations cannot be asked to disarm, unless they obtain guarantees for their security, which render armament superfluous and eliminate the motives and pretexts for war.

Experience has shown that when treaties lose their binding character, nations take recourse to arms. International institutions must, therefore, be created to safeguard the respect of treaties and, which is equally important, to modify them in accordance with the changing of conditions in the relations between states.

The lack of international institutions of this character in the world today has given free play to the selfish policy of individual powers at the expense of others. States must accept the principle of collaboration in the family of states. From their free and loyal acceptance of this principle, a new international juridical order will be born. The respect for the personality of the individual states demands that the international institution be based on a principle of equality. Thus the will which should regulate international relations will not be hegemonic (the will of the stronger), nor the will of groups which pursue particular interests, but, instead, the expression of the institution, itself.

The institution should be composed exclusively of sovereign states, inasmuch as protectorates or vassal states have no freedom to act. This Federation of States would be rendered more efficient by the establishment of a Court of Justice empowered to arbitrate between nations. The Hague Court merely handed out opinions on international questions and disputes at the request of the League of Nations. The Court of Justice should have far greater powers in order to impose compulsory arbitration, which, besides mediation or conciliation, means also the obligatory settlement of problems. This type of institution would not affect the principle of sovereignty, since the Court would derive its authority from the will of the member states.

RELIGION AND ITS INFLUENCE ON INTERNATIONAL RELATIONS

In the last point of his peace program, the Pope defended the rights of the religious conscience and of the spirit while asserting that religious freedom is a basic condition for the reconstruction of the post-war world.

According to the Pontiff, persecutions against religion cannot be compatible with the creation of a new world, because Faith is the most efficient factor in the safeguarding of an order based on moral principles. Faith, in so far as it affects the individual, also affects indirectly the state. Faith is regarded as the most efficient factor, inasmuch as it gives moral strength to life, makes him who believes in the law of Christ and in His preachings of love and brotherhood a powerful defender of the social order, and gives the spiritual energies of the Roman Catholic Church the opportunity to promote understanding and good will among peoples.

Because of its universality, the Church cements brotherhood among men and indirectly the solidarity among civilized nations, to which men belong. Because of this universal character, it opposes the narrow policy of national egoism, the struggle among nations. It tends to unify, not to divide. It regards all men as children of God and as such it is concerned with their material as well as spiritual welfare, regardless of class or race. The Catholic Church is the perfect example of that spiritual ideal which should inspire a family of nations.

* * *

It will be readily seen from the foregoing that the Pope's conception of peace does not conflict with democratic principles and implies indeed the condemnation of totalitarian policy as represented by Germany. The papal new order is in striking contrast with the so-called new order advocated by the Axis powers. While Germany trampled upon the rights of the small European states by invading Poland, Norway, Denmark, Belgium, Holland, Luxembourg, Greece and Yugoslavia, the Pope affirmed the right to life of all nations. While Germany methodically killed hundreds of thousands of people in the countries under her domination in pursuance of a policy that had as its cardinal principle the supremacy of the German master race, the Pope favored equality of rights of all ethnic groups. With regard even to his third point, which the Axis powers frequently publicized as a defence of their aspirations, the Pontiff made clear in several speeches that the policy of intensive military preparedness of which Germany was the outstanding exponent had been one of the main causes of the world-wide economic crisis. At the same time, his suggestion for the creation of an international institution again offered a contrast to the foreign policy of Japan, Germany and Italy, which were the first among the big powers to resign from the League of Nations. The allusion to Germany's anti-religious policy in the fifth point needs hardly an explanation. For in that country, millions of Christians were systematically persecuted.

Conversely, it is clear that the Pope sees the possibility of realizing his ideal post-war order only through a victory of the democratic powers which have already shown—as, for instance, in the Atlantic Charter, drawn by President Roosevelt and Mr. Churchill—a more humane and ethical understanding of international problems.

The Pontiff's past actions justify the belief that he will wish to contribute directly to the establishment of peace. What will be the concrete form of his contribution it is impossible to foresee at present, but it cannot be doubted that, as he acted diplomatically to stave off war in the summer of 1939, so will he act after the end of the hostilities to champion his peace plan.

Pius XII today is in a far more advantageous position to make the full weight of the Vatican felt in the world than Benedict XV, who reigned during World War I. The latter was seriously handicapped by two facts. First, the Vatican had based its policy on the assumption that the Central Powers would win, and changed its course only in the last few months of the conflict; second, the Roman question had not been solved, and Italy regarded the Vatican with suspicion, because she feared that the Pope might attempt to obtain territorial concessions through the intervention of the Allies.

No such situation exists today. The solution of the Roman question obtained with the signing of the Lateran Treaty between the Vatican and Italy in 1929, gave the former official international recognition as a sovereign state. Thus, the Pope today is not only a spiritual leader, but the head of a state as well, with the juridical attributes of any other lay monarch or president of a republic. By virtue of this dual role, he may intervene as any other neutral statesman in the settlement of the post-war problem. Since the Vatican is no longer seeking territorial aggrandizement, it will be the religious interests of the Catholic faith that it will wish to defend and make internationally recognized. Freedom of religion, already promised in the Atlantic Charter, will, therefore, be the cardinal interests of its policy after the war. Yet, the Holy See is the first to realize that freedom of religion would be threatened by a defective settlement of other purely political and economic problems, inasmuch as only a satisfactory solution will ensure a lasting peace. Consequently, its concern with non-religious issues, therefore, will be equally great. Of course, the Holy See knows that its intervention in the peace settlement may be fought to a certain extent by all the other churches, as well as by some of the lay governments, such as Russia, which do not favor Vatican influence on international affairs. How this problem will be solved no one can say, although it is expected that the Holy See will adopt a universalist attitude which, because of its loftiness and unselfishness, will tend to conciliate religious and lay rivals, and allay their diffidence.

As far as Europe is concerned, there can be little doubt that leaders of all religious denominations will find it politically advantageous to collaborate with England and the United States in the post-war settlement. The Vatican, as the directing and policy-making body of the most powerful and influential faith in Europe, has for many years clearly seen that the natural allies of the Catholic faith are the two Protestant Anglo-Saxon nations. At first glance this may seem paradoxical, but, as I have attempted to demonstrate earlier, the rise of pagan Nazism drew the papacy towards those powers which upheld a democratic system of government and permitted the free development of religious activities.

Admittedly, the two arch foes of religion are neo-paganism fostered by Nazi Germany, and atheism fostered by Communist Russia. The Holy See, however, regarded the former as its most direct enemy because Germany, in the years that preceded World War II, was the strongest power in continental Europe, and potentially capable, therefore, of imposing her anti-Christian ideology on other nations. This fear was justified after the outbreak of the war, when the Nazi juggernaut subjugated one country after another and sought to stamp out the Catholic Church in Europe.

With German power smashed by the United Nations coalition, it is clear that victorious Russia will replace Germany as the strongest power in Europe. She will, then, automatically become the most dangerous enemy, not only of the Catholic Church, but of all other faiths as well.

To counteract this long-foreseen danger, the Vatican will un-questionably support the post-war policy of England and the United States, the two conservative powers which, having gone to war twice during this century to prevent German hegemony of Europe, cannot conceivably accept Russian hegemony representing an equally strong threat to their future national security. The Vatican will be keenly interested in a settlement that will delimit the reciprocal spheres of influence of Washington, London and Moscow. In many speeches the Pope has supported the restoration of the independence of the smaller central and eastern European states, which would create not only a political but spiritual barrier against Communism and has also advocated the exclusion of foreign interference in the internal affairs of those states. For different reasons, Washington and London cannot but strive to promote a settlement with Moscow that will create a sort of no man's land between Russia and themselves in Europe. For, unless such an agreement is reached, the Anglo-Saxon powers on the one hand, and Russia on the other, will compete for domination in Europe and the stage will be set for a third world war.

The restoration of the independence of the smaller nations and the exclusion of foreign interference in their internal affairs, then, are the basic aims of the Vatican in post-war Europe, since such a solution would enable the Catholic Church to carry out its mission without the opposition of Communism—its deadly enemy.

The Roman Catholic Church, as well as all other churches, today is traversing one of the gravest crises in its history. The ultra-nationalist spirit, the exasperated passions, the unquenchable hatred, the bestial cruelty unleashed by the war have brought about the collapse of ethical and moral values and created a spiritual void in which the exhortations, appeals, prayers and diplomatic efforts of Pope Pius XII have been lost as those of his predecessor, Benedict XV, were in World War I. The voice of the Roman Pontiff, preaching love and good will among men, has been smothered by the clash of arms, the anguished cries of men dying on the purple-stained battlefields, and the oaths of the subjugated nations. These victims of the war find the moral strength to withstand the untold physical sufferings, humiliations, persecutions, mass murders threatening their survival, not, unfortunately, in their belief in God, but in the understandingly human, though far from laudable, prospect of re-venge after the defeat of their enemies.

This return to uncontrollable human passions kindled by the war is the spiritual crisis rending mankind today, and must be faced by both religious and lay leaders. There are a great many blueprints for peace, but the trouble with them is that their authors have con-ceived them in wartime, that is, when the human factor, in so far as it affects international co-operation, was checked by immanent considerations; namely, the necessity for defense against the enemy and for solidarity with the Allies. It will be a tremendous task to convince the Poles, Norwegians, Belgians, Netherlanders, French-men, Yugoslavs, Greeks, Russians and Chinese that they must forget the atrocities perpetrated in their territories by the Nazis and Japanese, let bygones be bygones, suffocate their desire for revenge, and start life anew under a system of international security, which, to be successful, involves collaboration with their former enemies.

The fact is often overlooked that this world is made up of individuals who have personal interests overshadowing those of the collectivity as a whole. Through no fault of their own, millions of these individuals have suffered; and suffering through injustice breeds hatred. Hatred is a single-track feeling that brooks no opposition, no matter from what quarter it may come; unless it abates, no lasting peace is possible. It is for this reason that Pius XII has pleaded scores of times, indeed in almost every one of his speeches and public pronouncements, for a just peace, and has warned against a settlement inspired by hatred and a spirit of revenge.

We Americans have had the good luck of being spared the humiliation, as well as the mental and downright physical torture, caused by invasion—which is the ultimate expression of the horror of war. Our attitude in regard to the conflict is influenced by that plain fact. Our troops went overseas "to do a job." They were told that, unless some powers were defeated, our mode of life, our democratic institutions, indeed, our nation, itself, would cease to exist as we know it today. If they felt any hatred for their enemies, it could hardly be compared with the one harbored by the victimized people of any of the territories conquered by Germany, Italy and Japan, because these human beings, unlike us, were personally affected by the war. Their homes were destroyed; children starved; women were attacked; property was seized; parents and relatives were shot or jailed.

The gap between our feelings and those of other peoples, including our allies, will be one of the greatest obstacles to the permanent establishment of peace. Americans, who have suffered less than anybody, are, in this sense, a minority. Those of us who have been directly affected by the treachery and savagery of our enemies are few, and cannot influence the entire nation. Instead, the hatred harbored by other nations is widespread; it is blind fury; it is the instinctive reaction caused by bleeding wounds—but because it is emotional, it is also irrational. To cite one example, the majority of the Americans do not hate the Italians. They thought Mussolini ridiculous, even though despicable and ruthless. But there were Italians I knew who hated the dictator far more fiercely than any foreigner, because he had ruined their lives. Their hatred was such that it overshadowed any other moral consideration.

We have, undoubtedly, the right idea as to what should be done in the post-war period. We want to eliminate future wars, ensure freedom of expression, freedom from want, freedom from fear and freedom of worship. It is an excellent platform and it cannot fail to be supported by the American people. However, the problem is how to apply it. Everybody agrees about permanent peace, but everybody disagrees as to the way it should be achieved.

Wars have been waged time and time again despite treaties and peace plans. The lessons of history are easily forgotten. If it were not so, the world would have had permanent peace long before now, after the devastations and suffering caused by countless wars. This failure is due to the fact that wars are not only the result of the clash of political, social and economic interests, but they are also the result of still-primitive morality, and unless moral changes take place in the hearts of men, they will continue to be waged.

If a citizen who has reached the highest possible standard of moral development is involved in a quarrel with another citizen, he will nearly always complain before a court of justice. An uneducated citizen, instead, will grab a gun and take the law in his own hands. Thus, one of the fundamental tasks facing the post-war world will be that of developing a higher standard of morality in the relations between states as well as between citizens. This is one of the aims of religion, which advocates tolerance, good will and collaboration, respect for law and the constituted authority, and seeks at the same time to improve man's moral standards. The support of religion and the promotion of its activities by the lay governments, then, will be one of the prerequisites for the attainment of a permanent peace.

INDEX